Property Of:
The Graduate Institute
701 North Street
Milford, CT 06460

Schooling in Sub-Saharan Africa

Reference Books in International Education
(Vol. 41)
Garland Reference Library of Social Sciences
(Vol. 952)

Schooling in Sub-Saharan Africa

Contemporary Issues and Future Concerns

Edited by Cynthia Szymanski Sunal

GARLAND PUBLISHING, INC.
A MEMBER OF THE TAYLOR & FRANCIS GROUP
New York & London
1998

GI
LA
1501
.S35
1998

Copyright © 1998 by Cynthia Szymanski Sunal
All rights reserved

Library of Congress Cataloging-in-Publication Data

Schooling in sub-saharan Africa : contemporary issues and future concerns / edited by Cynthia Szymanski Sunal.
       p.   cm. — (Garland reference library of social sciences ;
vol. 952. Reference books in international education ; vol. 41.)
    Includes bibliographical references and index.
    ISBN 0-8153-1645-3 (alk. paper)
    1. Education—Africa, Sub-Saharan.   2. School management and
organization—Africa, Sub-Saharan.   3. Education—Africa, Sub-
Saharan—Curricula.   I. Sunal, Cynthia Szymanski.   II. Series: Garland
reference library of social science ; v. 952.   III. Series: Garland reference
library of social science. Reference books in international education ;
vol. 41.
LA1501.S35   1998
370'.967—dc21   98–24283
                                                  CIP

Printed on acid-free, 250-year-life paper
Manufactured in the United States of America

Contents

Contents

Series Editor's Foreword

This series of scholarly works in comparative and international education has grown well beyond the initial conception of a collection of reference books. Although retaining its original purpose of providing a resource to scholars, students, and a variety of other professionals who need to understand the role played by education in various societies or world regions, it also strives to provide accurate, relevant, and up-to-date information on a wide variety of selected educational issues, problems, and experiments within an international context.

Contributors to this series are well-known scholars who have devoted their professional lives to the study of their specializations. Without exception these men and women possess an intimate understanding of the subject of their research and writing. Without exception they have not only studied their subject in dusty archives, but have lived and traveled widely in their quest for knowledge. In short, they are "experts" in the best sense of that often overused word.

In our increasingly interdependent world, it is now widely understood that it is a matter of military, economic, and environmental survival not only that we understand better what makes other societies tick, but also that we make a serious effort to understand how others, be they Japanese, Hungarian, South African, or Chilean, attempt to solve the same kinds of educational problems that we face in North America. As the late George Z.F. Bereday wrote more than three decades ago: "[E]ducation is a mirror held against the face of a people. Nations may put on blustering shows of strength to conceal public weakness, erect grand façades to conceal shabby backyards, and profess peace while secretly arming for conquest, but how they take care of their children tells unerringly who they are"

(*Comparative Methods in Education,* New York: Holt, Rinehart and Winston, 1964, p. 5).

Perhaps equally important, however, is the valuable perspective that studying another education system (or its problems) provides us in understanding our own system (or its problems). When we step beyond our own limited experience and our commonly held assumptions about schools and learning in order to look back at our system in contrast to another, we see it in a very different light. To learn, for example, how China or Belgium handles the education of a multilingual society; how the French provide for the funding of public education; or how the Japanese control access to their universities enables us to better understand that there are reasonable alternatives to our own familiar way of doing things. Not that we can *borrow* directly from other societies. Indeed, educational arrangements are inevitably a reflection of deeply embedded political, economic, and cultural factors that are unique to a particular society. But a conscious recognition that there are other ways of doing things can serve to open our minds and provoke our imaginations in ways that can result in new experiments or approaches that we may not have otherwise considered.

Since this series is intended to be a useful research tool, the editor and contributors welcome suggestions for future volumes, as well as for ways in which this series can be improved.

Edward R. Beauchamp
University of Hawaii

List of Contributors

Mohammed Kabiru Farouk
Associate Professor
Florida International University
Miami, Florida

Mary E. Haas
Professor of Curriculum
and Instruction
West Virginia University
Morgantown, West Virginia

Benson Honig
Assistant Professor
Tel Aviv International School
of Management
Tel Aviv, Israel

Gail Jaji
Associate Professor of Education
Jacksonville University
Jacksonville, Florida

Lazarus M. Jaji
Research Associate
Center for Higher Education
and International Programs
Ohio University
Athens, Ohio

R. Lynn Jones
Assistant Professor
of Science Education
University of Texas at Austin
Austin, Texas

Peter Okebukola
Vice Chancellor
Lagos State University
Lagos, Nigeria

Osayimwense Osa
Chair, Department of English
Mississippi Valley State University
Itta Bena, Mississippi

Cynthia Szymanski Sunal
Professor of Teacher Education
The University of Alabama
Tuscaloosa, Alabama

Dennis W. Sunal
Professor of Science Education
The University of Alabama
Tuscaloosa, Alabama

Overview of Schooling in Sub-Saharan Africa

Cynthia Szymanski Sunal

Given the extent of the difficulties faced in delivering both quantity and quality of education, sub-Saharan Africa may develop unique and innovative approaches in the quest for solutions to its educational problems that inform the other regions of the world. Quantity education involves universal access to education, referring to efforts to provide mass public education. Sub-Saharan African nations have been committed to providing at least a primary school education to all of their citizens since a continental conference in Addis Ababa in 1960. Quality education refers to efforts to facilitate each student's development of basic literacy and numeracy, knowledge of the cultural heritage, and thinking skills. It can, however, go far beyond these minimums. It is meaningful education, a difficult concept to define. Often it is defined operationally, through pass rates on exams, retention and promotion rates, and other formal and quantifiable means.

Both quantity and quality education require great commitment of resources and must compete with other demands, such as those for quantity and quality in public health services. These competing demands mean that educators and the citizenry usually recognize that more could be done, but efforts are constrained by resource limitations. In sub-Saharan Africa the provision of both quantity and quality education is more difficult to achieve than in other world regions. The stressors impacting sub-Saharan Africa and its educational systems are more extreme than in other regions.

Surging enrollments and heavy public expenditures for education have characterized schooling in sub-Saharan African nations for the past thirty years. Africans have supported the decisions of their governments to spend significant percentages of national income on education. There are concerns that the rapid expansion of basic education has resulted in a low quality of education. There is debate about quantity versus quality. These are not new concerns and they are not concerns relevant only to sub-Saharan Africa. These concerns have accompanied the development of public education in the nineteenth and twentieth centuries throughout the world. They continue to be relevant everywhere today (Snyder, Bolin, & Zumwalt, 1992). Thus, the struggles in sub-Saharan Africa to provide a high quality education to all children are representative of a worldwide struggle.

The situation is exacerbated in sub-Saharan Africa because of the extremity of the stressors impacting African nations and their efforts to provide education. Sub-Saharan economies are experiencing small amounts of growth relative to the rest of the world. In addition, other factors—such as warring groups within nations, desertification, rapidly expanding populations, limited health care and clean water, famine, and difficulties in the transportation and distribution of foodstuffs—are all stressing African nations.

Education has a role in the reduction of these stressors. It can help individuals understand health care precautions, factors contributing to desertification, and the arguments used by political factions. A functional literacy can enable people to read newspapers, information on new varieties of seeds, the directions for preparing oral hydration drinks, and other information sources. A functional numeracy can help individuals understand appropriate pricing so that they can recover their production costs and sell items at a profit. A functional understanding of science can help people take measures to protect their environment, understand health measures, and take proper precautions with electrical cords and appliances. Education can develop the knowledge and abilities that will reduce the extreme stressors acting upon people and nations in sub-Saharan Africa. However, concerns about the quality of education become important here. Is education of a high enough quality to produce such knowledge and abilities in most students? If not, what can be done to raise it to such a level? Again, as sub-Saharan Africa deals with these concerns, its insights may inform all other regions of the world since they, too, deal with these issues to varying extents.

An Overview of the Status of Education
at Different Levels

Formal education is available at all levels in many parts of sub-Saharan Africa. These levels include primary, secondary, and higher education available through public and private formal schooling. The informal sector of the economy also provides education. Thus, as it is elsewhere in the world, education is a complex and multifaceted enterprise in sub-Saharan Africa.

Education at the primary level is available to many of sub-Saharan Africa's children. However, about 12 percent will have no opportunity to go to school. Chapter 1 discusses primary education and the likelihood of its ability to serve all children in sub-Saharan Africa by 2050. An important issue in primary education is wastage—the lack of school completion by students. Thus, their enrollment in school is "wasted." Many children begin primary school, but a great number do not complete it. Those who do complete primary school often have to repeat grades and do poorly on examinations when compared to their peers in other regions of the world. So, primary schooling in much of sub-Saharan Africa is faced with the dual problems of quantity, serving all children, and of quality, enabling children to learn important content and thinking processes. The cost of educating a child and the lack of perceived job-related benefits from that education are factors slowing enrollment increases in many sub-Saharan primary schools. Other potential benefits of education, as suggested above, may not be perceived by the citizenry, since some primary school graduates may not be functionally literate and numerate, nor do they have a functional scientific literacy. Thus, primary education in sub-Saharan Africa presents numerous issues that must be addressed.

Secondary education has grown at a far slower pace than has primary education. Concerns are being raised in some countries regarding its efficacy in helping young people acquire good jobs, a knowledge base that will assist them in establishing their adult occupations and lives, and understandings that will help them contribute to national decision making about the stressors operating on their society.

Secondary education in sub-Saharan Africa often enrolls students who have passed an examination in order to attain a place at that level. These students may have a better primary education than do others or they may have greater intellectual ability. Frequently, they are among the better students in the nation. Even so, secondary schools are beset with many problems in working with their students. These include underqualified teachers, limited teaching practices focusing on memorization, and poor materials and facilities. Because far fewer students are served by secondary schools, their graduates have a greater likelihood of finding a job than do those with only a primary school education. But, many secondary schools do not offer an education that translates well to the world of work. A secondary education is not a strong guarantee of finding a job. The chapters examining issues in content areas, Chapters 4, 5, 6, and 7, discuss secondary schooling in sub-Saharan Africa. Some issues such as underqualified teachers and the inclusion of indigenous content and teaching examples emerge across these chapters. A few, such as problems with obtaining current laboratory equipment for science classes are particular to a specific content area but relate to generic problems in finding appropriate teaching materials.

African nations have spent a relatively large portion of their education budget on higher education when compared to countries in the Far East and Latin America, although this level of education serves very few students. Despite these allocations, institutions of higher education generally are underfunded in sub-Saharan Africa. They struggle with questions regarding the type of coursework to be offered, the role of research and service, quality of teaching and advisement, student selection, and resources for learning such as library materials and computers. Higher education has expanded tremendously in the last thirty years. After independence sub-Saharan African nations began establishing new universities and expanding existing ones. Some nations, such as Nigeria, have a large system of universities, polytechnics, and teachers' colleges. Most African nations have per-pupil costs exceeding those in most developed countries. The rapid growth of higher education institutions in sub-Saharan Africa stands out from other regions of the world, where a much smaller portion of the national budget has been devoted to public higher education.

The fostering of higher education by African governments has resulted in the establishment of a group of highly educated Africans.

While "brain drain" to more developed areas of the world has occurred, many of these individuals have stayed in their home country and contributed to its development. Whether the rapid growth of higher education institutions has been the best use of scarce funds for education is a question being debated in the 1990s and will be a future concern. The status of higher education in sub-Saharan Africa is discussed in Chapter 2. As with other levels of education in sub-Saharan Africa, the concerns with which higher education deals are not unique to the region.

As the region is impacted by extreme stressors, the need for education for the informal sector grows throughout sub-Saharan Africa. There are many costs associated with formal schooling for families ranging from the purchase of school uniforms to the loss of the student's income-generating capacity during schooling. These costs keep some children from school. Schooling itself does not prepare students for many available means of generating income, such as trading. One unanticipated effect of the great expansion of educational opportunities in sub-Saharan African nations has been a significant reduction in the employment prospects for secondary school graduates and their self-employment in the informal sector doing trading, small-item manufacturing, and similar individual work. As a result, most individuals acquire some job-related education informally. Others participate in short-term formal training. They may attend a training meeting that helps them with bookkeeping or informs them about small-loan programs. The informal sector of the economy can be assisted by formal government education and business agencies. Such a relationship is developing in parts of sub-Saharan Africa. It suggests ideas and strategies that may be of value to other regions. A number of sub-Saharan nations have included informal sector "training" as part of their standard secondary curriculum, while vocational education has had measurably less success. Educational strategies are being developed and investigated for supporting training for the informal sector. Chapter 3 discusses the informal sector, how training related to it can be fostered, and its relationship to formal education.

The economic problems being experienced in sub-Saharan Africa have restricted the pace of educational growth, but also have created a situation where innovation occurs, where indigenous ideas are considered, and where unique solutions can be successful. Sub-Saharan Africa is composed of many cultures, each of which is addressing education in its own way. The variety of cultures found in the region creates a tremendous reservoir of perspectives and ideas from which African educational systems can derive ideas to address contemporary issues and future concerns. This wonderful variety means that sub-Saharan Africa is giving—and will continue to give—the world new ideas in education. As the period of European colonization recedes, sub-Saharan educators are looking inside their own cultures for solutions to their problems. Some elements of sub-Saharan educational systems, their curricula, and the instructional pedagogies used are adapted from elsewhere. But, when successful, their configuration and goals reflect the cultures of sub-Saharan Africa into which they have been introduced. The process of educational development occurring in sub-Saharan Africa enriches education in all parts of the world. This theme is discussed by the chapters in this book as they describe the ideas being generated from the variety of cultures in sub-Saharan Africa in their effort to address contemporary educational issues and future concerns

Contemporary Educational Issues and Future Concerns in Sub-Saharan Africa

Each of the chapters in this book addresses a set of contemporary educational issues and future concerns in sub-Saharan Africa as applicable to its topic. The authors jointly developed a listing of these issues and concerns based on a review of the literature and on their personal research efforts in sub-Saharan Africa. Of primary concern was the identification of educational issues that impact all of sub-Saharan Africa despite its diversity in culture, geography, and perspectives. A second criterion used was whether the educational issue was likely to be a future concern. The issues and future concerns that emerged from this collective deliberation are: (1) the objectives of mass education, (2) funding, (3) inequities in access to education, (4) curriculum, (5) instructional methodology, and (6) research needs and efforts. These issues and concerns are broad. The particular form they take and the level of difficulty within a specific nation will vary because of the differences among and within sub-Saharan nations. Yet, all of sub-Saharan Africa is dealing with these issues. The chapters in this book will consider both the difficulties being faced in the provision of quality and quantity of education in sub-Saharan Africa and the unique and innovative approaches developing to address those difficulties.

Section 1 contains a set of chapters that consider issues, future concerns, and innovations through the lens of level of schooling: primary schooling (Chapter 1), higher education (Chapter 2), and informal sector education (Chapter 3). Thus, the two endpoints anchoring the continuum of formal education are highlighted in this section. The issues and concerns outlined in the chapter on primary schooling often continue to affect education throughout all its levels. For example, instructional strategies fostered by cultural perspectives frequently are evident in primary schooling and set expectations among students for instruction throughout the rest of schooling. Students develop a view of their role in the classroom and the types of thinking abilities accepted in the context of the classroom that continues into other levels of schooling and is not easily reconstructed.

Higher education deals with issues at the opposite end of the educational experience from primary schools, yet the major issues remain much the same. Because higher education requires substantial funding and is important in training leaders in government, business, education, and health it has a strong impact on its society. Therefore, this book gives it separate consideration. Higher education affects other levels of education as, in turn, it is affected by them. A major impact occurs when it either directly trains teachers for other levels of education or educates those who will be the teacher trainers.

Informal sector education is the most difficult of the levels of education to describe. It exists widely, sometimes with and sometimes without ties to formal education. It is an important part of society, impacting it strongly, although its capacity to address the needs of the citizenry for training related to the informal sector is questionable and the status given to training for the informal sector is not high. Yet, the need is significant and there are efforts in sub-Saharan Africa that indicate formal education can play an important role in informal sector education.

The chapters in Section 2 look at the six major issues and future concerns through the lens of content-area teaching. Four major disciplinary curriculum areas of education are considered: science, mathematics, citizenship, and literature education. These provide a foundation of knowledge and thinking skills needed if the stressors faced by African societies are to be resolved. Chapters 4, 5, 6, and 7 discuss the issues and future concerns across all levels of education in some depth. Each also gives much consideration to two specific issues, curriculum and instructional methodologies. A major curriculum-related question being debated throughout sub-Saharan Africa is: How African in content and perspective should this discipline's curriculum be? A related question is: How specific to the local culture and its perspectives should this discipline's curriculum be? Another question is: Can there be such an entity as an African curriculum in this discipline when African societies are so diverse? Yet another question is: What portion of this discipline is worldwide in content and perspective, and therefore should be an important part of the curriculum for African students? Similar questions are raised in regard to instructional methodology. For example, inquiry-teaching and problem-solving approaches are prominent in the national standards for all disciplines that have been recently developed in the United States. These approaches are being given thoughtful consideration by educators throughout the world. Yet some societies in sub-Saharan Africa do not tradionally foster questioning by children. Such questioning is an important part of inquiry-teaching and learning. So educators in the region debate the extent to which teacher trainers should attempt to foster inquiry-teaching among educators in sub-Saharan Africa. Educators are debating which instructional strategies provide a best fit for their students, for their societies, and for the accomplishment of the development goals of their societies.

Author Perspectives

As institutions of higher education in sub-Saharan Africa train doctoral-level researchers, the volume and diversity of research generated throughout the region can be expected to grow. A number of the authors in this book have conducted research in Nigeria which has, for several decades, produced a large amount of educational research in sub-Saharan Africa. Several other nations in the region, such as Zimbabwe, Kenya, and South Africa, also have extensive educational research programs. The relative wealth of Nigeria makes it different in some respects from many African nations, yet its cultures and history mark it as African.

The authors have striven to examine the research from all of sub-Saharan Africa, comparing it to their own research, where applicable, and to their experiences in a number of nations throughout the region. Each chapter considers the broad spectrum of research on its topic throughout sub-Saharan Africa. Research in other regions of the world is sometimes used to highlight the connections between the issues being explored in sub-Saharan Africa and the considerations of those issues elsewhere. The authors generalize from their own research and are aware of its limitations. However, they have studied the regional research literature, have lived in several of the region's nations, and realize that for all its differences, sub-Saharan Africa has a distinctive common background and set of perspectives that make it a unique region. As Africans share much, studies in any African country can inform other nations in the region and may have relevance for the rest of the world as well.

Overviews of the Issues and Future Concerns
The Objectives of Mass Education

Sub-Saharan Africa continues to struggle with identifying the objectives of mass education. This is a struggle repeated throughout the world. As the world continues to change rapidly, this issue will continue to be considered. Among the questions related to this issue as it is being debated in sub-Saharan Africa are the following: Is the attainment of a basic literacy and numeracy by all the objective of educational efforts? Many Africans have few or no reading materials available. Many jobs in the informal sector do not require literacy. Schooling is often of such low quality that those who pass through the schools are barely literate. So more questions must be asked: Is the expense of schooling to families and governments worth the results? Are the objectives of mass education different in African societies than in other societies? Must the objectives of mass education in sub-Saharan Africa be those of developed nations if the populace is to be competitive on world markets? These are questions being asked by the general populace, educators, and government officials. There appears to be a consensus that basic literacy and numeracy are empowering accomplishments all individuals should attain. A consensus is not evident on the other questions related to the objectives of mass education.

Much sub-Saharan education as demonstrated through curricula and instructional methodologies is preparation for the next level of education. This appears to be an existing objective of mass education. Since few students participate in secondary education and far fewer participate in higher education, is education focused on preparation for the next level justifiable?

Some have identified vocational education as an appropriate objective of sub-Saharan mass education. Chapter 3 examines the limited efforts to involve students in vocational education. Such efforts seem to have potential for delivering education that has immediate applications. But the costs are high, the training is poor, and it has not been well received by parents. The populace perceives education at one level as a means of obtaining entrance to a higher level, with a university education and a fine job with high salary and status as the end results.

Education also is viewed throughout much of sub-Saharan Africa as having the promotion of citizenship as another objective. This is important in nations whose colonial rulers paid no attention to ethnic groups when deciding the boundaries of the colony. As a result, ethnic groups are split among countries and one country may contain portions of several large ethnic groups. Education is perceived as the vehicle through which a national identity and national loyalty are established. Chapter 6 discusses citizenship education efforts. The persistence of wrangling and even warfare among groups within various sub-Saharan African nations suggests that education has not been highly successful in accomplishing this purpose.

Rationales given for the expansion of educational opportunities in sub-Saharan Africa and for the funding required to deliver those opportunities frequently state the following as the major objectives of mass education: basic literacy and numeracy, citizenship, preparation for the next level of education, and vocational development. Other objectives, such as the enabling of the fullest development of an individual's potential, also are stated. Because of the need for national development, stronger economies, and the attainment of a strong political voice in the world's affairs, the objectives of education most often are seen in practical terms—the ability to facilitate. As Africans debate and weigh the import of decisions regarding such objectives, their decisions and the criteria used in decision making may be of interest in other regions of the world.

Funding

Education in sub-Saharan Africa has significant funding, accounting for 5.2 percent of national budgets in 1980 and 4.6 percent in 1990. This percentage of national government spending was surpassed only by the Arab States in 1990 (5.5 percent) and the most developed nations such as Austria, Canada, Israel, and New Zealand (5.3 percent) (UNESCO, 1993). Continuing such expenditures suggests rapid economic growth—something that eludes sub-Saharan Africa.

Of all the world's regions, African economies rank last in wealth as well as in rate of growth. The population is burgeoning. This combination of rapidly growing populations and slowly growing economies means that funding for educational purposes will become more and more limited. Structural adjustment policies expect families to take on an increasing share of the costs of education at a time when individuals find themselves with limited incomes due to weak economies. With increasing population growth it will be difficult to continue to enroll the same percentage of the cohort. Some nations are attempting to offer universal education beyond the primary school. However, the percentage of children enrolled in primary schooling has dropped in the 1990s. Financial difficulties, cultural reservations, and child health problems due to inadequate funding of public health delivery systems are related to this drop in enrollment, and are discussed in Chapter 1.

The funding of education will require hard decisions in the next century. Universal education is a goal that cannot be reached in the near future in most sub-Saharan African countries. Each nation will have to decide how to apportion the limited available funds among the growing numbers of potential students in order to achieve the best possible balance between quantity and quality in education.

Inequities to Access in Education

As severe funding problems continue, educational inequities in access to education in sub-Saharan Africa are exacerbated. In the past thirty years rural children and girls, particularly Muslim girls, have been most underserved (see Chapter 1). Nomadic groups have presented special problems in the delivery of education and have been largely left out of the educational process.

As more of the costs of education are turned over to parents, lower income children increasingly will be unable to attend school. Parents have become aware of the inability of primary and sometimes secondary education to guarantee a good job. Fewer children may be enrolled by those parents for whom education requires great economic sacrifice or who have cultural and/or religious concerns. Inequities in educational attainment in terms of both quantity and quality can be expected to increase as funding becomes stretched and access to education is limited. These issues are discussed in Chapters 1, 4, and 5.

Inequities in access to education exist in all societies. The factors influencing reduced access to education are many, but, frequently, rural children, children with low socioeconomic status, girls, and children from specific nonmajority cultural groups are those for whom access to education is limited. Thus, African societies share a worldwide problem and may generate solutions viable elsewhere.

Curriculum

Curriculum is a fourth major issue and future concern with which sub-Saharan African nations have been dealing. Colonial, European-focused curricula have been standard throughout the region. In the last thirty years there has been a gradual increase of locally developed curricula. Chapters 4, 5, 6, and 7 address issues related to the development of indigenous curricula.

African educators are strongly influenced by movements and theories originating in other regions of the world. Many have advanced degrees from overseas institutions and publish their research in international journals. They are part of a worldwide community of scholars. Two questions being considered are: How much should curricula reflect international, often European and North American–based, ideas, and how much should it reflect local cultural values and interests? and Should the primary school curriculum be more locally based than the higher education curriculum? There is no set formula for these balances. Chapter 1 discusses these issues in relation to the primary school. Other chapters, such as those on mathematics education (Chapter 5) and using indigenous literature in education (Chapter 7) discuss these issues in relation to a specific content area.

The perceived objectives of education will influence the curriculum, whether it be toward basic literacy and numeracy, vocational development, preparation for the next level of education, or citizenship. There can be no single balance that adequately serves all of sub-Saharan Africa, a region diverse in cultures, languages, religions, and political systems. The curricula in each of the world's regions should be suitable to its needs. The processes and criteria established for the goals and content of African curricula may be useful elsewhere.

Instructional Methodology

A fifth major issue and future concern for education in sub-Saharan Africa is instructional methodology. Traditional pedagogy in the region focuses on lecture and memorization, using oral transmission as the main vehicle through which learning occurs. Both indigenous and foreign educators promote the use of discussion, problem solving, and inquiry. These sometimes do not fit well with traditional views of appropriate behavior among children. National development experts often support the fostering of problem-solving and decision-making skills among the populace. However, in traditional families and in nations that are not democracies, such skills are not valued, and they threaten the current structures in society. African educators are looking to the past, examining the role of traditional instructional methodologies, and looking to the future, considering how traditional methodologies can be incorporated into a broader pedagogy that incorporates tradition while preparing students to live in a rapidly changing world. Chapters 4, 5, 6, and 7 address issues related to instructional methodologies, the choices available, and the decisions to be made.

Underprepared teachers generally do not have the ability to foster higher-level thinking skills. Professional teaching materials are scarce in the region and underprepared teachers do not know how to use available local resources such as oral literature, traditional architecture, and traditional native plants in teaching. They fall back on lecture and memorization because these require limited teaching skills and can occur with limited teaching materials. Chapters 1, 3, and 4 discuss the problems of underprepared teachers and the means being explored to increase their effective use of a range of instructional methodologies.

Traditional instructional methodologies are established in each culture. The problems sub-Saharan Africa faces with underprepared teachers are severe. All nations work with the issue of how best to prepare teachers to utilize innovative instructional strategies. African solutions created to address a severe problem may be informative to nations that face similar problems and to those whose major concern is not underpreparedness of teachers per se, but the directions and goals of the preparation for the use of nontraditional instructional methodologies.

Research Efforts

The sixth major issue is a lack of educational research. Because of limited accessibility to higher education in the region, there are few trained researchers in education. Without such individuals it is difficult to collect baseline data. It is even more difficult to analyze existing problems, propose solutions, test those solutions, and analyze the implications of the results of those tests. The determination of which questions should be asked and which strategies should be investigated is difficult when few researchers are available.

Life in the region is not easy. Trained researchers have limited access to the work of other researchers. Many have few opportunities to work with others in their field. They face technical problems ranging from the inability to have a computer repaired to finding transportation to a site so that research interviews can be carried out. Low salaries due to weak national economies are common as are health problems and frequent interruption of water and electrical service to homes and offices. Researchers in the region face many obstructions to their scholarly productivity. Because there are so many limitations on the research that can be done, questions remain unexplored. Solutions will not be offered as frequently and will take longer to test than in many of the world's regions. Chapter 2 discusses the problems of higher education and the difficulties facing researchers.

All researchers face some limitations, but in much of sub-Saharan Africa those limitations are extreme. Yet, educational development requires a foundation of valid research if informed decision making is to occur. Both the successes and failures of African educational research should be informative to the rest of the world. The extremity of the situation of many African researchers is likely to result in creative solutions. These solutions will be of interest and possibly of assistance to educational researchers everywhere.

Solutions

Given the population growth and resource conflicts evident in most of sub-Saharan Africa, educational expenditures are likely to be too small to enable the system to adjust in an optimal manner. Careful direction and evlauation will be necessary to ward off the most adverse effects on education of the stressors impacting countries in the region. A range of strategies are being implemented to solve the issues existing in sub-Saharan Africa and to reduce the likelihood of their continuance as future concerns. Each chapter discusses some of these strategies and analyzes their current and potential impact.

Because of the diversity of the region, each nation and all areas within a nation will have to find its own way. The range and depth of cultures in the region are a great resource. Educators in the region may find some or most of their solutions within their own cultures. The region's diversity should result in a wide range of solutions to the six major issues that have been identified in this overview to the book. The potential solutions, the processes created to derive those solutions, the rationale used to support them, and the level of success or failure of each solution: all will have import for the rest of the world and may be adaptable elsewhere.

References

Snyder, J., Bolin, F., & Zumwalt, K. (1992). Curriculum implementation. In P. Jackson, (Ed.), *Handbook of research on curriculum* (pp. 402–435). New York: Macmillan.
UNESCO (1986). *Statistical yearbook.* Paris: Author.
UNESCO (1987). *Statistical yearbook.* Paris: Author.
UNESCO (1993). *World education report.* Paris: Author.

Section 1

The Education System

Primary Education

Primary school education is widespread throughout sub-Saharan Africa. It has grown rapidly in recent decades in terms of sheer numbers of children attending primary schools. Yet, researchers have predicted that some African children will never attend primary school. There are concerns that, although the numbers of children in school will increase due to rapid population growth, the percentage of children in school will decrease.

A rationale must be built to explain the purposes for primary education in any society. African nations must articulate their rationale for the large investment in primary education. Chapter 1 considers the state of primary education in sub-Saharan Africa, as there seem to be ever more children and ever less money. The purposes of primary education, its cost, its enrollment prospects, and the potential for successful alternatives to formal schooling are discussed.

There are many factors placing stress upon the effort to deliver a high quality of education at the primary level. Teacher and classroom factors are of major importance. These have an effect on the daily delivery of primary schooling. In all parts of the world teacher factors such as teacher training and salaries and classroom factors such as the availability of classrooms, resource materials, and electricity have an effect on quality of education. Student factors also are of extreme importance throughout the world. Health, nutritional, and home factors, in particular, can influence the ability of the student to attend school and to learn. Chapter 1 examines the status of such factors and their effects on primary education in sub-Saharan Africa. Stresses associated with these factors are extreme in the region. They require diverse and unique solutions. The specific case of primary education in Nigeria is examined in depth. All six issues and future concerns identified in the introduction overview are addressed in the chapter in terms of all the nations of the region and the specific example of Nigeria. The Nigerian case suggests that solutions are being sought. It indicates that some unique ideas are emerging and that other ideas are being adapted from outside the country to the national setting. It also indicates that some of the ideas emerging may be useful elsewhere.

Higher Education
Recent decades have seen an expansion of higher education. Polytechnics, agricultural universities, teacher training colleges, and other types of institutions have been established, along with more traditional academic research institutions. Graduate programs have grown. Special evening and weekend programs, such as an external master's of business administration, are found at some institutions. The range and depth of higher education have increased rapidly within the region, with several patterns discernible. These are described in Chapter 2.

The six major issues and future concerns identified in the introduction overview exist in higher education in sub-Saharan Africa. Higher education in the region has strong ties to higher education elsewhere, particularly in Europe and North America. Ties between higher education institutions within the region are developing. The exchange of ideas is increasing within the region and may facilitate the development and implementation of solutions to the issues that exist.

Higher education in sub-Saharan Africa suffers from the same basic problem that faces primary education, a burgeoning population resulting in greater numbers of students seeking admission while the economy grows slowly and less money is available to support the institution. Enrollment has increased in some institutions while others have kept a level enrollment. Because of slow economic growth, often accompanied by inflation and/or a decline in the value of the national currency in the world market, even institutions that have kept enrollment level have less real money with which to operate.

Quality of education is debated throughout higher education. Among the questions asked are the following: Can quality be maintained if enrollment is increased? Can it be maintained even if enrollment is kept level? What is the best balance between teaching, research, and service? Where should doctoral-level faculty be trained? How can adequate library and research resources be obtained and maintained? What is the relationship of the institution of higher education to national development? What forms should instruction take? What is the role of the student's adviser? All these questions, and many others that are being asked and debated, relate to the six major issues and future concerns identified by this book as impacting education in sub-Saharan Africa.

These questions are not relevant only in sub-Saharan Africa, but are debated elsewhere as well. As higher education institutions adapt to a changing world and serve the communities that support them, such questions always must be asked. While there is not likely to be one final, definitive answer in a changing world, there are solutions that better adapt the higher education institution to its students, the nation, and the world. The difficulties of higher education in sub-Saharan Africa are extreme, but the extremity appears to be creating a diversity of ideas that may suggest alternatives for higher education elsewhere.

Chapter 2 discusses factors such as World Bank recommendations that have impacted higher education to some extent throughout the region. Regional and country examples are cited. A case study from Nigeria, an African nation with one of the most complex systems of higher education, is used to illustrate potentials, problems, solutions, and consequences.

Education for the Informal Sector

With the expansion in recent decades of educational opportunities in sub-Saharan Africa, an unexpected effect has been a significant reduction in the employment prospects for secondary school graduates. The generally slow-growing economies found in much of the region have not kept pace with the more rapidly growing educational levels of the populace. This is particularly true of large manufacturing enterprises. The growth that has occurred has been in microenterprises including everything from vehicle repair to vending to freelance computer programming. Such enterprises employ about half of the urban labor force in the region. They are termed the informal sector of the economy. Chapter 3 discusses the relationship of formal education to the informal economy. The chapter addresses all of the six major issues and future concerns identified in the introduction overview. A central issue is the relationship of the informal sector economy to the objectives of mass education. Formal mass education can provide specific training for eventual work in the informal sector such as bookkeeping. It also could alter the expectations students and their families have regarding work possibilities following the completion of education at the primary, secondary, and higher education levels. Formal education can work to foster the status and desirability of informal sector employment.

Vocational and informal sector training by formal education exists to varying extent throughout the world. Generally, such training is not as high status as is academic training, whose goal often is preparation for the next level of education. Many countries have a thriving informal sector of the economy that can provide jobs for primary and secondary school completers. The informal sector is adaptive and can be rapidly changing. Formal education worldwide has found it difficult to respond quickly to the changing needs of the informal sector. African responses could suggest workable strategies that might be implemented elsewhere.

The chapters in Section 1 use level of education as a lens for examining education in sub-Saharan Africa. Each chapter considers the diversity of the region and the innovations that can come from such diversity as various levels of education strive to find solutions to the six major issues and future concerns identified in this book. They identify patterns and trends found in educational development within the region.

Chapter One
Primary School Education in Sub-Saharan Africa

Cynthia Szymanski Sunal

The provision of primary education to children in sub-Saharan Africa will present formidable problems at the beginning of the next century. The numbers of children will have grown rapidly, with a 90 percent increase in attendance expected in the fifteen-year period between 1985 and 2000. In the year 2000 there will be 125 million students in primary school in sub-Saharan Africa. They will represent about 20 percent of primary students in the world's developing nations, an increase from 14 percent in 1985. Despite this rapid increase in the numbers of children in school, some (about 12 percent) will never receive any formal schooling (Lassibille & Gomez, 1990). Delivering a primary school education to these rapidly increasing numbers of children will stretch limited national budgets.

As the numbers of children grow, African governments continue to try to provide primary education for all. They honor a commitment made at a continental conference in Addis Ababa in 1960. At that conference, African nations set 1980 as the target year for the achievement of universal primary education. This goal was not met and will probably not be met by the year 2000. But the sheer number of children in primary school was far greater in 1980 than the projections had suggested it would be. It had been projected that 33 million children would be enrolled in African primary schools in 1980; instead 59 million were enrolled (UNESCO, 1961, 1986, 1987). The goal of universal primary education has been an elusive one in sub-Saharan Africa as populations rapidly increase and strain available resources.

More Children, Less Money: The State of Primary Education in Sub-Saharan Africa

Purposes for Primary Education

Since it is extremely difficult to deliver primary education to burgeoning populations in sub-Saharan Africa, its nations must articulate valid purposes for the effort and expense they have undertaken. Two purposes are usually cited: (1) primary education can make citizens literate and numerate to the extent that they can deal with problems encountered at home, and (2) it can provide a foundation for further education (Lockheed & Verspoor, 1991, p. 1). These purposes are not fully accomplished in sub-Saharan Africa for several reasons. First, some groups are unlikely to attend school. These typically include girls, rural students, and the poor.

Second, while many African children begin school, a large proportion of them do not complete their schooling. Primary school completion rates declined in the lowest-income countries (those with an annual per capita income of $450 U.S. or less) during the 1980s. This decline can be traced to dropping out of school early and also to high rates of repeating grades. Lack of school completion is also related to a third factor; the content of the curriculum presented to children while they are in school is often too limited to accomplish its purposes. For example, most Chadian students spend two years in first grade. They repeat first grade because they have not learned the material that is considered to be the content of the first grade curriculum. In their classrooms the actual curriculum is much more limited than that intended in the national curriculum. Although national curricula have been developed that provide guidelines for an education of high quality, several factors found throughout sub-Saharan Africa result in a curriculum that is often too limited to accomplish its purposes. These include: high student–teacher ratios, underqualified teachers who have limited teaching strategies available to them, few books and teaching materials, and teachers who do not plan because they are tired from traveling long distances to school or working more than one job as a result of a low salary (Cornia, Jolly, & Stewart, 1987; Graham-Brown, 1991; Lassibille & Gomez, 1990; Sunal, Osa, Gaba, & Saleemi, 1989).

Fourth, those who do complete their primary education often

do not perform as well as their peers in developed nations on international assessments such as that of the International Association for the Evaluation of Educational Achievement (IEA). This is particularly true of the lowest-income nations. It is also true of many lower-middle-income countries, whose annual per capita income is between $450 and $1500 U.S. The IEA assessments contain items that address content found worldwide but the items are geared toward the national curriculum of the nation in which the assessment is occurring.

Their poor results indicate these students are not meeting international standards. Nor are they meeting national standards (Lockheed & Verspoor, 1991). Malawian students, for example, achieved a median score of 34 percent on the first IEA reading achievement test, and Nigerian students achieved a median score of 33 percent on the first science assessment in comparison to the international median of 54 percent. In both testings, however, there was a wide range of scores within each country suggesting that some schools are far more successful at teaching content than are others. Testing that utilizes higher-order problems asking students to apply knowledge to new situations has found even lower median scores among sub-Saharan African students. Orivel and Perrot (1988) report 70 to 80 percent of sub-Saharan African students tested had basic numeracy but only 26 percent in one country and 44 percent in another country could solve problems where they had to use two operations such as multiplication and division, in contrast with 78 percent of French students.

Fifth, many students begin school at a late age (Gajraj & Schoemann, 1991). These students' families may have had to wait until they saved enough money to cover uniforms and school materials. Or, they may have had to save enough money to be able to go without the student's income-producing activity for a while. In some cases, the student is an adult who previously did not have access to primary schooling. These students may not complete their primary education due to the same factors that caused their late enrollment.

The Cost of Primary Education

Primary education is expensive even though it is neither meeting national purposes nor serving all children. African countries spent

9 percent of their capital expenditure on education between 1975
and 1987, allocating a greater share of their resources to primary
education (1.43 percent of their gross national product) than did
countries in Latin America or Asia.

The economies of sub-Saharan Africa are weak. The average
gross national product of African countries is expected to grow about
0.3 percent a year. This will be low compared to other areas such as
Latin America where a 1.4 percent growth is expected and Asia,
where a 4.7 percent growth is expected. The large enrollments expected in Africa will cost the equivalent of $10 billion U.S. by the
year 2000. If all children were served through university primary
education the cost would be $13 billion U.S. as expenditures in-
creased annually by 6.7 percent. Universal primary education would
result in an almost 60 percent cost increase over what was spent in
1985 (Lassibille & Gomez, 1990). A relatively large proportion of
sub-Saharan national budgets is spent on education. Yet in absolute
terms the amounts of money spent on education in developing nations is small when compared to the money spent by developed nations, because the total national budgets are small (Graham-Brown,
1991, p. 33). When the money available is not large, teacher salaries
are relatively low, fewer educational facilities can be built, fewer textbooks and materials can be purchased, and less curriculum development can occur. Since materials such as paper and scientific equipment may be imported by developing nations, costs are higher than
in many developed nations. When economic problems occur, any
cutbacks that are made have severe effects because, in U.S. dollar
terms, the national budget is small. Economic problems have occurred with increasing frequency throughout the 1980s and into the
1990s. Mozambique, Sudan, and Zambia are severely indebted low-
income countries. Zimbabwe is a lower-middle-income nation that
is moderately indebted. The high population growth in sub-Saharan
Africa makes the economic situation ever more difficult.

Enrollment Growth

Both enrollment and the school-age population grew rapidly into
the early 1980s. But declines in the percentage of enrolled students
became obvious as the 1980s progressed, although sheer numbers
increased. This was particularly true in low-income countries, but

also became evident in lower-middle-income countries. Those countries that experienced war and a rapidly declining gross national product had the greatest declines. These included Ethiopia, Mozambique, and Somalia (Gajraj & Schoemann, 1991). Other countries' enrollment growth rate slowed because greater percentages of the population were served by primary education, and the elusive goal of universal primary education moved closer.

Those still unserved were often poor, lived in isolated rural areas, or were girls from traditional families (Gajraj & Schoemann, 1991). These girls were viewed by family members as eventually having responsibility for passing the culture on to their children. Their families viewed primary schooling as a mostly foreign process that might change their daughters' ability to pass on the culture. Many of these families also became concerned about the length of primary schooling. As their daughters approached and entered puberty, they worried about the possibility of pregnancy. In some cultures, daughters are married at puberty. Marriage was thought to be incompatible with continued primary school attendance. These families were likely to withdraw their daughters from primary school as they approached puberty. They were also more likely to refuse to ever enroll them because of the concerns they would have in the later years of primary schooling (Adesina, 1982).

Solving the problems presented by hard-to-enroll segments of the population requires financing programs that address all aspects of the lives of these people. Some countries may not make a strong effort to enroll those who are underserved. This is most likely to happen when they do not have enough facilities or enough trained teachers to handle these children, should they enroll in primary school. The Ivory Coast, Liberia, and Nigeria are examples of those countries that do not have the capacity to enroll 80 percent or more of potential students. Surging population growth reinforces efforts to continue to enroll children from families who are already supportive of enrollment and provides a rationale for placing less effort on the enrollment of other segments of the population.

Alternatives to Formal Schooling
Since formal schooling is not reaching all children, alternatives have been tried. These experiments included rural education centers in

Burkina Faso, Koranic schools in Mauritania, and distance education through television and radio in several nations (Christensen, 1990; Coombs, Prosser, & Ahmed, 1973; Lebby & Lutz, 1982). There was very limited success. In general, the public did not accept these innovations and demanded a formal primary education program. The alternatives were viewed as having less potential for helping children achieve academic success and as carrying lower status.

Teacher and Classroom Factors in Formal Schooling
Teacher–Student Ratio and Teacher Salaries
In the formal settings supported by the public, there will be an estimated thirty-seven students per teacher in sub-Saharan African nations in the year 2000. A reduction in the student–teacher ratio would greatly increase the cost of primary education, since the population of potential primary school students is growing quickly. The cost of a decrease in student–teacher ratio could be lowered by hiring less qualified teachers and paying them 70 percent of the salary of those currently in the teaching force. This means of reducing the student–teacher ratio has been suggested but has not been given much consideration in sub-Saharan Africa. Instead, wage forecasts suggest that average teacher salaries will increase by the year 2000 and in the years beyond (Lassabille & Gomez, 1991). Yet, between 1980 and 1985 real salaries declined in all but two sub-Saharan countries. In eleven countries the decline was 10 percent or more. Among these countries were Kenya, Zambia, Zimbabwe, and Senegal (Zymelman & De Stefano, 1989, p. 35).

In Nigeria during the early 1980s, many teachers were not paid for periods of up to eighteen months because of revenue shortfalls from a rapid drop in oil prices. In Cameroun teachers have waited a year to be paid at various times in the 1980s and early 1990s. Because of the economic crises occurring in much of sub-Saharan Africa between 1983 and 1986, over 80,000 teachers found other work or were laid off because there was no money to pay them (IDS, 1989). Even if the present student–teacher ratio were maintained, a 15 percent increase in the current outlay would have to occur. It would have to be increased by 45 percent to provide universal primary education (Lassabille & Gomez, 1991). The weak economic situation in sub-Saharan Africa suggests the financing of universal primary education is unlikely. There will be difficulty in maintaining the present student–teacher ratio either with teachers who have qualifications similar to those now teaching or with those who have lesser qualifications.

Classroom Settings and Instruction

The classroom setting and teachers' quality of life profoundly affect instruction. A survey of fifty-one primary schools in Botswana concluded that students with adequate classrooms, desks, and books perform significantly better on tests than do those without adequate facilities and materials (Mwamwenda & Mwamwenda, 1987). Students in many African countries purchase textbooks at local bookstores. Often one or a few copies of different textbooks are offered for sale. As a result, students bring to class a variety of textbooks. Textbooks and instruction manuals structure the curriculum and ensure that specific material is covered during the school year (Sunal, Osa, Gaba, & Saleemi, 1989). Without standardization of textbooks it is more difficult to ensure that specific material is covered.

Improving working conditions enables teachers and students to perform better. When students perform better, the teacher's motivation is reinforced, as is classroom practice (Lockheed, Vail, & Fuller, 1986). This is particularly important when teachers are not well trained and have few inservice programs available to them.

Instruction in sub-Saharan countries is often authoritarian and places students in a passive role where recall of information is the expected result of student learning. Observations of classes in Botswana found students listening to lectures for 54 percent of the observed instructional time and participating in oral recitation without discussion of material for 43 percent of the time (Fuller & Snyder, 1991). These are teaching strategies used in many traditional societies. They are strategies that teachers with limited training can utilize. They are also strategies that require little preparation time on the part of the teacher. Graham-Brown (1991, p. 40) reports an even more limited strategy. Teachers write a section of a textbook on the chalkboard and ask students to copy and memorize it when there is just one copy of a textbook available.

Overt classroom assessment has been rarely observed. Ali and

Akubue (1988) found continuous assessment techniques used 10 percent of the time in Nigerian primary classrooms, while in Botswana students took tests only 1 percent of the time (Fuller & Snyder, 1991). The lack of continuous assessment may be related to inherited European colonial traditions where assessment is focused on year-end exams, particularly at the secondary school and university levels. Continuous assessment does occur in traditional societies where learning is apprenticeship based. The trainer constantly evaluates the skills and knowledge of the trainee and sets new tasks that challenge the trainee to move to the next attainable level. Continuous assessment in a formal school setting requires the teacher to have a deep understanding of both content and pedagogy. Teachers with limited training do not have such deep understanding nor do they have enough training to enable them to comprehend the necessity for continuous training and readjustment of the curriculum and pedagogy to the needs of their students.

Student Factors

Instructional strategies and classroom conditions have a strong effect on children's learning. However, health and nutritional status and the home environment must be adequate if even the most effective instructional strategies are to be productive in terms of student learning. In Burkina Faso, 90 percent of primary school students have been reported to have parasites, and 29 percent suffer from chronic malnutrition. In Kenya, nearly 39 percent have an iodine deficiency, 25 percent suffer chronic malnutrition, and 35 percent have parasites. In Zaire, 55 percent suffer chronic malnutrition and 45 percent have parasites. In Zimbabwe, nearly 15 percent suffer chronic malnutrition and 63 percent have parasites (Graham-Brown, 1991).

Most children return from school to homes that are crowded. Extended families live in large compounds. In families with multiple wives, common throughout much of sub-Saharan Africa, each wife has her own dwelling and often her own cooking fire. These are both places around which her children gather. Often they play with their siblings and half-siblings in the compound. Many people live together and create the noise and activity found with groups that average twenty or more people. This setting does not lend itself to quiet study. Many children cannot find a private spot to study without interruption, nor a place where they can store school materials (Mazrui & Levine, 1986; O'Connor, 1983).

Children have chores to do and are likely to be involved in family enterprises. They may care for younger children in the compound, draw and haul water to the compound, weed fields, hawk peanut oil or snacks produced by their mother, or collect the sheep. All of these activities are essential to the economic survival of the family. Children's work is highly valued. However, it limits children's study time and the energy available for study (Graham-Brown, 1991; Ungar, 1986). When children also are malnourished or have parasites, studying is difficult and learning is less likely.

Financial Factors

The economic crisis experienced throughout sub-Saharan Africa has placed additional burdens on families and has resulted in a debate about financing of primary schools (Ozigi & Ocho, 1981). Prior to independence there were many private schools. Frequently these were founded by missionaries and churches. Well-funded public schools were few (Amucheazi, 1985; Taiwo, 1981). In many countries private schools were taken over by the independent nation. As this occurred these schools became subject to the same shortages of qualified teachers, books, and materials that were prevalent in the new public schools. Students and their parents documented a decline in the quality of education with the growth in public education. In the effort to advance universal primary education a debate ensued over quantity versus quality education. Those who experienced a decline in teacher quality and availability of teaching materials wished for a return to the days of private schools. Some parents who could afford private schooling for their children were particularly angry when private schools were not permitted. Arguments of elitism and mediocrity ensued.

Earlier, private schools, usually colonial, often taught a limited curriculum. Some subjects were emphasized and others not included. The breadth of national curricula after independence was not found in earlier colonial private schools. However, these schools were often free or low cost and the quality of education, while biased, was stronger than it appeared to be in many of the new public schools (Graham-Brown, 1991).

As public schools suffer from the weak economic situations in their country, parent–teacher associations are often formed to provide extras for schools. These associations might buy a map, books, or chalk, or build a classroom onto a school. Family-based funding has always been common in education throughout sub-Saharan Africa (Carnoy & Samoff, 1990). Many schools in recent years depend heavily on such funding for supporting the cost of everything other than teacher salaries. In some cases special teachers for the arts, a foreign language, or other areas are hired on a part-time basis through parent funding. Generally it is expected that families will pay for writing materials and textbooks. When uniforms are required, families pay for them. As the economic picture weakens, families pay for more and more of the costs of education both directly and through parent–teacher associations. Poor families are faced with tough choices when the limits of their finances are reached. The percentage of poor children who are not in school can be expected to grow.

Primary Education in Nigeria

As part of the movement toward universal primary education in sub-Saharan Africa, Nigeria began working toward a six-year level of basic primary education in 1976. While accepting the common purposes given for universal primary education, Nigeria also was responding to a felt need resulting from a civil war. The civil war had caused extensive destruction of life. Primary education was seen as a means of creating unity and a stable nation out of many ethnic groups who spoke different languages, practiced different religions, and came from widely divergent cultures. While most sub-Saharan nations have not endured a civil war since independence as Nigeria has, most contain a multiplicity of ethnic groups and are striving to create unity. Primary schooling in Nigeria was intended to reduce inequities in education while it fostered an understanding of and respect for the many cultures contained within the country. It was recognized that some Nigerian children were receiving an excellent primary education while many others were not. This and other imbalances had contributed to the civil war. Universal primary education could redress some of these imbalances (Adesina, 1982; Ozigi & Ocho, 1981). Most Nigerians endorsed a national commitment to universal primary education (Casapo, 1981, 1983).

Despite a large national commitment of personal and financial support, many problems occurred as primary education became available to large numbers of Nigerian children. Many millions of children received a primary education but it was often of low quality (Bray, 1981). Inspectors responsible for primary schools were surveyed a decade after the initiation of the effort to achieve universal primary education. They indicated that conditions in primary education were continuing to be such that quality education was difficult to obtain (Sunal et al., 1989).

Most research studies carried out in Nigeria used government statistics or focused on the reports of administrators. As has been true elsewhere in Africa, little data have been available from those who teach primary school students. A study carried out by Sunal and Sunal (1994) interviewed primary teachers and attempted to build a profile of the status of primary education as it was experienced and perceived by those who taught at that level.

Universal primary education (UPE) in Nigeria was designed to educate children aged 6 to 12. At the time it was instituted, those receiving a primary education tended to be male, urban, well-to-do, and residents of a southeastern or southwestern state in Nigeria. These education imbalances were thought to increase the stresses already experienced by a nation with over 200 ethnic groups speaking many languages and practicing Christianity, Islam, and traditional religions. It was thought that education could promote children's view of themselves as Nigerian citizens first and then as members of an ethnic group. It could also equalize opportunities, as citizens all received a basic level of education (Fafunwa, 1982; Ozigi & Ocho 1981).

Problems occurred as the UPE effort was initiated (Casapo, 1981, 1983; Urwick, 1983; Wilson, 1978). First, there was an initial large underestimation of enrollment. Second, there was a need for huge expenditures of money, much more than had been estimated because of the much higher than expected initial enrollment of students. Large amounts of money were spent. Education expenditures ranked first in state and second in federal budgets. Despite this large commitment, there was not enough money to finance the extensive needs of primary education. A third problem became evident over the first three years. This was a continuing lower percentage of enrollment of northern children. These children belonged to groups that had been underrepresented in primary education prior to the civil war.

The research studies relating to the early years of the UPE effort were followed by a study that described conditions in primary schools a decade into UPE as reported by 147 school inspectors (Sunal et al., 1989). Some positive change seemed to be occurring in Nigerian primary education, although many limitations were present. They noted that much progress had been made in the construction of facilities, training of teachers, and development of curricula. But it was almost impossible to meet the needs of a rapidly growing population. Crowding, resulting in some classes being taught outdoors; a great shortage of textbooks and basic teaching aids; the presence of many teachers who did not meet minimum qualifications; and a lack of basic amenities such as access to health care, resulting in difficult living conditions for many teachers, were among the limitations. Positive changes noted were: larger numbers of qualified teacher's-college graduates beginning careers by teaching in the primary schools, and continuing large portions of state and federal budgets being assigned to education. The findings suggested quality education was occurring in some settings, a cadre of trained teachers was developing, and the potential for quality mass primary education did exist. The view of these inspectors was one of cautious optimism.

Research studies examining the development of Nigeria's efforts to implement universal primary education during the first ten years of the program used federal and state education statistics and interviewed administrators, such as school inspectors. Classroom teachers were not given a voice in these studies. Those who are teaching can provide information that is central to the examination of conditions as they are encountered on a daily basis. First-hand information from primary school teachers reveals both positive and negative aspects that might not be evident in government statistics or administrators' reports. Teachers describe those conditions they know best, their own. Their perspective will be influenced by many factors. These include the events they identify as being of major importance in determining the direction of their teaching, the cultural background they bring with them, and their own expectations. While each teacher has his or her own biases, a random sample could overcome part of the problem resulting from personal biases.

The study was conducted in order to build a portrait describing the status of the Nigerian universal primary education effort during its second decade as experienced by a sample of classroom teachers. It identified those portions of the educational process in which quality education was continuing or evolving at the local level despite the stresses imposed by quantity education and limited financing. Several questions were considered: How adequate are primary classrooms? How adequate are supplies of teaching aids and materials? How adequate is the level of teacher training? What is occurring in terms of basic teaching practice? and How adequate are teaching salary and living conditions? The first four questions address areas that directly determine quality of education in practice. The fifth question addresses an area of indirect impact, teacher salary and living conditions.

Methodology

The study surveyed 149 primary school teachers in Nigeria and interviewed 65 percent (n = 96) of this group. More teachers were male (67 percent) than female (33 percent). The larger percentage of male teachers was a representative sample of Nigerian primary schools. There was a wide age range among the teachers in the sample, between sixteen and forty-nine, with an average age of twenty-seven. All parts of the nation were represented, but the group was somewhat skewed toward those who practiced Islam (60 percent). These teachers' parents had little or no education. Just 5 percent of their fathers and 2 percent of their mothers had had a six-year primary school education. The average teacher had taught for seven years and was responsible for a class that averaged thirty-four students. Slightly more than half (52 percent) taught in a village school. The rest taught in large towns and cities.

The Primary Education Survey (PES) was hand delivered and individually discussed with each teacher (Sunal et al., 1989). Versions of the instrument were available in Hausa, Arabic, English, Yoruba, and Ibo. The interviews were conducted by university faculty members and tape recorded. The PES contained eighty-six multiple choice and short answer questions related to the study's five research questions. The interviews encouraged teachers to discuss the five research questions in depth. The data collected were subjected to cross-tabular analysis.

Results

The results of the study were reported in five categories corresponding to the research questions: school facilities, teaching materials, teacher qualifications, teaching practice, and quality of the teacher's life.

School Facilities

The study surveyed primary school needs with regard to the provision of basic classroom facilities and furniture, since researchers have indicated these are not always available in sub-Saharan Africa and do have an effect on student learning. None of the teachers reported being without classroom facilities, but they felt crowded. Often students doubled or tripled up at a desk, which made taking notes difficult. There was little difference between teachers reporting on conditions in different parts of the nation. Most thought economic conditions would not improve and that there would be little effort to enlarge or improve existing schools. Some suggested that there is more graft to be made by officeholders when a new school is built and that these are often not built in locations where they relieve overcrowding at existing schools. Instead, they are built in locations where they will garner support for the officeholder from a new segment of the population. The new school may fulfill a need if an area has been unserved. But, it might serve few children, while an addition built on to an existing school in a heavily populated area would serve many more children.

Schools were often reported to be in poor condition because money was not allocated for maintenance. Also, schools were often built with materials that were not indigenous and were difficult and costly to maintain. Most teachers (96 percent) suggested that adaptations of indigenous design be used when modifications were made to schools or when new schools were built, because these would be easiest and cheapest to maintain. The teachers also mentioned that schools built with indigenous materials and designs did not look modern and so might not be considered of high status, but that this viewpoint could be overcome in time. The furnishings of schools, such as desks and chairs, were also often not maintained, so many were unusable. Again, they were frequently built of materials that were hard to maintain. Indigenous materials would be sturdier.

While schools were generally electrified, an inadequate national generating capacity meant that frequently there was no electricity available. So, students needed enough windows to have an adequate supply of light and air flow. Technology from the simple (an overhead projector) to the complex (a computer) could not easily be integrated into the curriculum, because much of the time the electricity was not available to operate such equipment. Widely fluctuating energy levels were hard on equipment, so that frequent repairs were needed. Often equipment was not repaired because spare parts were expensive and technicians were located far away.

Teaching Aids and Materials

Some teaching materials such as textbooks and chalk are considered basic to primary school education. Fewer than half (47 percent) of the teachers reported that their students had textbooks. Significantly more southeastern and southwestern teachers ($F = 6.69$, $p < .01$) reported their students as having textbooks than did northern teachers. Generally, textbooks were purchased by the student's family and represented what was available in bookstores at the time of purchase. As a result, students had different textbooks. Teachers viewed textbooks as a resource for an individual student, not as an integral part of the curriculum, because of their limited availability. Teachers did not always have a textbook in each area they taught. Most (75 percent) had a mathematics textbook, while fewer (37 percent) had a science textbook. A regional disparity was noted, with fewer northern teachers (69 percent) reporting having a mathematics textbook ($F = 6.23$, $p < .01$) in comparison to 80 percent of teachers in other areas.

The national syllabus for each content area was considered to be the curriculum and included: mathematics, science, social studies, religious knowledge (Christian or Islamic), language arts, arts and crafts, and physical education. The syllabus was supplemented in some states with sets of recommended objectives, activities, and instructional procedures. Most teachers (71 percent, $n = 104$) reported trying to follow the syllabus, but said they had problems resulting from a lack of textbooks and resource materials and their own inadequate knowledge of the content areas they taught.

Few materials were available to provide additional resources for teaching the curriculum. Teaching aids typically were purchased at the time the school was built and furnished. Only 5 percent of teachers reported the later purchase of teaching aids. Chalk was the most commonly available instructional aid, but only 69 percent reported having adequate supplies of it. When it was not available, teachers purchased it or took up collections from parents to buy it. In 21 percent of the schools many teaching aids were available because the schools had an active and affluent parent–teacher association. These schools were most likely to be in the northern part of the country ($F = 1.42$, $p < .05$).

Teacher Qualifications
The minimum qualification for primary school teachers has been the Grade II teacher's certificate. The certificate was awarded following the completion of the course of study in a teacher's college, a secondary school preparing primary school teachers. Since 1981 the federal government has worked toward having all primary school teachers obtain the National Certificate in Education (NCE) (Federal Government of Nigeria, 1981). The NCE is achieved by completing a two-year postsecondary program at an advanced teacher's college. Most of the teachers in the study (86 percent) had completed a Grade II teacher preparation program, a much higher percentage than had been reported in an earlier study (61 percent) by Sunal et al. (1989). The NCE was held by 9 percent. A few teachers (5 percent), all from the north, had certification at the Grade III level, representing a program no longer in existence which required only a junior secondary school level of training.

A large percentage (48 percent) of those teachers at the Grade II level had not passed their Grade II examinations. More (63 percent) were from the north than from other regions of the nation ($F = 5.43$, $p < .05$). They were identified as Grade II "failed" teachers in contrast to Grade II "passed" teachers. Grade II failed teachers were employed because of a shortage of fully qualified primary school teachers, but they were paid less than Grade II passed teachers. All of the teachers thought it would be a long time before all primary school teachers held the NCE, because the funding needed to accomplish the transition to the NCE for all teachers was not available and would not be available for a long time.

In recognition of the weak qualifications of many primary school teachers, the federal government established an inservice program (Federal Government of Nigeria, 1981). However, 42 percent of these teachers said they had never participated in an inservice. Those who had not participated in an inservice were often the first- and second-year teachers in the sample. A mean was found of one inservice experience every two years. Inservice programs are typically held in a central location within a state over a period of several days. Teachers' expenses are covered by the local education authority. In recent years, the local education authority has taken over education costs that were once covered by the federal government. As a result, less money is available for the support of inservice programs. Teachers reported crowded inservices with working groups that were too large, often twelve to eighteen people. All the teachers who had attended inservices reported a shortage of materials so that not everyone had access to them. As a result, some felt they would have difficulties carrying out activities or reproducing materials, since they did not have hands-on experience with them.

Classroom Instruction

Memorization and recitation were the instructional strategies most used (61 percent) in teaching. This is consistent with research on primary school instructional strategies reported elsewhere in Africa. In comparison, research studies from the United States indicate that lecture is used daily by 20 percent of primary school teachers, while discussion is used daily by 60 percent (Superka, Hawke, & Morrissett, 1981). Other types of strategies such as discussions were reported by small percentages of the teachers.

While homework was given every day or nearly every day by 57 percent of the teachers, 20 percent rarely or never gave homework. Fewer teachers in the north (44 percent) than in other parts of the country (72 percent) gave homework ($F = 10.01$, $p > .01$). One teacher who did not give homework said, "My students have other duties when they go to their house. They should not do homework when these other duties must be done." Another said, "At home, there is no place to study." A third said, "Most of my students' parents are illiterate. They do not understand what homework is. There will be no place to do homework and there will be nobody who can make sure the student is doing the homework as it should be done."

Homework typically involved memorization of material to be recited in class the following day.

Lesson plans were sometimes developed by 72 percent of the teachers, while 28 percent reported never planning for teaching. Teachers in the southeast and southwest (79 percent) reported planning significantly more frequently than did teachers in the north (68 percent) ($F = 3.99$, $p > .05$).

The primary school curriculum in Nigeria utilizes the major indigenous language in the local area as the medium of instruction. English is the medium of instruction at the secondary school level. These teachers favored the use of the indigenous local language in primary school instruction. They expressed concern for those students from minority groups with small representation in an area or with small representation nationally. These students were not instructed in their home language. Many small minority groups had few, if any, textbooks or other instructional materials written in their language.

Many teachers ($n = 73$) reported uncertainty about replacing English as the primary school language of instruction with indigenous languages. They resented the dominant position of English in the country because of its association with the colonial era. Nevertheless, they thought a high proficiency in speaking English gave a person many opportunities for advancement.

Teacher's Quality of Life

Most teachers walked to school (59 percent). Transportation for those who lived a distance from the school was a problem, one that often caused them to be late to school. With the long decline in oil revenues in the nation, spare parts for vehicles and tires have become much more costly. The price of new vehicles has risen quickly. As a result, the small, operator-owned vans that used to provide cheap transportation are far less available and dependable.

Most teachers (80 percent) thought their salary, about one-third that of secondary school teachers, was insufficient for their needs. So, most (96 percent) had a second job. They belonged to a union, but noted that the union had not been able to obtain salary increases sufficient to keep up with their needs, nor had the union tackled the problems of inadequate school facilities and materials.

They felt that as primary teachers their status was low. They also thought that the power was in the hands of the secondary teachers, and that fewer efforts would ever be made on their behalf. Yet, they supported the union because it was their best opportunity for having some voice in decisions concerning them.

When asked about basic amenities, many reported access to them. Slightly more than half (57 percent) lived in homes with access to electricity, although it was often not available due to national power sharing. Thirty percent of the survey respondents indicated they had access to piped water, generally the source of the cleanest water. Most frequently water was available by pipe, then by purchase, less often from wells, and least often directly from the river. Half (51 percent) thought health care was easily available to them. Hospital care (including outpatient care) was most often available. Pharmacies carried many drugs even in small towns. Differences were evident between the north and other parts of the country, with a higher level of care reported available to teachers in the north ($F = 3.13$, $p > .05$).

Conclusions and Implications

Serious problems continued to be found in Nigerian primary education during its second decade. However, fewer differences existed among various sections of the country. Where problems were noted in an area, they tended to be found in the north. A major continuing problem in the north was the greater numbers of underqualified teachers. These differences were expected, since there were considerably fewer teachers and schools in the north when the universal primary education (UPE) program was initiated.

While serious problems continued in primary schooling, positive change had occurred. Most importantly, a greater percentage of qualified teachers was indicated in all areas of the country than had been found in the Sunal et al. (1989) study describing the status of primary education at the end of the first decade of UPE. A reduced need for textbooks, teaching aids, and basic furniture was also reported. Some improvement had occurred in teachers' access to electricity, clean water, and health care, particularly in the north.

Although large amounts of money have been spent, there still are many needs to be met. Nigeria's rapidly growing population will continue to require the expansion of facilities, services, and the teaching force at a time when the global economy has seen years of declining oil revenues for heavily oil-dependent nations such as Nigeria.

Basic needs continued to exist in school facilities, furnishings, and teaching materials. Crowded and deteriorating facilities were common among the schools represented in this study. Teachers suggested improvements that could be made with minimal allocations of funding. Their focus was on inexpensive and easily maintained improvements, often incorporating the use of indigenous architectural design such as shutters rather than window glass. They were pessimistic about the ability and desire of officeholders and union officials to address problems of overcrowding and deterioration, the continuing shortage of textbooks and teaching aids, and low teacher salaries. They viewed themselves as having little power, being ordinary people in an occupation with minimal prestige. Their view of themselves resulted in their low expectations. All teachers, but particularly those with minimal qualifications, need the additional support provided by teaching materials. However, support materials, including textbooks, are not available to all students and teachers in Nigeria's primary schools.

Teachers need a means for identifying professional problems whether they relate to curriculum, facilities, teaching materials, enrollment, or any other concern at their school site. They also need a means for offering suggestions for the amelioration of problems to local education-authority administrators. Primary school management boards have been initiated in many states. These boards oversee and set policy for primary schools. Because of their role, board members are likely to have greater contact with primary-grade teachers and schools. If communication between teachers and board members can be fostered, teachers may have a greater voice in the decisions made and may develop enhanced status. The inclusion of some teachers on these boards would increase the likelihood that the needs and concerns of primary teachers and their students are addressed. This would also increase the likelihood that a higher quality of education might be delivered to children. However, the relatively low status and level of qualifications of primary school teachers makes it unlikely that a teacher presence on such a board would be welcomed. Teachers' unions have not advocated for such a presence.

Underqualified teachers affect all aspects of Nigerian primary education. They also limit possible solutions to the problems of primary education. A larger number of Grade II qualified teachers were reported in comparison to earlier reports. With better-qualified teachers, more solutions to existing problems can be tried and a higher quality of education becomes possible.

Falling birth rates may eventually occur and stabilize the need for new teachers. Many countries, such as Nigeria, offer short-term solutions by paying most or all the costs of training for teachers. This has been a successful strategy, as is evident from the reported increasing size of the cadre of qualified primary school teachers. Higher salaries have not been implemented as a strategy for attracting prospective teachers. Nor have there been efforts to increase the prestige of primary school teaching. Continuing problems with low salaries and low prestige make primary school teaching unattractive. Nigeria has made relatively quick progress in establishing a teaching force because of its relative wealth. Nevertheless, it has been necessary to wait out the time needed to train teachers. Other sub-Saharan African nations do not have Nigeria's wealth and must work with reduced expectations and the much longer time frame induced by having less money available.

Inservicing is a route followed in many countries to help teachers advance their knowledge (Choy, Bobbitt, Henke, Medrich, Horn, & Lieberman, 1993, p. 52). In nations with large numbers of underqualified teachers, inservicing offers an opportunity to upgrade limited skills. In Nigeria inservicing appears to be minimally functional. The frequency of inservicing has increased and suggests that even a less than optimal inservice experience can have some positive effects. Because of its greater expense, it is unlikely that efforts to upgrade a large number of primary teachers through the NCE certificate will be completed soon.

An effective inservice program offers a means of upgrading a teaching staff. It is a money-saving alternative to making it possible for all primary teachers to obtain the NCE. Nigeria is a lower-middle-income nation with many resources, but it has been unable to develop and implement a well-coordinated inservice program. The continuing need to provide initial training for new teachers, to build additional school facilities, and to develop curricula has meant that inservice training is not a first priority. Low-income sub-Saharan nations with fewer resources will find it even more difficult to develop and initiate effective inservice programs.

Teachers' quality of life has improved in some areas and declined in others. Federal efforts to provide services such as hospital care and electricity have reached many teachers. Such services have had a direct impact on teachers' lives. Economic stresses resulting from the nation's heavy dependence on oil production have eroded the quality of teachers' lives in many ways. Their salaries have not kept up with the costs of living. To provide for their family's needs, Nigerian primary school teachers often have a second and even a third job. Teachers in other nations, including the United States, have also taken on second jobs when salaries are low (Choy et al., 1993, pp. 42–44). The lack of time and the fatigue incurred by these extra jobs means that teachers cannot devote adequate time to preparation for instruction. This study found limited planning and the heavy use of easily implemented instructional strategies such as memorization and recitation. Inservicing and an NCE may have a reduced impact on the quality of teaching if teachers don't have adequate preparation time.

The low amounts of planning and emphasis on memorization and recitation may also be due to a lack of skill. Underqualified teachers often do not have the skills necessary to use other, more creative teaching strategies (Stallings & Stipek, 1989). The use of memorization and recitation as a teaching strategy also reflects tradition, particularly in areas with a strong oral storytelling heritage. Finally, another influence supporting this strategy is the limited availability of textbooks and teaching aids. With limited availability of materials teachers, particularly those who are underqualified, are likely to resort to memorization and recitation. Utilizing other strategies requires skill and the commitment of large amounts of time for planning and developing resource materials.

Most teachers in this study were the first generation in their families to obtain a formal education. Because primary school teaching has not required extensive formal education, it has offered individuals an occupation with some prestige and a modest but relatively secure salary. These are characteristics that have attracted individuals to primary school teaching in other countries as well. It has often been a first step in families to which formal schooling is new. Because it is often a first step, teachers may treat it as an entry-level position that is easily left when a more lucrative or higher-status opportunity presents itself. In sub-Saharan Africa, better-qualified teachers move into secondary school teaching when possible or into another occupation. Because secondary schools throughout sub-Saharan Africa have not been built at anywhere near the rate of primary schools, such teaching positions are fewer. Slow economic growth has limited other occupational opportunities. As a result, primary schools in Nigeria have held on to some better-qualified teachers, but these may be holding down another job as well. Higher prestige and/or higher salaries might keep better-qualified teachers in primary schooling. Perhaps sub-Saharan nations will be able to find a way to provide one or both of these to their primary school teachers.

Primary Education in Sub-Saharan Africa: The Future

A major international goal, the provision of a basic primary school education to all children in sub-Saharan Africa, will not have been met as the twenty-first century begins. Another prominent goal, the eradication of illiteracy, will also be unmet. The achievement of these goals is closely linked. As long as sub-Saharan Africa cannot enroll all its children in primary school, the ranks of the illiterate will grow as the population grows. The social and economic health of individuals and nations will be limited by the continuing lack of schooling among large segments of the population. Economic development today and in the foreseeable future is dependent on the ability of a nation to increase its agricultural and industrial production. Both of these are linked to technology. New technologies in agriculture may have a low level of sophistication. Perhaps a new type of hand-driven water pump is what is best for local irrigation of crops. Those who design such a pump, identify cheap materials for its construction, and find ways to easily repair it will need a degree in engineering. Others will have to analyze the existing situation and brainstorm possible solutions to the problems that are found. Still others will have to train farmers in the use and repair of the technology. The successful introduction of a simple new technology requires the existence of several individuals with high levels of education and experience.

A workforce with primary schooling is important if new technologies are introduced in order to expand agricultural and industrial production. Primary schools need to help students develop skills beyond rote memorization and recitation. Workers need a higher level of skills if they are to effectively use new technologies. Convergent instructional strategies such as memorization and recitation hamper the development of critical thinking, reflective thinking, problem solving, and decision making. Underqualified teachers train students in strategies that do not focus on the application and synthesis of knowledge (Chi, Glaser, & Farr, 1988). These are overall thinking skills necessary in citizens whose nation is competitive in the larger global society (Bricker, 1989; Copa, Hultgren, & Wilkosz, 1991; O'Reilly, 1991). International competitiveness requires flexibility. It needs workers who can be retrained, can handle abstract complex tasks, and can cope well with change. It has been predicted that sub-Saharan Africa will see less economic growth in the near future than will other parts of the world. Without an effective cadre of workers, quick economic growth cannot occur. Without economic growth, it will be impossible to fund the training of teachers and the development of materials that foster the growth of overall thinking abilities in students. A dilemma exists and it is a grave challenge to Nigeria and to other sub-Saharan African nations.

Nigeria is one of the wealthiest African nations, yet it has not achieved universal primary education despite intensive efforts to accomplish this goal. African nations generally share Nigeria's problems in providing facilities, well-trained teachers, and curricula appropriate for the nation. However, few African nations have the wealth and resources possessed by Nigeria. So, there is little likelihood of a continuing expansion of educational opportunities or an increase in the quality of education delivered.

Despite the gloomy economic forecast for sub-Saharan Africa and the limitations that will be imposed by it on educational development, much thought has gone into a consideration of what might be done with what is available (Graham-Brown, 1991; Lockheed & Verspoor, 1991). A major effort should be aimed at the improvement of the quality of education for those children in school. Inservicing of teachers is probably the most cost-effective means of

accomplishing this goal. This can be accomplished either by bringing teachers to a regional meeting, as is currently done in Nigeria, or
by taking short two- to three-day workshops out to individual schools.
Regional meetings are costly in terms of providing for the transportation, housing, and maintenance of teachers while they are at the
meeting. Inservices conducted in primary schools would be cheaper
in most cases, although more trainers and vehicles for their transportation would be needed.

Inservice workshops held at the local level should result in smaller
working groups. These would enable teachers to participate directly
in the workshop's activities. Enough money should also be available
to insure that each teacher has the materials with which to work.
There should be an emphasis on demonstrating and practicing instructional strategies that go beyond memorization and recitation.
Cookbook directions on a specific topic or set of topics in the curriculum are needed by teachers with minimal qualifications. When
combined with cheap, easily replaced materials, even those teachers
with minimal qualifications are able to follow through. There have
been a number of curriculum projects in areas such as science and
mathematics education that have developed cheap instructional
materials for use in developing nations. These resources should be
used as inservice curricula are developed.

Teachers do need to be warned that students may find a transition to more active learning difficult. They should not give up when
this is the case. Both teachers and students cannot be expected to
move from a memorization-recitation–oriented program into a
hands-on, minds-on curriculum for a short period of time, and then
return to the memorization-recitation–oriented program. Therefore,
teacher trainers should not expect great change. The inservice workshop is likely to be most effective if it focuses on a specific topic or a
limited set of topics. A workshop cannot deal with an entire syllabus
in the short time it has available. The inservice should be directed at
small increments of change that can be accomplished. If teachers
remain in primary school teaching for several years and are inserviced
yearly, they will gradually add more and more pieces of higher quality teaching to their program.

Because of the attrition that occurs within the ranks of primary
school teachers, new inservice workshops should not build upon

previous workshops. They will need to be self-standing modules. Each will have to review the basic instructional principles that are deemed critical to the program. Over the long term, as teachers receive good training at both the preservice and inservice levels, a cadre of better-qualified teachers can be built and less review will be necessary during inservice workshops.

In most low-income nations the reallocation of education funds for inservicing will require very tough decisions. It will mean, among other things, that teachers are not given raises, or that buildings are not built, or that fewer materials are available. These tradeoffs are not easy to make. Each choice has a strong negative impact on primary schooling. But, nevertheless, the choices will have to be made.

Distance education is an alternative means of providing inservicing for teachers. In Africa distance education projects have been successful when applied to teacher education (Bray, Clarke & Stephens, 1986; Lockheed & Verspoor, 1991). Both correspondence courses using the postal service and radio and television courses have been used. Distance education courses require self-motivated individuals who can structure their time consistently and set and meet goals. When a certificate is given for completion of a distance education course, and when this certificate results in an increase in salary, it is most likely that African primary school teachers will become involved in distance education. Like other inservicing, it appears that distance education is most effective when it is used to achieve a limited, short-term objective (Bray et al., 1986). A benefit of distance education for primary teachers is that they are able immediately to apply new ideas and strategies in their own classrooms (Lockheed & Verspoor, 1991). The opportunity for immediate implementation provides the practice needed for new ideas and strategies to become part of the teacher's professional repertoire. Distance education varies in costs (Taylor, 1983). Greenland (1983) has estimated a cost of approximately one-third that of residential education. No cost comparisons have been found between regional or on-site inservicing and distance education. Distance education requires a large initial outlay of money to purchase equipment and materials, to design curricula and train trainers, and to advertise the availability of the program. To make it cost effective, distance education must inservice large numbers of teachers. It is important to involve individuals with primary school teaching experience in the development and administration of both distance education and other forms of inservice programs. Experience enables the planner, trainer, and administrator to develop and implement a program that addresses needs with materials and curricula that are practical and easily used. Neither distance education nor on-site inservicing can replace high-quality teacher education institutions. But, with the economic constraints faced by sub-Saharan nations, and with the need to increase the quality of teaching in primary schools, inservicing is a feasible option.

The identification of mentor teachers who present preservice teachers with good models should be an important part of any program to upgrade or initially train primary school teachers. Mentor teachers can provide training for selected groups of primary school teachers who exhibit initiative and interest in upgrading these schools. These teachers can be sent to the classroom of the mentor teacher for a short apprenticeship, perhaps one week to one month in duration. Upon returning to their own school, the mentees can begin to adapt the strategies used by the mentor to their own situation. Successful teachers can be used as mentors for other local teachers. If each mentor trains ten teachers, and each of these teachers trains ten more teachers, a training pyramid has been established. More and more local trainers can be developed. These teachers can also serve as cooperating teachers working with preservice teachers. The identification and development of a cadre of effective mentor teachers is a relatively inexpensive option for inservicing. It is also an effective means of initially training higher quality teachers.

Once preservice and inservice teachers have had an opportunity to work with an effective mentor, a system should be established to maintain contact between mentors and those they have mentored. An annual visit by the mentor to the classrooms of the mentees is one option. A regional two- or three-day meeting at which new ideas and strategies are presented to all is another option. Such a system can be less expensive than one that brings teachers back to residential schooling. It can be combined with distance education or other forms of inservicing as well. It is likely to be a cost-effective means of upgrading the quality of primary schools because it also works with preservice teachers and provides opportunities for long-term communication between teachers that focuses on increasing the quality of primary schooling.

It will be important to protect the mentoring program from political influences. It will also be important to put in place criteria that initially identify appropriate mentor teachers. Regular evaluation of mentor teachers, perhaps on a three-year cycle, should also take place. Some teachers may not be able to keep up with the demands of mentoring. Others may tire of the role and need a few years off. Some may have initially been misidentified and may not be the effective models needed. The mentoring role should be established as a temporary position, which is regularly evaluated and either re-awarded or withdrawn, and from which the teacher may withdraw as he or she wishes. It will be important to consider the local culture and its ability to understand and support the mentorship role as one that is temporary, subject to evaluation, and resistant to political influences.

The best evaluators for teacher mentors may be exemplary primary school teachers. This is not a job to be given to a university graduate who has been unable to find other employment. These individuals would have to receive advanced training to prepare them for their role, particularly in staff development. They would also need support in terms of transportation, maintenance while traveling, and continuous further training.

The effective management and administration of a program whose goal is the increase of quality in primary education is difficult. Many sub-Saharan African countries lack a pool of skilled administrators who have substantial relevant primary school teaching experience. Those individuals with advanced training often move directly into secondary school teaching, into teaching positions at teachers' colleges, or into public school administration. They are likely to have minimal primary school classroom teaching experience. Administrative positions may be influenced by politics. The administrator may not be the best person available, but rather the individual with the best political connections. School administration can be a political prize, because money from school construction and other contracts can be skimmed off as graft. In such situations, effective educational management is unlikely. Without such management, adequate inservicing and preservice training are difficult to implement. The government that is willing to commit a large percentage of its budget, as many sub-Saharan nations have, needs to make sure those scarce funds are well spent. Lockheed and Verspoor (1991) recommend systematic staff development programs for managers, clear career paths with opportunities and incentives, and the establishment of systems of assessing managerial performance. A competent and effective public school administration has proven difficult to achieve in developed nations. African nations, beset by problems in all areas and faltering economies, will find it extremely difficult to develop and preserve effective school administrations. Yet, without them effective primary school education programs cannot exist.

The creation of an administrative board focused on the improvement and oversight of primary schools could be an effective means of increasing the quality of primary education. Nigeria has experimented with primary school management boards. A similar model might be used. The administrative board should aim at developing an effective, lean, cost-efficient administrative structure for primary schools.

Teachers and parents should be a part of such a board. Parent representatives must include those who are from rural areas, crowded low-income urban neighborhoods, and other typically low-status and underserved elements of the population. The problem of enrolling underserved and underrepresented portions of the population is best addressed by those who are a part of these groups. Representation by those who have a big immediate stake in the improvement of primary education, parents and teachers, should bring accountability to the actions of a primary school administrative board. Issues in curriculum, facilities development and improvement, materials, teachers' salaries, and costs borne by parents must be addressed by the board.

Real administrative power requires financial and political support. An effective board will have financial control. It will also have incentives for cost-effective practice. The national government will need to structure local boards who have financial power. The size of the region for which the local board has responsibility will have to be determined by each nation and should be dependent on local conditions, particularly population density and distances. Local problems can be addressed only with strong representation of those who live and work in the region. To facilitate effective administration, oversight would be needed by the appropriate national government officials, but care must be taken to eliminate politically driven decisions. The bulk of the decision-making power and finances must be in the hands of the local primary school administrative board.

There are many possibilities for the improvement of primary education in sub-Saharan Africa. The most effective strategies will be locally generated. While advisers from developed nations, international organizations, and other African nations may be helpful in a particular country, only those individuals who live in the nation will completely understand the potentialities and problems associated with any strategy. The unique problems of sub-Saharan Africa require unique, locally based solutions. Tradeoffs will have to be made. However, the goal should always be to provide universal primary education of high quality. With this goal in mind, tradeoffs can be made that work toward the goal and do not become mired in the status quo or in a feeling of hopelessness when considering all of the problems a particular trade-off represents. The nations of sub-Saharan Africa have made great efforts to provide quality primary education to all their children. This goal is yet to be achieved, but progress toward it has been made.

References

Adesina, S. (Ed.) (1982). *Planning and educational development in Nigeria.* Lagos, Nigeria: Board Publications, Ltd.

Ali, A., & Akubue, A. (1988). Nigerian primary schools' compliance with Nigeria's national policy on education: An evaluation of continuous assessment practices. *Evaluation Review, 35*(2), 625–637.

Amucheazi, E.C. (1985). *Readings in social sciences: Issues in national development.* Enugu, Nigeria: Fourth Dimension Publishing Co., Ltd.

Bray, M. (1981). *Universal primary education: A study of Kano state.* London: Routledge and Kegan Paul.

Bray, M., Clarke, P., & Stephens, D. (1986). *Education and society in Africa.* London: Edward Arnold, Ltd.

Bricker, D. (1989). *Classroom life as civic education: Individual achievement and student cooperation in schools.* New York: Teachers College Press.

Carnoy, M., & Samoff, J. (Eds.). (1990). *Education and social transition in the third world.* Princeton, NJ: Princeton University Press.

Casapo, M. (1981). Religious, social and economic factors hindering the education of girls in northern Nigeria. *Comparative Education, 17,* 311–319.

Casapo, M. (1983). Universal primary education in Nigeria: Its problems and implications. *African Studies Review, 26*(1), 91–106.

Chi, M., Bassok, M., & Lewis, M. (1988). *The nature of expertise.* Hillsdale, NJ: Erlbaum.

Chi, M., Glaser, R., & Farr, M. (1988). *The nature cf expertise.* Hillsdale, NJ: Erlbaum Associates.

Choy, S., Bobbitt, S., Henke, R., Medrich, E., Horn, L., & Lieberman, J. (1993). *America's teachers: Profile of a profession.* Washington, DC: U.S. Department of Education.

Christensen, P. (1990). *Educational radio: A conceptual framework.* Paper presented at the African Conference on Radio Education, Harare, Zimbabwe.

Clegg, A. (1991). Games and simulations in social studies education. In J. Shaver (Ed.), *Handbook of Research on Social Studies Teaching and Learning* (pp. 523–529). New York: Macmillan.

Coombs, P., Prosser, R., & Ahmed, M. (1973). *New paths to learning for rural children and youth.* New York: United Nations Children's Fund, International Council for Educational Development.

Copa, P., Hultgren, F., & Wilkosz, J. (1991). Critical thinking as a lived activity. In A. Costa (Ed.), *Developing minds* (pp. 188–192). Alexandria, VA: Association for Supervision and Curriculum Development.

Cornia, G., Jolly, R., & Stewart, F. (Eds.). (1987–1988). *Adjustment with a human face* (Vols. 1–2). Oxford: Clarendon Press.

Doyle, W. (1992). Curriculum and pedagogy. In P. Jackson (Ed.), *Handbook of research on curriculum* (pp. 486–516). New York: Macmillan.

Fafunwa, A. (1982). *History of education in Nigeria.* London: George Allen & Unwin.

Federal Government of Nigeria. (1981). *National policy on education.* Lagos, Nigeria: Federal Government, Ministry of Education.

Fillmore, L., & Meyer, L. (1992). The curriculum and linguistic minorities. In P. Jackson (Ed.), *Handbook of research on curriculum* (pp. 626–658). New York: Macmillan.

Fuller, B., & Snyder, C. (1991). Vocal teachers, silent pupils? Life in a Botswana classroom. *Comparative Education Review, 35*(2), 274–294.

Gajraj, S., & Schoemann, K. (1991, March). *Primary education: The excluded: Statistical issues.* (ERIC Document Reproduction Service No. ED 343 711) Paris: UNESCO.

Graham-Brown, S. (1991). *Education in the developing world: Conflict and crisis.* New York: Longman.

Greenland, J. (Ed.). (1983). *In-service training of primary teachers in Africa.* London: Macmillan.

IDS. (1989). Adjusting education to economic crisis. *IDS Bulletin, 20*(1), 1–32.

Lassibille, G., & Gomez, M. (1990). Forecasts of primary-education expenditure in developing countries in the year 2000. *Prospects: Quarterly Review of Education, 20*(4), 513.

Lebby, S., & Lutz, J. (1982). Education and productive work: The Bunumbu approach. *Prospects: Quarterly Review of Education, 12*(4), 485–493.

Lockheed, M.E., Vail, M., & Fuller, W. (1986). *Primary education in developing countries.* Washington, DC: World Bank.

Lockheed, M.E., & Verspoor, A.M. (1991). *Improving primary education in developing countries.* New York: Oxford University Press.

Mazrui, A., & Levine, T. (Eds.). (1986). *The Africans: A reader.* New York: Praeger.

Mwamwanda, T., & Mwamwanda, B. (1987). School facilities and pupils' academic achievement. *Comparative Education, 23*(2), 225–235.

O'Connor, A. (1983). *The African city.* New York: Africana Publishing Co.

O'Reilly, K. (1991). Infusing critical thinking into United States history courses. In A. Costa (Ed.), *Developing minds* (pp. 188–192). Alexandria, VA: Association for Supervision and Curriculum Development.

Orivel, F., & Perrot, P. (1988). *Mobilization and management of financial resources for education.* Paris: UNESCO.

Ozigi, A., & Ocho, L. (1981). *Education in northern Nigeria.* Winchester, MA: George Allen & Unwin.

Sierra Leone. (1974). *Sierra Leone government national development plan 1974* (p. vii). Freetown, Sierra Leone: Government of Sierra Leone.

Stallings, J., & Stipek, D. (1989). Research on early childhood and elementary school teaching programs. In J. Wittrock (Ed.), *Handbook of research on teaching* (3rd edition, pp. 727–753). New York: Macmillan.

Sunal, C.S., Osa, O., Gaba, B., & Saleemi, A. (1989). Status of primary education in Nigeria following the initiation period of universal primary education. *Journal of research in childhood education, 4*(1), 30–39.

Sunal, C.S., & Sunal, D.W. (1994, December). Primary schooling today with implications for tomorrow: A case study from Nigeria. *African Studies Review, 37*(3), 1–27.

Superka, D., Hawke, S., & Morrissett, I. (1981). The current and future status of the social studies. *Social Education, 44*(5), 362–369.

Taiwo, C. (1981). *The Nigerian education system: Past, present and future.* Lagos, Nigeria: Nelson.

Taylor, D.C. (1983). The cost-effectiveness of teacher upgrading by distance teaching in southern Africa. *International Journal of Educational Development, 3*(1), 14–28.

UNESCO. (1961). *Statistical Yearbook.* Paris: Author.

UNESCO. (1986). *Statistical Yearbook.* Paris: Author.

UNESCO. (1987). *Statistical Yearbook.* Paris: Author.

Ungar, S. (1986). *Africa: The people and politics of an emerging continent.* New York: Simon & Schuster.

Urwick, J. (1983). Politics and professionalism in Nigerian education planning. *Comparative Education Review, 27*(10), 323–241.

Wilson, D. (1978). Universal primary education, Nigeria: An appraisal of plan implementation. *Canadian and International Education, 7*(12), 28–52.

Zymelman, M., & De Stefano, J. (1989). *Primary school teachers' salaries in sub-Saharan Africa.* (World Bank Discussion Paper No. 45). Washington, DC: World Bank.

Chapter Two
Issues for Higher Education in Sub-Saharan Africa

Dennis W. Sunal and Mary E. Haas

National benefits from higher education are twofold: the creation of governmental, economic, and social leaders and problem solvers; and service as a unifying force within the nation. Higher education contributes to economic growth by providing knowledge and training that increases productivity in both human and capital resources. Education and research develop knowledge that increases the ability to locate, extract, and process natural resources. Because these increase the availability of products and the demand for workers, more people find employment and have the potential for purchasing goods and services and creating new goods and services for consumers. The availability of additional goods and services helps to stimulate social development throughout all levels of society.

Higher education is a capital investment for a nation. It represents the largest single-budget item in African national economies. States and nations willingly contribute to the education of citizens, with most developing nations devoting large proportions of budgets to education.

Education acts as an agent of unification by establishing common languages and values and through training civil servants and employees to provide governmental services. In the increasingly interconnected world of today, all nations need leaders for the diplomatic and business communities who can communicate with representatives from other nations. Such leaders use skills and knowledge largely acquired through higher education. Individuals and corporations, as well as governments, benefit in similar ways from education, especially from higher education. While numbers in the highest leadership positions remain relatively small, there is a large increase in middle-level positions requiring a seemingly ever-increasing number of specific skills. Providing enough workers with this growing set of skills requires graduates of higher education and specialized schools. New schools requiring regular updating of technological equipment are costly endeavors. Yet, higher education is of prime importance to Africa's future in providing educated people and quality research on which to base policies and programs to enact the social and economic changes needed for the future. The Organization of African Unity affirmed this need in policy statements issued in 1981, 1985, and 1986 (The World Bank, 1988).

Today, global change through transfer of ideas occurs as cultural elements move from one country to another. The rate is highest in developing nations. In Africa, the pace is even greater, after thirty-five years of underdevelopment has created discontent with the current educational institutions. Sub-Saharan African nations find their existing higher education facilities and staffs unable to change curriculum and resources at the rate events require. This results in graduating students who are not finding positions that adequately use their skills. Yet, the desire and need for higher education is present among the young people who are crowding into the few classrooms. The focus of this chapter is on the concerns and issues in: (1) the search for models of higher education that will facilitate development and quality of life in sub-Saharan Africa, and (2) the future of African development through education.

Sub-Saharan Africa is large, diverse, and complex. It is not the intention of this chapter to document this diversity. Instead, specific cases will be used to underline the status of higher education and its complexity in specific regions of sub-Saharan Africa. In this discussion and analysis regional and country examples will be cited, but Nigeria, the African nation with the largest population and one of the most complex systems of higher education, will be used as a case study to illustrate potentials, problems, solutions, and consequences. Nigeria was one of the first major anglophone African nations to respond to local forces and needs in creating changes in its higher education system. Similar problems and concerns may also apply to other regions and nations in sub-Saharan Africa. However, the reader should be cautious in generalizing to other regions where special additional issues such as historical apartheid may supersede the issues examined here.

History and Status of Sub-Saharan African Higher Education

Higher education in sub-Saharan Africa today reflects its history. That history has impacted the rationale and role for higher education, curriculum, teaching, financing, staffing, and students. The motivation and strategies for starting and changing higher education institutions came from external forces. Global politics, colonialism, the struggle for independence, attempts at implementing unified central governments in multiethnic nations, and attempts at diversifying economies all affected African higher education. Today's problems reflect the results of various changes enacted to solve the problems of the past half century as well as newly developing problems.

In approaching independence sub-Saharan African nations adopted models for higher education similar to those of the colonial powers. In 1948 both Uganda and Nigeria established universities (University of Makerere and University College, Ibadan) as colleges of the University of London. The courses of study and examinations were to be approved by the University of London. Degrees were conferred by the University of London. The predominant model for higher education throughout anglophone Africa was a research university granting undergraduate degrees with majors in one of the liberal arts. Technological training, when provided, was at separate technological universities. The great need for teachers was often filled by special schools rather than universities. Ties with the traditions of former colonial rulers remained strong, but external political and economic forces, the unique needs of African lifestyles and values, and increasingly diversified societies led higher education to "Africanize" its focus and to consider uniquely African and local issues.

In Nigeria higher education assumed the important role of training future leaders and an assisting role in helping government extend literacy to key adults in society. In its early years higher education was largely isolated from African interests and tended to provide a route to employment within the government. University students and graduates were a new elite. While African, their scholarship directed their thinking away from Africa and into the theoretical ideas of their academic disciplines, which were dominated by developed-Western-world thinking. In theory, higher education in Africa should provide scientific knowledge and training to assist the government with internal development projects and training, particularly in agriculture and health care. In practice, the research was often a detached scholarly analysis not directly applicable to the problems and goals of the nation. Research requirements and rewards failed to encourage research of benefit to African planning and goals (Aminu, 1986).

Sub-Saharan African governments built and staffed universities, creating small communities with all services provided for staff and students (Hughes & Mwiria, 1990). Campuses included classrooms, laboratories, grounds, student and faculty housing, and municipal services such as power, water, and sanitation. As qualified students came from throughout the nation, governments also provided students with full academic services, social services, and living expenses.

Student admission was usually through the examination system, taking place at the end of secondary school, and was modeled after the colonial European system. For some others, graduation from secondary school was the requirement, with early examinations providing the selection factor for entry into the secondary school. The quality of university graduates was controlled through the use of a yearly examination system allowing passage to the next level, rather than through a continuous assessment scheme.

Universities, originally staffed with a few nationals and many expatriates, provided salaries, services, and living quarters for academic staff. Originally, universities awarded only the undergraduate degree. In an effort to include more nationals as lecturers, degree programs at the master's and doctoral levels were established, with full scholarships for the most promising bachelor's graduates enabling them to attend universities in developed nations. As more nationals received advanced degrees and returned home, graduate degrees were more often received at in-country institutions. Over time the availability of student openings in higher education in sub-Saharan Africa has increased. In 1960 one in 168,000 inhabitants graduated from a tertiary institution, but by 1983 the ratio improved to one in 5,800 inhabitants (World Bank, 1988, p.70).

Since the 1970s national and world economic problems have negatively impacted higher education everywhere, but especially among developing nations. Recently, African nations have shifted national economic priorities to balance growing trade deficits. Droughts and other natural disasters have severely damaged many African economies. Meanwhile, some African nations increased military budgets to deal with insurrections and ethnic unrest. Inflation has taken a toll on salaries, maintenance, and development. African civil servants, university faculties, and students all feel inflation's impact. In 1992 the real values of salaries for Nigerian university employees declined to only 10 percent of their 1978 value. In 1990 Ugandan lecturers received the equivalent salary of $19 U.S. per month. Throughout sub-Saharan Africa the average expenditure per university student declined during the 1980s from $6,300 to $1,500 U.S. in real terms (World Bank, 1994, p.17). Faculty members have responded by finding employment in other fields and treating their university positions as part-time employment, by seeking employment in other nations, and by striking for higher wages and benefits (Olashi & Hengst, 1988). Expatriate staff responded by leaving, and graduate students studying abroad have not returned to Africa to work.

Higher education which, since independence, often has received one of the government's greatest budgetary allotments is under great stress at a time when more and more students are seeking admission (Hughes & Mwiria, 1990). In some nations enrollments are being maintained at previous levels, but in many nations enrollments are being greatly increased. The large increases place a strain on the physical facilities, supplies, and remaining staff. Libraries are not being maintained and laboratories are overused or without necessary supplies and equipment. Where university students are coming in increased numbers, it is not uncommon for only a few textbooks to be available and for students to be limited in the amount of time they can use books in the library. As an example, at the University of Dakar the planned capacity of 3,500 was overextended in 1991 to nearly 20,000 students. The first budget items to be cut drastically at universities under stress are academic services such as the hours libraries are open and the numbers of books and periodicals purchased. Thus, budget cuts immediately impact quality of education. Learning becomes even more focused on rote memory from lectures provided to overly large classes. Emphasis on higher-level thinking skills and the ability to use and generate knowledge declines (World Bank, 1994).

Commonly, long-term plans for educational and capital improvements are being eroded to meet immediate operating expenses (Hughes & Mwiria, 1990). In Africa an average of less than 2 percent of total recurrent public funding is available for maintenance of university building and grounds maintenance and supplies. Replacement of faculty who leave with faculty of a similar level of expertise is a significant problem and a major limitation to the quality of higher education (World Bank, 1988, p. 24). The professional output of scholarship is also being impacted in most areas and is particularly evident in the scientific, medical, and technical areas, where technology is required during teaching and research. Science is being taught without demonstrations or students' experimentation. Equipment in technological fields is often more than thirty years old and not in working condition. The World Bank reports that declines in the number of scientific publications in national and international journals took place in Ghana, Uganda, Ethiopia, and the Sudan between 1977 and 1987 (1994, p. 22).

For all of its problems, higher education in Africa has provided nations with educated government employees, staffed the professions, and produced many teachers. In fact, one of the more recent problems is the inability of students to find jobs upon graduation from the university. Universities need to begin preparing students to create and fill new jobs to match the needs of their changing economies and societies. Yet, in most African countries, and particularly in francophone Africa, graduates seeking white-collar positions greatly outnumber the jobs available each year (World Bank, 1994).

During the 1970s and 1980s university students used political activism to protest against deteriorating conditions in universities. Complaints ranged from protests over the quality of food being served to the loss of benefits and the institution of cost-sharing fees. Often their protests turned political, addressing concerns of other groups such as civil servants and workers. Ethnic issues and movements toward more representative democracy were also the focus of student protests. Student activism prompted the closing of the universities, mass reapplication for admittance, arrest of leaders, and confrontations with the military, which in several instances resulted in student deaths. Student behaviors ceased to be peaceful as vandalism, destruction of physical property, and loss of life resulted. Protest by students is not a new phenomenon; indeed, many of the student leaders became some of Africa's early political leaders, and in recent years student protests have played a role in attacks on governments' domestic and foreign policies, as well as education policies. As one of the few organized groups in nations where organized opposition is being removed, protests today are concerns of both the faculty and the government (Nkinyangi, 1991). Closings of universities and damage to facilities reduce quality of higher education; threats of larger social protests can threaten the continuation of governments.

Major Problems

Money and the allocation of funds to improve education is the major problem facing higher education today (Hughes & Mwiria, 1990). Reforms, changes in past policies, and new sources of money will remain a problem for many years. Solving higher education problems in developing nations usually requires funding. There are few sources of capital, since higher education already receives large portions of national budgets. A large part of the solution to problems in education will require changes in the present allocation policies. Requests by higher education for increased funding are potentially a divisive force in African nations because many students are from the families of the wealthy, and free higher education creates a situation in which the children of the rich are recipients of a large portion of the national budget (World Bank, 1994).

African higher education as presently structured has many hidden costs (World Bank, 1994). Individual schools are often small and duplicate curriculum and physical facilities. The cost of public higher education for African students averages more than six times the costs in Asia and nine times the costs in Latin America. Typically, francophone nations have much higher costs than anglophone nations.

Factors contributing to the high costs of African tertiary education include: small institutions, subsidies for staff, large staffs, subsidies for students, and inefficient use of resources. In most African nations students pay no fees, and housing, food, and social services are provided by the government. Fellowships to students constitute half of the public expenditures on higher education in a number of

African nations (World Bank, 1988, p. 77). The number of non-teaching staff in university employment is very high, and at times has exceeded the number of students. Increasing funding for higher education will require finding new and creative sources of money and a reordering of spending priorities, along with reforms in management and organization.

Changes and Reforms in Higher Education in Sub-Saharan Africa

Presently, there is a widespread acceptance of the need for comprehensive reform in higher education. The World Bank recommends four categories of changes that it believes will improve the functioning of African higher education. Their recommendations have been criticized by many for emphasizing a goal of increasing economic development over all other potential objectives. Several critics of the World Bank recomendations have focused on the fact that universities have several roles to play in society, and that many other institutions and factors have a role as important or more important to economic development than do universities (Hughes & Mwiria, 1990; Van Den Bor, & Shute, 1991).

Following an extensive analysis of the experiences of developing nations, the World Bank suggests that the goals of greater efficiency, quality, and equity in higher education can be achieved through implementing reforms in the following categories:

1. Encouraging greater differentiation of institutions, including the development of private institutions
2. Providing incentives for public institutions to diversify sources of funding, including cost-sharing with students, and linking government funding closely to performance
3. Redefining the role of government in higher education
4. Introducing policies explicitly designed to give priority to quality and equity objectives (World Bank, 1994, p. 4)

Recommendations from a major funding source can have an impact on higher education in Africa. However, each nation can be expected to implement them in their own way and time. In some African nations such reforms are already underway. The reform effort has produced successes, controversies, and deep reactions. Reforming higher education will be difficult. Faculties are organizing to protect their interests, as are the students. One of the more difficult problems is likely to come from the fact that many students whose education is being funded by their country come from affluent families. Therefore, they can be expected to use their political and economic power to preserve their own economic advantages of free schooling and better jobs. Indeed, in 1988 and 1989 Nigerian students joined forces with other groups in fighting against World Bank and International Monetary Fund structural reforms (Nkinyangi, 1991).

Both faculty and students have much to gain and much to lose. Although they benefit from political stability, they are caught in the middle of the political problems. As potential contributors to reforms, both can be blamed by either the government or social and economic reformers for the failure to bring about changes. Solving problems in higher education will cost and benefit both faculty and students. If students can quickly find meaningful employment upon graduation, they will be encouraged to complete their educations in a timely fashion. Likewise, if they or their individual families are required to invest in their own education, students may be motivated to complete their education through the shortest and least expensive route. Students will also demand from the universities a curriculum and teachers who will provide an education that leads to a good job. If, however, the goal of attaining meaningful employment and opportunities is not likely, students may feel justified to milk the system for all they can get and may delay completion of their educations because of the benefits the present system gives to them. They can be expected to devote energies toward protest for broader social, ethnic, and religious goals. They will also fail to view government property as their own, but instead see it as an object of disdain and something to destroy rather than preserve.

Faculty members who see their efforts respected by students, society, and administrators will be more inclined to work to implement needed reforms and devote their energies to being full-time workers in higher education (Sunal & Sunal, 1994). However, those who fail to have their needs and ambitions fulfilled are likely to use their best talents in the private sector of the economy or in more rewarding parts of the public sector.

Diversity in Higher Education

The greater the diversity within a nation, the more potential for diversity of higher education institutions (Hughes & Mwiria, 1990). Higher education has the potential for short-term classes and for offering education in specific skills, especially those associated with the use of technology and other fields undergoing rapid change. These offerings are rare now in sub-Saharan Africa. If the traditional universities do not offer services such as training or updating in skills to business and governmental agencies, private institutions can fill the gap and may develop into institutions of higher education with special emphases.

In sub-Saharan African nations where there is a scarcity of student positions in the public universities, there is a market for private higher education. One additional group that may provide a market for private institutions of higher education is women. In nations with large Muslim populations, for example, families may prefer to have their daughters attend schools exclusively for women. The current policy of most sub-Saharan African universities is to use the facilities of the university only during the daytime with no classes during extensive yearly breaks. Night classes and classes offered during the "vacation" period would make use of available physical facilities for additional types of training. Universities, particularly in large cities, have an opportunity to provide physical facilities for evening, weekend, and short-term classes for temporary and part-time students. This is rarely done now.

Diversity in Sources of Funding

A large proportion of university funding currently goes to the support of students. This portion of the budget is likely to face revision. Funds for room and board on campus, or allowances for off campus living are considerable, and greatly increase the cost of higher education to the government. Several sub-Saharan African nations have begun to phase out this type of support. Students in some nations are now required to pay some fees. Other changes being considered are scholarships based upon need as determined by family income, or scholarships being converted to loans that are repaid when graduates are employed. Both options are rarely implemented now. Another new alternative is to grant full or larger scholarships to those seeking degrees in the most needed fields and limiting the number of scholarships to students in fields where there is an oversupply or anticipated surplus of graduates. Continuous evaluation of student progress toward completion could be required for renewing scholarships from year to year. This is rarely done now. Currently between one-third and two-thirds of the students who begin tertiary education do not graduate, or require additional time to graduate (World Bank, 1988, 1994). The poor record of completion raises the costs of higher education to society and cuts the potential benefits. Although rarely done at present, universities could sell research or training services to businesses and governmental institutions through grants and contracts. This type of change holds out possibilities for providing additional money and incentives to faculty and departments.

Redefinition of the Government Role in Higher Education

Administratively, the high degree of funding for higher education by national governments creates close ties between academe and government that can have negative impacts (Van Den Bor & Shute, 1991). Academic freedom to criticize governmental policy can result in cutting funds, dismissals, and closing of the university. Governments usually appoint the highest members of university administration. Students come into conflict with the government and find that government may respond by using the power of the purse or by sending in troops to assure order. On occasion, the university is not able to function because of student protests that have little to do with the responsibilities of the university or its staff.

Having full ownership of higher education has given the government the opportunity to exert great control over the goals and procedures of higher education (Aminu, 1986; Nikinyangi, 1991). Economic efficiency has not been a necessity for higher education survival. Political influence has more control over the direction of higher education than have economics and market forces. Duplication of facilities and services tends to predominate. Delays are frequent, slowing or eliminating attempts at change because of the necessity to deal with many governmental agencies, all with power to approve or change individual programs. Multiple institutions of higher education with identical missions are often dispersed throughout a nation, rather than establishing larger more economical facilities at fewer locations. Eliminating duplication in physical facilities, faculties, administrations, and overlapping governmental jurisdictions can save money and bring about higher quality in education by concentrating human resources where they more readily cooperate on academic tasks.

Equity and quality in higher education have been concerns since independence (Sunal, Sunal, Rufai, & Inuwa, 1995; Van Den Bor & Shute, 1991). The number of females in higher education in Africa is lower than in other developing nations. Some ethnic groups are underrepresented. Training in the types of skills that would be economically and socially helpful to large portions of the people often is not available. Establishment of specific shorter-term goals rather than typical abstract, global goals for educational development can assist higher education in diversifying and meeting specific needs. Allowing more freedom to institutions to take more of a part in planning their own goals and distribution of funds also can assist in improving higher education by allowing market forces to play a role in program development and continuation. Monitoring quality will remain a necessity as long as governments provide funds to higher education. One outcome of governmental control is monitoring the quality of graduates by examinations scored by outside readers, however little else is done. Accreditation organizations outside the control of government can provide such services if their reports are open for public assessment.

Future Trends
Administrative Restructuring
To administrate universities that are not completely financed by the national government, it will be necessary for academics to acquire more attitudes and skills associated with business management. All staff will need to act in ways that add to the efficiency of the university. Restructuring will be required, as will changes in the size of departments and regular availability of full-time staff (World Bank, 1994).

Creating regional institutions for advanced degrees or degrees in fields requiring costly technological equipment will require cooperation between nations and careful monitoring and confronting of ethnic and national issues. If these institutions are to be cost efficient for African nations, duplication of programs beyond basic needs must be avoided. Standards should be high so that existing institutions will be willing to close small departments and work in cooperation with regional institutions. Ease in transferring credits between a national university and a regional institution can save on costs. Temporary faculty exchanges might also be used as a way of providing some courses and ensuring that the school remains representative of the nations it serves. Procedures for assuring faculty of the importance and security of their regular positions should be carefully negotiated and enforced, as should acceptance of exchange faculty.

Outreach Programs

Outreach programs have a potential for new service and new funds. They must match the needs of individual communities, and these require a staff and faculty that have the time to devote to the systematic examination of individual programs. Universities will need to rethink faculty assignments and rewards if they are to broaden their outreach programs. Time must be available to work with all cooperating agencies. Workable objectives must be negotiated for each project. Funds have to be available to maintain an office to guide projects and serve as a planner and contact for potential clients. Interests and abilities of faculty members and departments must be constantly monitored to ensure that resources of the university staff are effectively used and encouraged. To be successful, faculty members must be as encouraged and rewarded for research related to practical application problems as they are for working with theoretical problems. Outreach programs will need to be self-sustaining financially. Over time, they might become a source of additional funds. Universities will need to use outreach funding to reward all who are contributing to the program, and to benefit departments not related to outreach research projects.

Relations with Non-African Institutions

North–south cooperation programs between universities also hold strong promise to improve educational quality. Only when the goals of the program are jointly developed and agreed upon can both parties gain something from the exchange. Since each school is unique, no one model of working together is feasible in all situations. The key is the partnership and input from all parties. In some instances teaching exchanges will be needed, while in others research, management, or a combination of benefits might result. People are only one form of exchange. Equipment must also be included when it is needed to accomplish the task. Another important factor is training personnel to use and maintain the innovative practices needed to properly sustain or develop a program. Granting institutions must recognize this need and encourage the exploration and funding of such undertakings.

Curriculum Changes

Curriculum changes need to be reflective of the needs of the nation. Systematic assessments of the learning needs of the students and the course content should be undertaken. Student failures can be reduced through student remedial centers located at the institution. Skills and knowledge of entering students are not always adequate because of weaknesses found in overextended and poorly funded student primary and secondary schooling (see Chapter 1). The first-year orientation and remedial course program now existing at many universities should be strengthened to assure student success in year one of university-level courses. Technology could play a large role in remedial work by focusing on prerequisite language and mathematical skills and by becoming an integral part of courses taught through distance learning. Correspondence courses and self-directed study programs using radio, television, and/or computers can play a role in introductory and low-enrollment courses and in reaching students in remote locations. Multimedia course work and distance-learning classes do require equipment, but, more importantly, they require regularly available power and mail service. Both are not always dependable in sub-Saharan Africa (see Chapter 1). Many faculty members do have skills and experience using computers. The computer and related media have the ability to provide a fast return in learning opportunities and improvement. Computer laboratories using quality software need staff but do not require the presence of senior faculty. Many universities throughout the world, including some in Africa, are already using media laboratories.

Individual courses and complete programs of study can be made relevant to the needs of the jobs available to graduates. Cooperation with employers in planning new programs and courses of study is imperative. New programs must have students interested in pursuing degrees. Students need to be made aware of new and needed academic majors beyond the traditional liberal arts majors that have dominated the curricula of the past. Vocational counseling of students should begin early and even precede their entry into institutions of higher education. Programs for secondary schools should be developed in cooperation with the national and local government, business, and institutions of higher education. When individual institutions are granted the opportunity to establish their own admission requirements and control their course offerings, they will need to recruit students from secondary schools who are aware of the types and numbers of positions in various majors, and the availability and requirements for new majors and programs.

Improvement in Staff

Staff development must strive to encourage the acquisition of new, appropriate skills by faculty members and the hiring of staff that fill departmental and program needs. In the past foreign universities provided the most common way for staff to acquire doctorates. This method fails if students do not return to their universities or if the training of returning scholars cannot be used to the benefit of the students and the institution. More staff are now being educated in sub-Saharan African institutions than in the past and the numbers are increasing.

Inservice staff development to improve teaching and research skills is generally rare or ineffectual (Inuwa, 1991). Often lecturers have gone directly from the role of undergraduate student to teaching graduate student to university lecturer with only their own student experience and senior lecturers to guide them as teachers. The importance of interactive instruction and techniques in preparing laboratory exercises and in leading discussions and investigations, if learned at all, have been learned through trial and error over time. Success of such efforts depends upon teacher attitudes toward learning and change. Inservice staff development needs to be available to expand knowledge of the needs of the learner, instructional methods, and effective assessment methods, and to broaden experience with various media. In a study on the attitudes of lecturers in two universities in Nigeria, Inuwa (1991) found that beginning faculty felt their jobs would be threatened by educational television, as it would serve as a substitute for lectures. However, experienced teachers who worked in outreach programs in agriculture and medicine viewed the use of educational television differently, seeing greater potential for its use.

Research

Research is one of the traditional roles for universities and a requirement for personal advancement of staff. Universities hold the potential of assisting governments with research that matches governmental plans for development. With the increased number of university graduates in the civil service, the opportunities for cooperation between the government and university researchers are better today than at any time in the past. The Africanization of higher education requires the Africanization of the research questions, procedures, and funding for the research role of the university.

Action research must be practiced and given equal credit with theoretical research. Research should take a holistic approach and include participation from local constituencies and researchers in framing problems, making decisions, and evaluating the success of projects. The application of research toward the solution of problems must become a part of the study. Such views are necessary if research in Africa is to have economic and social benefits (Sunal & Sunal, 1994). The following extended description of a research study by one of the authors provides a model and an example of results useful in describing the present status, documenting the effects of change, and determining future policy at sub-Saharan African universities.

Effective Teaching in African Universities—
A Nigerian Case Study

A general assumption, in sub-Saharan African countries (as in the United States), is that university lecturers are more interested in the scholarly research aspects of their roles than in teaching—that teaching may indeed be a burden to be endured in supporting other more important work. The work of Eble (1974), Ladd and Lipset (1975, 1976), and Sunal (1989a, 1989b) indicate this description is a role myth. Over 75 percent of sub-Saharan African and U.S. university faculty surveyed and interviewed in these studies indicated a greater commitment to teaching than to research. Eight lecturers were found heavily devoted to teaching for every one heavily devoted to research. These reports concluded that most faculty are primarily concerned with teaching. They also concluded that teaching-development programs must provide services to support them in teaching. Although planned and intermittent development activities occur at most institutions, those in the sub-Saharan African nations typically deal with concerns of the administration (eg., budget or grade policies), and not with addressing the more central concern of teaching: What is actually happening in the classroom?

Higher education classroom methods and activities generally have not been addressed in literature through description and analysis of observed occurrences in the classroom, type of instructional innovations, or increasing alternative instructional methods. Doubt and conflict surround the need for change in teaching (Eble, 1983). Questions too infrequently asked in sub-Saharan African higher education are: How do we motivate lecturers to teach effectively? and, How do we motivate them to try something different or to participate in a professional development program? Regardless of the level of precision, the answers to motivation practices are necessarily vague, especially for sub-Saharan African institutions. Obtaining information about the instructional perceptions of sub-Saharan African lecturers or students can more realistically point to a systematic organization of developmental practices leading to motivation and to more effective ways to change patterns of behavior.

For sub-Saharan Africa, as well as other developing regions, the importance and uniqueness of classroom teaching have been advocated in the very limited amount of literature available. Orientation courses in the past have been required for new lecturers at the University of Ife (Fafunwa, 1975). Problems of teaching in higher education in Africa and differences from universities in developed nations have been reported. The problems involve curricula that fail to integrate with the actual needs of the country, unfavorable teaching conditions, and different rewards for teaching and research (Berendt, 1981). Different systems of education for different purposes have been explored (International Association of Universities, 1977). The importance of goals and objectives, characteristics of instructional problems, and the need for supportive infrastructure have been outlined (University of Science, Penang, Malaysia, 1979). However, general dissatisfaction with conditions of university teaching, in countries of which Nigeria is typical, exist (Faghaniye, 1981). Yet, teaching goes on.

Purpose

The purpose of this study was to develop a model for assessing teacher motivation and instructional development needs for a sub-Saharan African university system with unique characteristics. Regionally and nationally, sub-Saharan Africa is made up of many such cultural and subcultural systems. From within the context of motivation, researchers investigated the importance and interrelationships of factors related to classroom teaching in a model setting, a subsample of Nigerian universities. Thus, the focus was on philosophy of teaching, rewards for professional achievement, professional goals, interests of students and lecturers, and perceived teaching responsibilities. A comparison of these factors was made with observed classroom indicators of effective teaching, classroom instructional methods, student learning outcomes, and teaching-development needs. Portraits were constructed and relationships between these factors were explored through four basic research questions.

1. Can factors related to motivation provide a coherent and identifiable model, a portrait of characteristics, for a sub-Saharan African university lecturer?
2. What relationships exist between model-lecturer motivational factors and indicators of effective teaching?
3. Are model-lecturer motivational characteristics comparable with their student characteristics and student-expected indicators of effective teaching?
4. What teaching staff development needs are perceived as useful by model lecturers of varying motivational portraits?

Procedure

The universities sampled were from a similar cultural area of a developing African university system. The selected area, northern Nigeria, had a dominant Hausa-Fulani cultural pattern and included eight states with five federally funded universities. All universities had been established by 1977. Many university departments in this region comprised lecturers of different nationalities and cultures. A majority of the lecturers had received terminal degrees in European or North American universities. Most of the others had received degrees from Asian and other African universities. This pattern was similar to that found in other developing African regions with nationally funded university systems. The administrative structure of Nigerian universities follows a traditional pattern, with power held at the vice-chancellor and department-head levels. Increasing enrollment is planned in each program area for each year, although most actual enrollment figures are one-half to two-thirds of projected amounts. Total enrollment in Nigeria grew from 53,000 in 1978 to just under 100,000 in 1995 at thirty-three state and federal universities in Nigeria. Degree offerings at Nigerian universities are quite extensive, with arts, sciences, and education offered at all institutions.

The population for this study included only Nigerian full-time lecturers, at the rank of lecturer and above (or equivalent), and students in departments of education from five federal universities in the northern Nigerian cultural region. Non-Nigerians made up less than one-third of the total of these sixty-five lecturers. Education students made up about 20 percent of undergraduate and 25 percent of graduate university population for a total of about 3,000. The population was more narrowly selected to establish a clearer indication of lecturers who have a long-term commitment and who reflect the increasing majority (i.e., Nigerians). A single department was selected because it reflected more unified needs and goals. The Department of Education was selected because of its potential for the greatest impact on the largest number of citizens (i.e., graduates taking positions in secondary schools) and the highest student–teacher ratio. The ratio in education is 22 to 1, compared to 11 to 1 in science and arts, and creates a potentially more important instructional role. Other departments may have very different goals and, thus, may not be grouped together without washing out or blurring relationships existing in single departments.

The sample selected for participation in the study included eighteen Nigerian lecturers and 855 students in their respective classes during the last term of the academic year. Each lecturer was asked to participate in the study by completing an interview and volunteering a typical class for further data to be gathered from students. The students in these typical classes were asked anonymously to complete a detailed questionnaire similar in content to information gathered from lecturers. The questionnaire items were read to the students, pausing for questions on terms or meaning if needed. University instruction is in English. Additional observations were made of the classroom teaching of each lecturer to determine the reliability of the data obtained from students and lecturers. The "University Teacher and Student Questionnaire" examining motivational factors and indicators of effective teaching was adapted from the work of W. Bergquist and S. Phillip, *A Handbook for Faculty Development,* (1977), published by the Council for the Advancement of Small Colleges.

Analysis of lecturer and student responses and observations of classroom data used descriptive and inferential statistics—means, standard deviations, t-tests, chi square, and factor analysis. Significance was set at $p < 0.5$. Agreement was noted when two-thirds or more of the subjects reported similar responses.

To simplify the reporting, the results of the study were consolidated to address the research questions in the following format. Descriptions were made of four basic contexts:

1. portrait of a Nigerian lecturer
2. portrait of a Nigerian student and comparison of student and lecturer characteristics
3. relationship of Nigerian lecturer motivational factors and indicators of effective teaching
4. analysis of motivational factors and indicators of effective teaching as a process model for future Nigerian university department self-studies, teaching development activities, and possible reorganization

Results

Portrait of a Nigerian Lecturer

The characteristics of Nigerian lecturers where agreement was strongest represents, in general, a traditional and encouraging set (Table 2-1). The lecturers interviewed believed that more than one style of effective teaching exists and can be learned the way a craft is learned, to improve their teaching. Scholarly research was seen as leading to more exciting teaching. Characteristics relating to philosophy, beliefs, and other areas did not demonstrate a significant consensus.

Professional goals in this portrait involved a strong commitment to students' goals. Preparing students for careers and developing intellectual skills represented strong common views. Also, there was consensus that most lecturers were interested in student academic progress, and desired academic interaction beyond the classroom. The typical class size was sixty students.

Rewards for achievements were compatible with the other motivational characteristics. These included publishing professional works and being a knowledgeable, conscientious adviser. Little reward was seen for institutional governance activities and participation as a consultant and scholar beyond the institution.

Effective teaching was identified with a passive role for students, with emphasis on listening and thinking. Lecturers used independent study (i.e., assignments) and discussion, and made efforts to include relevant student interests and social problems as additional activities. There was consensus on only two student learning outcomes: understanding methods or procedures, and clear expression of ideas. Disagreement existed on all other possible outcomes.

Teaching-development needs most highly desired by lecturers concerned improvement of techniques and skills most closely related to classroom teaching. All development areas were found to be of value by the lecturers. Less desirable needs, however, related to knowledge about teaching or activities indirectly related to teaching.

Portrait of a Nigerian Student and Comparisons with Lecturers

Nigerian students appeared more traditional in regard to perceptions of teaching than their lecturers. Some aspects were significantly more so. Rather than describing a complete portrait, highlights of

Table 2-1. University Teaching—Portrait of Nigerian Lecturer
Motivational Factors

Beliefs

Agreement exists on

there is more than one style of effective teaching.

teaching is a learned set of activities and lecturers can learn to improve their effectiveness.

involvement in scholarly research leads to far more exciting teaching.

good teaching is an art, not a science.

Disagreement exists on

knowledge of discipline makes best teachers.

effect of sabbaticals and leaves on teaching.*

the necessity of student interest.*

whether students are the best judges of how to teach.*

whether learning can be measured.

whether teaching should be judged on student changes.*

Goals

Agreement exists on

preparing students for careers.*

developing student's intellectual skills.

Disagreement exists on

helping students clarify their ideas and relating to others.

further scholarship and research.*

improving the institution, communities, and society.*

providing students breadth of course work and preparing them in an academic concentration.*

Interest

Agreement exists on

most lecturers are interested in academic progress of students.

most lecturers are interested in development of students beyond classroom instruction.*

Disagreement exists on whether

students are interested in academic affairs and

relationships with lecturers beyond the classroom.*

Rewards (Importance of lecturers' achievements in obtaining tenure, promotion, or salary decisions)

Most believe important

publishing professional works.

being a knowledgeable, conscientious adviser.

Most believe of little importance

participating in departmental and institution-wide governance affairs.

participating as a consultant, scholar, and leader beyond the institution.

Mixed perceptions

being a demanding and challenging teacher.

exercising innovativeness in teaching.

---

*differs from student responses significantly $p \leq .05$.

significant departures from lecturers will be described. Students believed that greater knowledge distinguishes the best teachers. In addition, students did not feel that they could judge good teaching. Students, however, believed good teaching involved the need to arouse student interest and that judgment of teaching should involve its effect on student learning or satisfaction.

Students disagreed with lecturers and with traditional professional goals for lecturers in the areas of research, institutional governance, and breadth of coursework. The dominant goal of lecturers was seen as developing students' intellectual skills. Student interests generally reflected academic concerns but were definitely negative toward nontraditional academic relationships involving advising or class work.

General indicators of effective teaching differed from lecturers in that students felt class time should not involve learning activities. They preferred passive learning. Students also differed in stating that subject matter should relate to students' own lives and interests.

Relationship of Motivation Factors and Indicators of Effective Teaching

Interrelationships between philosophy and goals and the diversified role of university teachers involved definite patterns or teaching styles among Nigerian lecturers. Through use of factor analysis procedures, the dominant teaching styles were found to converge on what can best be described as content-motivated and student-motivated motivational patterns. About two-thirds of the lecturers were found to be best described as content motivated. Beliefs about teaching for each group are shown on Table 2-2. The patterns represented polar positions on many responses. Lecturers representing each style also represented a unique set of goals toward which they performed their professional duties. The content-motivated teaching style prepared students for future responsibilities in specific roles. The student-motivated teaching style planned for alternative futures by developing a broader base of knowledge skills and ideas.

Interests of lecturers and students were viewed in ways that reflected the content- or student-motivated orientation of the overall pattern. In many respects, the lecturer who displayed a student-motivated style had views opposed to those of the students on factors where the students had a consensus. Student responses were significantly different on each of the three interest areas reported for the student-motivated lecturer group. These lecturers perceived low interest in areas where students reported high interest, especially in academic affairs. The lecturers expected high student interest in relationships with students outside of the classroom in advising, discussion, and tutoring. Their students reported that very few (0 to 20 percent) students would have interests in out-of-classroom professional contacts. Lecturers with a content-motivated style matched their students' interest expectations in all areas.

The motivational aspects of the two teaching-style patterns were strongly related to specific indicators of effective teaching. The teaching methods for both groups involved primary emphasis on listening, remembering, lecturing, and reading assignments. The content-motivated lecturers, in addition, relied on independent study assignments with some discussion and rare student activity occurring during class time. Student-motivated lecturers relied more strongly on discussion, team teaching, and involving students in activity and learning problems during class time.

Table 2-2. The Differing Beliefs of Northern Nigerian Lecturers with Different Teaching Styles

Content-Motivated Lecturers' Beliefs	Student-Motivated Lecturers' Beliefs
*Best teacher is one who knows the most about the subject	Best teacher is not the one who knows the most about the subject
*Teaching cannot be improved by sabbaticals and leaves	*Teaching can be improved by sabbaticals and leaves
*Involvement in scholarly research leads to exciting teaching	*Involvement in scholarly research does not lead to exciting teaching
*Good teaching is a science not an art	*Good teaching is an art not a science
*Good teaching does arouse student interest	*Good teaching does not arouse student interest
*Students are not the best judge of teaching	*Students are the best judge of effective teaching
*Any method is acceptable if it results in desired student change	*Any method is not acceptable even if it results in desired student change
*The most important learning results cannot be measured	*The most important learning results can be measured

*differences between teaching styles significant at $p \leq .05$

Table 2-3. Differing Effective Teaching and Learning Methods of Northern Nigerian Lecturers with Different Teaching Styles

Content-Motivated Lecturers	Student-Motivated Lecturers
Teaching Methods	
Specific Emphasis	
Rely primarily on lecture and readings	Don't rely primarily on lectures and readings
Don't meet with students out of class	Frequently meet with students out of class
Rely on independent study for part of work	Rely on small group techniques to increase interaction
Don't use small group techniques to team teach course	
Don't involve students in deciding learning outcomes	Involve students in deciding learning outcomes
Student Learning Options	
Emphasis	
Master facts, terms, and other specific information	Integration of subject matter from other disciplines, from current social problems, or from students' own lives
Comprehend principles or generalizations	
Acquire skills or techniques	
De-emphasis	
Little understanding of methods or procedures	Little comprehension of principles or generalizations
Little integration of subject matter from other disciplines, from current social problems, or from students' own lives	Little analyzing of ideas or issues
Little examination and judgment of course material or methods	Little original or creative thinking
Little emphasis on expression and clarity of ideas	Little emphasis on acquiring skills or techniques

Expected student outcomes reflected teaching methods (Table 2-3). Mastery of facts, items, and specific information was strong for all lecturers. Except for lecturers with high emphasis on development of intellectual goals in students, there was little if any expectation of comprehension of principles or generalizations, critical analysis of ideas, or creative thinking. Student-motivated lecturers expected students to be able to relate subject matter to other fields of study,

social issues, and their own lives. Content-motivated lecturers expected students to be able to examine and make value judgments of
factual material and acquire specific skills and techniques. Students,
however, reported high expectations in mastery of facts; comprehension of principles and generalizations; making relationships with
the subject matter to other discipline areas, social issues, and their
own lives; and making judgments using actual materials. Students
differed significantly from both lecturer styles on expectations of
learning outcomes.

Rewards perceived for professional achievements related to lecturer motivational factors and to indicators of effective teaching.
Content-motivated lecturers generally expected rewards resulting
from most of the areas relating to professional competence. Somewhat less reward was expected from a strong emphasis on teaching
and participation in university governance. Student-motivated lecturers, on the other hand, generally expected little reward for achievements in any of the categories except strong emphasis on teaching.
Table 2-4 reports a summary of the findings.

Table 2-4. Rewards Expected for Achievements by Northern Nigerian
Lecturers with Different Teaching Styles

Content-Motivated Lecturers	Student-Motivated Lecturers
*publishing professional works	*less likely for publishing professional works
*less likely for being a demanding and challenging teacher	*being a demanding and challenging teacher
*less likely for participating in institution governance affairs	*less likely for innovativeness in teaching
*exercising innovativeness in teaching	*less likely for being a knowledgeable, conscientious adviser
*being a knowledgeable, conscientious adviser	*less likely for participation as adviser, consultant, scholar, and leader beyond the institution
*participation as consultant, scholar, and leader beyond the institution	

*significant difference between teaching styles $p \leq .05$

Teaching development and training needs of Nigerian lecturers
were strongly desired and related most closely to areas of classroom
activity. The highest-priority areas, for all lecturers were in:

1. developing new and redesigning old courses
2. developing personal, organizational, management, and leadership skills

Virtually all lecturers reported these as the greatest needs. In addition, motivational factors of content-motivated lecturers related to needed development in six other areas, listed in order from strongest to weakest:

1. learning about students' learning styles, characteristics, and needs
2. improving instructional skills by experimenting with different teaching techniques
3. learning about teaching in a new academic specialty within or outside of own field
4. learning about higher education generally
5. having others criticize teaching
6. sharing attitudes and values about teaching with my colleagues

Student-motivated lecturers did not regard any additional area as a developmental need other than the two highest-priority items above. Two areas were selected as not valuable by most of these lecturers. The areas of little interest were:

1. learning more about course and teacher evaluation
2. learning more about student advising

With the typical class size of about sixty students, effects of very large classes were related most strongly to factors of motivation and indicators of effective teaching. In general, the responses of students and lecturers in classes above 100 became more traditional and restrictive. Large classes produced similar responses from both students and lecturers, indicating lower motivation. Both also reported factors associated with less effective teaching. These included a focus on passive learning with little interaction between students and teachers. Rewards perceived for achievements were related to non-teaching activities. Teaching development was perceived as less necessary when class sizes were very large.

Summary of Results

A comparison was made of factors of motivation and indicators of effective teaching among Nigerian lecturers and students in a developing African university system. A summary is given in Table 2-5.

An identifiable portrait of typical Nigerian lecturer characteristics was constructed. The various components of teacher motivation were consistent within and between subparts. The portrait supported a traditional teaching pattern with strong concerns for student academic progress. Motivation for teaching for Nigerian lecturers was similar to expectations of students in their classes. Differences, when they occurred, involved student views that were more traditional and more narrowly concerned with their own learning needs.

Relationships between teaching motivation and indicators of effective teaching were found with the lecturers. Grouping motivational aspects of Nigerian lecturers through factor analysis resulted in two coherent teaching styles, content motivated and student motivated. Each style was strongly related to specific teaching methods and student learning outcome expectations. These methods and outcomes were similar in content and process to the emphasis of the motivational factors making up each teaching style. However, the two styles were not equally compatible with typical expectations of the students in the lecturers' classes. The content-motivated teaching style was closely related, whereas the student-motivated style was significantly different in most areas of methods and learning outcomes expected from university students.

The developmental needs of Nigerian lecturers were significantly

---

Table 2-5. Summary of Results Relating Lecturer Instructional Goals, Responsibilities, and Rewards in Northern Nigerian Universities

Identifiable portraits of typical Nigerian lecturer motivational characteristics can be constructed.

The various components and relationships between motivational factors of Nigerian lecturers and indicators of effective teaching are consistent with motivational theory.

Specific patterns of motivational factors among Nigerian lecturers have varying compatibilities with student expectations and needs.

The teaching-development needs of Nigerian lecturers can be predicted from variations in lecturer motivational characteristics.

related to their teaching motivations. Content-motivated lecturers desired additional training and experience in a number of areas directly related to classroom teaching. Student-motivated lecturers expressed needs in few areas and in training that did not directly relate to classroom teaching.

Conclusions and Implications

The purpose of the study was aimed at developing a model for assessing teacher motivation and teacher development needs for a developing sub-Saharan African university system with unique regional characteristics. See Table 2-6 for a summary of conclusions. The results from the sample investigated indicated that teaching-motivation theory effectively described Nigerian lecturer motivational factors and their relationships with indicators of effective teaching and with needs for training in teaching. Assessing motivational factors provided useful information on expected performance and needs of university lecturers. See Beeman (1981); Scott, Halpin, and Schnittjer (1974); and Armes and Watkins (1983) for similar results in developed university systems.

The application of motivation theory to northern Nigerian universities resulted in a different set of portraits for lecturers, but similar relationships when compared with developed university systems. Results from universities in the United States demonstrated a greater diversity and less dominance of any one style (Loadman, 1976; Mann, 1970). Content-motivated and student-motivated styles were found

---

Table 2-6. Summary of Conclusions Using Motivational Theory As a Means of Fostering Education for Development in Africa

Teaching-motivation theory effectively described relationships in lecturers between motivational factors and effective teaching.

Assessing motivational factors provides useful information on extent and type of teaching-development training needs of lecturers.

Lecturers in developing African universities have different motivational patterns than do lecturers in universities in developed countries.

Satisfaction with work as predicted by motivation theory is a better indicator of effective teaching than dissatisfaction levels with work conditions, under normal circumstances.

Short-, mid-, and long-range practices are suggested for increasing effective teaching at African universities using data relating to motivation theory.

to be present along with a number of other motivational styles. Relating university teaching styles to appropriate teaching methods found in other countries may provide additional developmental training possibilities to enhance teaching in the most receptive lecturers. A sample classification of styles and compatible teaching methods is found on Table 2-7. Without significant changes in general student needs and expectations or the university curriculum, some styles such as interaction-based patterns may not be applicable.

Dissatisfaction with work conditions was reported by Fagbamiye (1981) to be generally strong and spread throughout Nigerian universities. Abei (1972) earlier described work conditions as the strongest source of dissatisfaction. Also, Abei described the strongest source of potential work satisfaction to be related to the work itself, teaching. In this study, strong satisfaction was found in the positive teaching-motivation factors of Nigerian lecturers. Thus, dissatisfaction with work

---

Table 2-7. Classification of Instructional Methods

Content-Motivated Instructional Methods
    Lecture
    Question and Answer/Recitation
    Reading
    Programmed Instruction/Computer-Assisted Instruction
    Audiovisual Technologies
    Audiotutorial Laboratory
    Personalized System of Instruction (Keller Plan)

Student-Motivated Instructional Methods
    Tutorial
    Independent Study
    Learning Contract
    Field Placement: Sheltered/Real
    Student-Generated Course: Faculty Led/Student Led/Jointly Led

Interaction-Motivated Instructional Methods
    Seminar/Discussion Group
    Laboratory/Studio
    Symposium/Debate
    Team Teaching
    Case Study/Socratic Method
    In-class Discussion: Learning Cells, Small Groups
    Simulations On Paper/Participation/Computerized
    Role Playing: Faculty/Student

conditions did not relate well to satisfaction with work itself. Teaching motivational factors were better indicators of effective teaching and developmental needs than ratings of dissatisfaction for Nigerian lecturers. Exceptions to this relationship may exist when work conditions become extreme. Large classes, with more than 100 students, engendered dissatisfaction. This was indicated through detrimental changes in motivational factors, effective teaching indicators, and developmental needs in the typical lecturer portraits. The same relationship may exist with extremes in other work and work-related conditions (e.g., administrative relationships, salary, housing).

Lecturers with motivational styles different from their students need special attention. Correction of extreme work conditions may produce the desired positive effects on teaching (e.g., specific actions aimed at the work of the lecturer—teaching—could produce stronger effects for all in the short term). Suggested activities include but are not limited to:

1. more compatible reward systems directly related to classroom teaching (Thorne, Scott & Beaird, 1976);

2. direct emotional and resource support for teaching and classroom lessons;

3. nonthreatening information and training available on teaching styles of lecturers and learning styles of their students. This should be coupled with readily available consultants who can help lecturers remediate self-diagnosed or observer-noted deficiencies;

4. changes in degree program curricula and voluntary workshops and seminars should be offered students to explore and develop alternative learning styles compatible with those of lecturers;

5. establishment of a course and lecturer evaluation system in each department, unrelated to administrative control or access, to provide lecturers with objective information on the relevance of their degree program content, teaching styles, and student expectations and needs;

6. establishment of a needs assessment system obtaining information directly from the communities and states served by the university. Information on the types, characteristics, and numbers of graduates needed to support continued national development should be sought;

7. establishment of a university inservice teacher development program for lecturers designed to be responsive to their perceived needs and other information obtained from within and outside the university (see Eastmond, 1975; Shveard, 1978).

Using information suggested by assessing teaching motivation, relevant and practical information can be obtained as a starting point for increasing effective teaching in developing sub-Saharan African university systems. Lecturers most favorable to teaching-development efforts can be targeted for short-term changes. Other efforts related to motivational theory are suggested for mid- and long-term development of teaching with lecturers, students, and institutional processes. The long-term goal for developing sub-Saharan African university systems would involve a model of teaching development based on motivational factors. The model provides direction for one part of the broader problem of education for development in Africa.

References

Abei, C. (1972). The application of Herzberg's motivation-hygiene theory to college educators as tested by two different methodologies. (Doctoral dissertation, University of Michigan, Ann Arbor) *Dissertation Abstracts International, 33/08,* 2979-A.

Aminu, J. (1986). *Quality and stress in Nigerian education.* Maiduguri, Nigeria: University of Maiduguri and the Northern Nigerian Publishing Co.

Armes, N., & Watkins, K. (1983). The shadow side of teaching: An analysis of personal concerns. *Community College Review, 11*(2), 13–19.

Beeman, A.L. (1981). *Toward better teaching.* Indianapolis, IN: Lilly Endowment, Inc. (ERIC Document Reproduction Service No. ED 208 792)

Berendt, B. (1981). *Improving teaching and learning in higher education.* Bonn, Germany: German Foundation for International Development. (ERIC Document Reproduction Service No. ED 215 599)

Bergquist, W.H., & Phillip, S. (1977). *A handbook for faculty development* (Vol. 2). Washington, DC: The Council for the Advancement of Small Colleges.

Davis, R., Strand, R., Alexander, L., & Hussain, M. (1982). The impact of organizational and innovative variables on instructional innovation in higher education. *Journal of Higher Education, 53*(5), 568–586.

Deci, E., & Ryan, R. (1982). Intrinsic motivation to teach: Possibilities and obstacles in our colleges and universities. *New Directions for Teaching and Learning, 10,* 27–35.

Eastmond, N. (1975). Instructional development under the microscope. Logan: Utah State University. (ERIC Document Reproduction Service No. ED 112 882)

Eble, K. (1983). The joy of teaching. *Change, 15*(6), 12–19.

Eble, K. (1974). *The craft of teaching.* San Francisco: Jossey-Bass.

Fafunwa, A.B. (1975). The preparation of teachers for African universities. *West African Journal of Education, 19*(1), 159–168.

Fagbamiye, E.O. (1981). *The organization and administration of Nigerian universities and the satisfaction and motivation of lecturers in some of these universities.* Paper presented at the American Educational Research Association, Los Angeles, CA. (ERIC Document Reproduction Service No. ED 201 266)

Freedman, M. (Ed.). (1973). *Facilitating faculty development.* San Francisco: Jossey-Bass.

Hughes, R., & Mwiria, K. (1990). An essay on the implications of university expansion in Kenya. *Higher Education, 19*(2), 215–238.

International Association of Universities. (1977). *Differing types of higher education* (IAU Paper No. 14). Paris: International Association of Universities.

Inuwa, A.R. (1991). *A plan for expanding the use of educational television in northern Nigerian universities.* Unpublished doctoral dissertation, West Virginia University, Morgantown, WV.

Jabker, E.H., & Halenski, R.S. (1978). Instructional development and faculty rewards. *Journal of Higher Education, 49*(4), 316–328.

Ladd, E.C., & Lipset, S.M. (1975, October 14; 1976, April 19). The Ladd-Lipset Survey. *Chronicle of Higher Education, 11,* 2; *12,* 8.

Loadman, W.E. (1976). *Identifying the characteristics of the ideal professor: An application of multidimensional scaling.* Paper presented at American Educational Research Association, San Francisco, CA. (ERIC Document Reproduction Service No. ED 129 865)

Mann, R. (1970). *The college classroom: Conflict, change, and learning* (pp. 1–19). New York: Wiley.

Maslow, A.H. (1954). *Motivation and personality.* New York: Harper & Row.

McKeachie, W.J. (1982). The rewards of teaching. *New Directions for Teaching and Learning, 10,* 7–13.

Nkinyangi, J.A. (1991). Student protests in sub-Saharan Africa. *Higher Education, 22,* 157–173.

Olashi, T., & Hengst, H. (1988). University faculty and administrator morale: A case in Nigeria. *International Review of Education, 34*(4), 508–514.

Rathgeber, E.M. (1988). A tenuous relationship: The African university and development policymaking in the 1980's. *Higher Education, 17,* 397–410.

Schneider, B., & Zalesny, M. (1982). Human needs and faculty motivation. *New Directions for Teaching and Learning, 10,* 37–46.

Scott, D., Halpin, G., & Schnittjer, C. (1974). *Student characteristics associated with student perceptions of college instruction.* Paper presented at the National Council on Measurement in Education, Chicago, IL. (ERIC Document Reproduction Service No. ED 090 263)

Shveard, A.R. (1978). Educational development at a moderate sized university. *New Directions for Higher Education, 6*(4), 1–13

Sunal, D.W. (1989a). *Analysis of motivational factors and indicators of effective teaching in lecturers in African universities.* Paper presented at the annual meeting of the American Educational Research Association, San Francisco.

Sunal, D.W. (1989b). *Overview of a model for enhancing educational effectiveness of an African university.* Paper presented at the annual meeting of the African Studies Association, Atlanta.

Sunal, D.W., & Sunal, C.S. (1994). *Effective teaching in African universities—a Nigerian case study.* New Orleans: American Educational Research Association.

Sunal, D., Sunal, C.S., Rufai, R., & Inuwa, A. (1995). *Equity in primary and secondary education.* Tuscaloosa: University of Alabama (ERIC Document Reproduction Service No. ED 383 812)

Thorne, G.L., Scott, C., & Beaird, J. (1976). *Assisting faculty performance.* (ERIC Document Reproduction Service No. ED 132 955)

University of Science, Penang, Malaysia. (1979). International conference on the teaching–learning process in universities. (ERIC Document Reproduction Service No. ED 192 631)

Van Den Bor, D., & Shute, J.C.M. (1991). Higher education in the third world: Status symbol or instrument for development? *Higher Education, 22,* 1–15.

The World Bank. (1988). *Education in sub-Saharan Africa: Policies for adjustment, revitalization, and expansion.* Washington, DC: Author.

The World Bank. (1994). *Higher education: The lessons of experience.* Washington, DC: Author.

Chapter Three
The Significance of the Informal Sector to Education in Sub-Saharan Africa

Benson Honig

Beginning with the end of World War II, newly independent African countries expanded educational opportunity at tremendous rates, more than tripling enrollments (United Nations, 1970, 1980, 1987; World Bank, 1988). One unanticipated effect has been a significant reduction in the employment prospects for secondary school graduates, particularly those of lower classes and rural backgrounds. This apparent surplus of better-educated unemployed youths may lead to economic disincentives that undermine student and parental decision making concerning educational investment. The potentials for spillover effects concerning health, fertility, nation building, and labor force capability are so disruptive that the unemployment issue now commands attention at the highest levels of government.

Despite a remarkable advance in the annual growth of educational enrollments, the economies of sub-Saharan African countries have failed to keep pace. During the post-independence years of 1965–73, the mean growth rate for primary education was 7.1 percent, while gross domestic product (GDP) grew at a robust 6.4 percent. By the following decade (1973–1984) primary growth rates had dropped to 2.9 percent and gross domestic product (GDP) growth to only 1.3 percent, significantly below the 2.8 percent rate of overall population growth (World Bank, 1988). Although all economic sectors of sub-Saharan countries have experienced dramatically reduced growth, the manufacturing sector was particularly hard hit, with mean growth rates being reduced over the two decades from 8.8 percent to 2.3 percent (World Bank, 1988). This reduction reflects the limited growth of job opportunities in the nonagricultural formal sector—the preferred employment location for the vast majority of school leavers.

Although employment growth in the formal sector continues to be severely limited, self-employment in both manufacturing and services is increasingly becoming the most viable occupational opportunity in sub-Saharan Africa. Today, microenterprise employment represents the largest share of job growth, comprising 40–60 percent of the urban labor force of most African countries, including well over 20 million individuals (Fluitman, 1989).

Definition of the Informal Sector

The "informal sector" is a broadly defined term that encompasses an ubiquitous and heterogeneous phenomenon: the labor of small firms and individuals, often with minimal resources; operation in the "gray" areas with respect to legality; and employment of a wide range of activities and services. The celebrated 1971 Nairobi conference organized by the International Labor Organization (ILO) provided the following characteristics of informal activity (Haan, 1989):

1. ease of entry
2. reliance on indigenous resources
3. family ownership of enterprise
4. small scale of operation
5. operation in a semipermanent or temporary structure or in a variable location
6. acquisition of skills outside the formal education system
7. operation in unregulated and competitive markets

A number of African governments, in attempting to understand and support the phenomenon of self-employment, have codified informality for the purposes of systematic study and assistance. The Kenyan government, for example, defines informal activity as follows: "Small-scale manufacturing, retail trading, building and construction, and the provision of services. Manufacturing activities include the fabrication of metal goods (often using waste materials from the formal sector), furniture making, tailoring, shoemaking, and handicrafts. Trading activities include street hawking, operations of food and retail kiosks, sale of charcoal, etc. The services include shoeshining, repair work (clothes, shoes, vehicles, watches, furniture), newspaper vending, barbering, car-washing, etc. (Republic of Kenya, 1983, p. 211).

Viewed as a sector, informality encompasses a broad range of activities spanning the entire range of economic activity, from the most basic to more advanced, highly specialized occupations. The informal sector is heterogeneous, crossing gender and class backgrounds, engaging individuals with a highly diverse set of educational properties. It should be emphasized that informality can occur at the highest levels of education, and may include consultants, accountants, programmers, and other highly educated individuals, who may be operating in the "gray" areas of legality due to preference rather than necessity.[1]

Formal Education and the Informal Sector

Throughout Africa, governments have sought to institute curricular programs reflecting both the demographic and the labor market shifts of their countries, while acknowledging the importance of the informal sector. The result has been a strong interest in various types of vocational education. Their activities are typically justified by one or a combination of four goals:

1. acknowledging that the state has a responsibility to provide employment for all of its citizenry, accompanied by a belief that vocational education helps individuals attain and create employment
2. addressing issues of equity, by deflecting criticisms that academic pursuits promote a white-collar bureaucratic mentality
3. addressing issues of development operating under the assumption that economic advancement is technology led, justifying the necessity for schools to enhance worker training beyond traditional apprenticeship programs
4. stemming the tide of rural to urban migration[2]

The vocationalization of education typically focuses on one of two alternative strategies. Either attempts are made to strengthen separate vocational institutions, usually at the secondary level, or efforts are aimed at introducing curriculum diversification programs, which introduce prevocational subjects to primary and secondary students. The latter is often justified by asserting that dropouts and repeaters (who make up a significant component of the informal sector) will benefit. Unfortunately, labor market considerations have rarely informed these investment strategies (Middleton & Demsky, 1989).

Relationship to Mass Education
In general, countries that have low levels of secondary school enrollment ratios tend to expand vocational schools, while those with over 50 percent secondary school enrollments favor diversification and nonformal education (Hultin, 1987). A good argument can be made to support this gradual transition: immediate demands for a technical labor force suggest the need for parallel vocational education. Once primary education becomes universal, and universal literacy and numeracy are achieved, the level of national development will most likely demand more middle-level laborers, such as technicians. Diversified secondary schools, offering a mixed curriculum with a range of adult and specialized technical education, are thought to be more suitable (and less expensive) for training the nonacademically oriented graduates of primary institutions (Hultin, 1987).

Thus, schools can play two roles in preparing students for the changing labor environment in sub-Saharan Africa. First, schools can provide specific training for eventual work in the informal sector: for example; bookkeeping, marketing, quality assurance, and finance classes taught at an appropriate level, including (but not limited to) adult education. Second, they can alter the expectations students and their families have regarding work possibilities. Currently, modern-sector employment carries the most prestige in Africa. New awareness of the informal sector and self-employment can enhance the desirability of microenterprise employment. This can be accomplished by developing ties between formal educational institutions and successful informal enterprises, as well as by conducting seminars and presentations regarding these possibilities.

Curriculum and Instruction
One of the more critical decisions that must be made by planners of the formal educational system is to identify when to begin instituting formal educational curricula in support of informal sector skills

acquisition. King (1977, pp. 36–37) argues in favor of the primary school level. He points out that one of the most significant aspects of primary schools in Africa is their "ordinariness," which reflects the probability of informal employment by the students. King characterizes these schools as popularly based institutions built of available materials in consonance with local village life. In this view, the transition from primary school to the informal sector is actually quite normal, and the formal educational experience beneficial in terms of enhanced communication skills and the desire for self-improvement.

Attempting to promote informal sector skills at the primary level certainly has a number of distinct advantages. First, it provides exposure to the largest educational segment of the population. Relatively few African students are able to participate in secondary education. Second, cost differentials are minimized. The level of instruction is typically the most basic, utilizing available materials and technologies. Third, it provides an opportunity to alter prejudices and misconceptions regarding the social status of informal sector activity. King emphasizes the merits of this last point, and refers to the validation offered through exam-based certification as follows:

The basic school finds it very hard to teach beyond the existing technology of the informal sector that surrounds it; and in practice, it very often falls far short of such expertise. Second, the informal sector clearly does not need any help from the schools in developing and reproducing expertise in the various trades; this happens through the sector's own systems of socialization. But third, by making practical work subject to national examination, attitudes towards productive work can gradually alter in ways that may be hard to quantify, but that are nevertheless important. (King, p. 28, in Fluitman, 1989)

Unfortunately, it is very difficult to systematically evaluate the social or economic returns to the African informal sector by curricular intervention at the primary school level. Aside from the lack of resources, there may be insufficient infrastructure and stability to undertake conclusive longitudinal studies at present. This certainly has been the case in the past. As with other specific investments in education, such as an expanded emphasis on science and mathmatics, support for the informal sector in the primary curriculum becomes an act of faith rather than a fully evaluated investment decision.

Vocational Education and the Informal Sector

Views on vocational education have endured cyclical periods ranging from deference to disdain: Benavot (1983) refers to this as the "rise and fall of vocational education." Today we are just emerging from a period of skepticism, so it is reasonable to anticipate a future rise of interest in vocational education. Bilateral and multilateral assistance organizations play a large role in promoting these educational trends. A recent World Bank policy paper provides an illustrative example: "The Bank faces a significant opportunity, and an equally significant challenge, in providing support for vocational education and training over the balance of the century. . . . The challenge is posed by the problems of developing cost-effective training systems in small low-income countries, notably in sub-Saharan Africa (Middleton & Demsky, 1988, p. ii).

Although there has been no conclusive study examining the role of education on economic growth in sub-Saharan Africa, for which much investment is predicated, there has been a limited amount of cross-national research that seems to suggest positive returns for vocational education during certain periods. For example, Benavot found that vocational education had a slightly stronger effect than general education on economic growth for all less developed countries during the period between 1955 and 1970; however, it had a small negative effect for the period between 1965 and 1980 (Benavot, 1986).

Funding

The institution of vocational education has been universally plagued with two major limitations: cost and relevancy. Critics often note the difficulty in obtaining suitably trained vocational instructors, and lament the lack of transferability of what is taught in vocational programs to the working world. Instructors are said to teach antiquated methods that have little marketability for the self-employed or informal sector production (Wright, 1986). A further complication pertaining to African vocational and nonformal education is that curriculum development is not typically a component of project development. Rather, there is a reliance on expatriate teachers and teacher trainers to design appropriate courses (Middleton & Demsky, 1989). This transference of curriculum from one environment (the expatriate's) to a radically different one (the host country) further divorces the relationship between the demands of the marketplace and the supply of newly skilled students.

Cost is arguably the major constraint in expanding African education. Pure vocational programs cost upwards of six times that of traditional schooling. Even supplemental courses are expensive. Industrial education courses in Kenya are twice as expensive as science, and eight times more expensive than math or Kiswahili in terms of initial development costs per student (Lauglo, 1986). Critics of African vocational education point to the high costs and lack of employability of the graduates (Middleton & Demsky, 1988).

Relevancy and Equity

One alternative to separate vocational schools is to incorporate vocational elements into the formal secondary education curriculum. This is often referred to as diversification. Such efforts are typically designed around issues such as relevancy, as well as equity. Because secondary school students are numerically and often socially an elite, there is a considerable political effort to imbue a sense of respect for manual labor that may be otherwise absent. The World Bank's enthusiasm toward diversification at times inspired educational policy that was inappropriately transferred to the countries in question. Scarce resources were used for the expansion of laboratories and technical and trade schools over general educational expansion (Middleton & Demsky, 1989; Wright, 1986). Much of the rationale for this expenditure in sub-Saharan Africa was either based on overly optimistic human resource surveys,[3] or on the desire to replace expatriate managers and technical workers.

The joint diversification goals of relevance and equity have produced arguably unfavorable results. Psacharopoulos and Loxley (1985) found in Tanzanian secondary schools that the students from lower-income backgrounds favored technical and agricultural programs while those from higher-income families chose academic and commercial programs. This class-based selection began at the secondary school level, where children of fathers with the highest levels of education (more than eight years) were six times more likely to be found in secondary school. Psacharopoulos (1986) was able to confirm a demonstrated gain in achievement in the particular areas of vocational specialization (such as agricultural, technical, and commercial achievement tests for these respective schools), controlling for a range of other factors.[4] The annual costs of diversified technical schools in Tanzania were about 14 percent higher than in the academic schools. Tracer studies conducted one year after graduation seemed to indicate little difference regarding a student's status—whether working, training, looking for work, or continuing on to higher education, despite the type of school attended.

Psacharopoulos also found that the vocational exposure of diversified schools seemed to have little if any immediate effect on either finding or creating employment. Only technical students seemed to show a correspondence between employment and their area of specialization. His research concluded that the economic returns for diversified education were negligible:

By any standard, the rates of return in Tanzania are low, ranging from two to six percent. The technical bias has the lowest return—a reflection of the higher unit cost associated with this bias. Conversely, the academic bias exhibits the highest rate of return. All that can be said at this point, is that the first indications do not corroborate the hypothesis that the introduction of pre-vocational studies into secondary schooling can be justified on the basis of their economic payoff being greater than for academic schooling. (Psacharopoulos, 1986)

A similar failure to identify a close correspondence between technical education and work was found in a study of Kenyan diversified schools (Jauglo & Narman, 1986). One year after taking their O-level examinations, students who had four or more years of Industrial Education (IE) displayed little variation with their non-IE counterparts regarding the ability to find work, undergo training, or continue with their education.[5] This study also found that those students who scored lowest in their fourth-form examinations were significantly more likely to obtain work. This apparent anomaly might be due to realizations based on lower expectations. Significantly, these findings undervalue both the effects of credentialling and of curricular exposure. The authors speculate that kinship and personalistic relations are the most significant components in obtaining employment.

Rates of return to education may reflect a salary bias rather than an inherent social inefficiency. For example, many sub-Saharan African bank clerks and secretaries are paid wages similar to or in excess of automobile mechanics, yet the costs of their education may be considerably less. In such conditions, rates of return might reflect a segmented labor market rather than the true social rates of return (Carnoy, 1980; Gordon, 1982). Labor market segmentation theory posits that the most lucrative jobs will be allocated according to criteria unrelated to productivity, such as ethnicity, gender, or social stratification. Empirically tested, occupational income will not be determined solely by productivity-compensating wage differentials.

Another critical issue is time lag. Individuals often start their own firms later in life. Others do not enter the informal labor market until well after formal education is completed. One study in Kenya found that only 6 out of 1,080 students were self-employed one year after their exams, limiting the applicability of IE considerably (Narman, 1988). A longitudinal study conducted three years later found little if any correlation between learning at an IE school and obtaining employment. The apparent failure of formal education to stimulate self-employment was also identified in a study of Sierra Leone, where less than 5 percent of the fifth-form (secondary) students planned to start their own business (Wright, 1986). Such findings seriously question the utility of current diversification strategies in Africa.

Nonformal and Informal Education and the Informal Sector

Nonformal education can be roughly characterized as out-of-school education that provides functionally oriented training or skill enhancement for specific subgroups, often aimed at productive employment. It is frequently cited as an alternative educational track for those who cannot continue with formal education. One of the major driving forces of nonformal education is the asserted irrelevancy gap between formal education and national development (Bock & Papagiannis, 1983; Coombs, 1968; Simkins, 1976). Formal education is cited as wasteful, rigidly structured, credential based, and hierarchical. Nonformal education, by contrast, is thought to be efficient, flexible, practical, and nonhierarchical.

The World Bank, which has supported many nonformal programs, characterizes African nonformal education as follows:

It serves mainly young adults, many of whom are the same age as their counterparts in the formal school; much of the activity is organized locally and takes place with little or no direct intervention and control from the state beyond some minimal registration and supervision; the young recipients (or their families) often pay for courses that are, in some sense, equivalent to those offered in the schools or in formal industrial training; even those who pay for instruction are typically drawn from the poorer elements of rural and urban society, and they are often obliged to combine their education or training with work; many of the courses taught, especially those organized through nongovernmental organizations, have been negotiated with the participants or their representatives and, to this extent, reflect the needs of the community. (World Bank, 1988)

By skirting the urban biases typical of African ministries of education, nonformal programs offer tremendous possibilities of effective skill development as well as social change. Because of the significant interaction between environmental and market forces and the curriculum itself, nonformal education presents a unique opportunity for promoting rural innovation. As Harbison (1973) states: "nonformal education often provides greater opportunity for innovation than centralized formal-education bureaucracies do."

There are a number of useful examples of African nonformal education relevant to the informal sector. For example, the village Polytechnics of Kenya, located in rural areas, are also designed to provide artisanal skills. The Vocational Improvement Centers in northern Nigeria were designed to improve the skills of artisans and journeymen workers. In Senegal, the Rural Artisan Training program develops and promotes skilled nonfarm work such as manufacturing and construction (McLaughlin, 1979).

Because of the local empowering nature of nonformal education, it often represents a challenge to the formal institutional arrangements associated with governments and ministries of education. Coles (1982) has identified four structural requirements for effective nonformal education, as follows:

1. Nonformal education must be regarded as an integral part of national development consonant with national objectives.
2. It should be viewed as a national service and be given an identifiable framework in which to operate.
3. Nonformal education must be an integral part of the education system.
4. The nonformal system must be adequately staffed with trained people.

The preceding structural requirements essentially highlight the shortfalls and weaknesses of most nonformal educational programs. They are typically directed by the adult education branch of the Ministry of Education, where resources are the most limited and staff the least professionally trained. All too often, such programs are brought out piecemeal under the direction of an external donor, only to collapse when the funding pipeline is shut. As a result, they are rarely provided the opportunity to fully integrate into national systems, nor are they seriously evaluated.

Empirical Research on Informal Sector Training and Skill Acquisition

To date, there has been very little research on the subject of skill acquisition in the informal sector, and even fewer attempts to evaluate the effectiveness and utilization of nonformal education on career activities. When specific programs are designed, they are typically small demonstration projects and lack sufficient resources for effective evaluation. For example, a number of training programs were set up for small craft producers in West African countries (Senegal, Chad, Upper Volta, Niger, Cameroun, and the Congo), with the assistance of the International Labor Organization. Most of these training programs were oriented toward farming-related crafts (e.g., bricklayers, blacksmiths), were very small, helping less than 1 percent of the producers, and involved primarily men (Trouve, 1984, p. 63). Another project, funded by the Swedish government, consisted of twenty-four seminars that trained 500 individuals in seven countries. As with many of the smaller projects, evaluation and monitoring components were not an integral aspect of the program, and it was not possible to confirm the relevancy of the curriculum or the impact on employment (Hultin, 1985).

When nonformal programs are large, they often focus on broad universal goals such as adult literacy. For example, the government of Tanzania attempted to develop adult education following the landmark Arusha declaration in 1967. The declaration was highly critical of Western assistance and the economic development paradigm, and stressed the need for self-reliance at the individual and local levels (Ravenhill, 1986). The historic dependence by the attending less developed countries on expatriate technicians and experts was cited as both the motivation and the inspiration to promote new types of mass education. Unfortunately, the Tanzanian population was not wholly convinced of the relevance of literacy: one study of village education found lack of attendance at adult literacy programs to be a major problem. Nationally, this pattern of poor attendance was well documented by the Ministry of National Education (Kweka, 1987). Unlike formal education, where the goal of certification is concrete and well established, nonformal education promises practical skills that may lack the imprimatur of a widely respected program. Participants in nonformal education are more likely to demand that their time and efforts are well spent in practical skill development. A failure to do so may encourage people to "vote with their feet," as in the Tanzanian case, providing very immediate feedback regarding the perceived utility of a particular program.

Any evaluation of the effectiveness of alternative educational investments must adequately reflect the variations in cost per student across the range of alternatives. Middleton and Demsky (1989) in comparing vocational costs in different parts of the world, found that the total investment costs per place were among the highest in Africa, particularly for nonformal and secondary education. The costs of World Bank–funded nonformal education in Africa exceeded that of secondary education by a factor of nearly six to one. Even considering that nonformal courses typically run one year, while secondary courses last two or three years, the nonformal programs still operate at costs of at least twice that of formal education. Student boarding costs in sub-Saharan Africa are one feature that explains the significantly higher vocational and nonformal educational costs (Middleton & Demsky, 1989). Boarding is normally justified in terms of equity issues, to ensure rural student participation. Considering the rapid growth and specific social and technological requirements of the informal sector in urban areas, there may currently be sufficient grounds to discount traditional rural–urban equity issues. Combined with innovative delivery systems, there is likely to be significant latitude in designing cost-effective nonformal programs. Thus, while traditional vocational programs have centered around providing formal sector skills to a heterogeneous student population, an alternative design might be to provide streamlined and perhaps more occupationally relevant training to students on location, in both rural and urban areas.

A Study of Microentrepreneurial Skill Acquisition in Sub-Saharan Africa

The most comprehensive African study regarding microentreprenurial skill acquisition is a recent World Bank study in west Africa that utilized an enlightening empirical approach to understanding the relationship between education and the informal sector (World Bank, 1992). Research teams surveyed over 1,500 microenterprise firms in four towns (Dakar, Senegal; Ibadan, Nigeria; Lome, Togo; and Niamey, Niger). Their objective was to learn how owners and employees obtained the necessary skills to function in their respective marketplaces. Their findings regarding skill acquisition are highly informative, and present the most accurate assessment of the demand for informal sector educational investments available to the region.

Although a limited number of microentrepreneurs obtain necessary skills and training in the formal sector, followed by informal self-employment, this is by no means the most typical career path (McLaughlin, 1979). The World Bank study found that the average time spent in wage work before starting a firm was about two years, of which most was spent in informal activities similar to the firms that they started. Considering the relatively limited size of vocational programs in Africa, it should come as no surprise that most informal sector microentrepreneurs and laborers obtain their skills by informal means, primarily through apprenticeship and on-the-job training. Only a small minority of the entrepreneurs surveyed (11 percent) were found to have any type of preservice training. The majority of those were in more technologically sophisticated trades such as automobile and TV repair, where barriers to entry and educational levels are much higher than with other trades, as well as in industries where local hygiene laws required specific courses, such as hairdressing and meal preparation (World Bank, 1992). A still smaller percentage (7 percent) had experienced inservice training beyond traditional apprenticeship practices. When asked to specify why they had not engaged in training activities, the entrepreneurs cited lack of training opportunities, lack of time, and lack of financial resources as the primary obstacles to continued nonformal education.

Interestingly, the demand for inservice training was fairly high: the majority indicated that they desired further training. Most of the respondents wanted to improve their technical skills, while less than 5 percent were interested in management, accounting, and marketing (World Bank, 1992). This finding underscores an important point, as many of the educational interventions offered by governments and nongovernmental organizations concentrate on accounting and marketing skills. It may be that such investments are inappropriate to the informal sector, reflecting biases introduced by the needs and experience of the formal small business sector.

The overall findings of the World Bank study can be interpreted as indicating that microentrepreneurs have few options, and are otherwise uninformed regarding potential training opportunities. The majority of individuals appear to have learned their skills through traditional apprenticeship; therefore, they consider this training the most valuable. Informal apprenticeship is one of the most ubiquitous components of the African informal sector. Most entrepreneurs felt that their most useful learning experience was apprenticeship (48 percent), followed by on-the-job training (27 percent), and school (11 percent). Apprenticeship was even more highly valued in the technical trades, such as auto and television repair, tailoring, weaving cloth, and metalwork. The relatively low identification of inservice and vocational training as a useful learning experience is most likely the result of limited exposure and opportunity. Significantly, in meal preparation, where a number of governments provide inservice training, 20 percent of those surveyed thought it was their most useful learning experience (World Bank, 1992). This points out a bias in the study, namely, an emphasis on subjective evaluation. Because microentrepreneurs simply believe that a particular education was the most beneficial does not make it so. An empirical test would be necessary to definitively compare and contrast the alternatives.

While the practice of apprenticeship is useful and economically rewarding for both the master and the apprentice (or it would otherwise not persist), the variation in both quality and costs will differ markedly between firms, sectors, and countries, in what is generally an unregulated activity. The subject of apprenticeship itself has not been comprehensively studied, so it remains unclear how effective and efficient the learning component is. The apparent satisfaction of the respondents could conceivably be an artifact of cognitive dissonance: having invested considerable time, money, and effort in the apprenticeship system, journeymen are unlikely to discount its value. The study did find a correlation between the level of formal education and the length of time necessary to start a business after completing the apprenticeship; however, there was no control for the socioeconomic advantages that the more-educated entrepreneurs probably enjoyed.

Alternative opportunities, such as vocational education and inservice training, were so rare as to be virtually insignificant in the study. As a result, when asked to evaluate their most useful learning experiences, responses were biased in favor of available opportunities, primarily apprenticeship and job experience. Over 50 percent of the microentrepreneurs surveyed by the World Bank responded that they would actively participate in skill advancement programs if available and affordable. Nevertheless, they indicated a preference for traditional educational platforms. Fully 73 percent of the firm owners preferred lectures and demonstrations as a mode of learning, over site visits by a specialist (18 percent) and correspondence courses, books, radio, and television. More than half of the sample preferred learning at a government center over nongovernmental organizations (17 percent), on the job (17 percent), or at home (22 percent). There are at least two explanations for this preference: it may simply be due to unfamiliarity with the alternatives; or there may be an underlying assumption that training at a government center will lead to some sort of government employment. The microentrepreneurs were also asked to evaluate the most important skills for their firms. Their overall rating was, in rank order, negotiations with customers, pricing, training staff, writing, designing, reading, advertising, utilizing new machines, and repairing machines (World Bank, 1992).

A set of questions were asked of entrepreneurs in different occupations. These included what were the most important skills they utilized, and where did they learn them. Reading and writing were almost universally acquired at school. Using a calculator was often identified as having been learned in a training course, on the job, or during apprenticeship, as were product design, preparing accounts, and pricing. By occupation, those with the highest levels of education, such as television and auto repair mechanics, indicated the greatest likelihood of learning how to use a calculator either in school or in a training class. These also tended to be the most lucrative enterprises in terms of income.

While the Bank's study presents a useful platform with which to begin evaluating future investment in education for the informal sector, there are still many issues that remain unresolved. For example, there is a need for measuring and evaluating various educational interventions from a less subjective viewpoint than that provided primarily through participant attitudes. Do some programs offer significantly higher rates of return than others? Are there particular apprenticeship arrangements that are more beneficial, producing more successful microentrepreneurs at lower costs? Is external intervention advisable, or is the sector better left to its own specifications, traditions, and relationships?

Possible Models for African Development

There is a general dearth of empirical research on nonformal education. However, insight can be gleaned from utilizing what available research there is, as well as extrapolating from other geographical areas.

In many ways, the Caribbean region represents a possible model for African development. Countries like Trinidad and Jamaica have populations with cultural backgrounds quite similar to that of many African countries; however, as middle-income[6] countries, they are wealthier than most in Africa. Perhaps they represent the future for those countries that are able to move up from low-income status. In any case, their situation is arguably insightful.

Jamaica has successfully implemented universal primary school education. As early as 1970, 96 percent of the labor force had completed at least five years of schooling (Honig, 1993a). This researcher interviewed over 250 microentrepreneurs during 1991 and 1992 with the objective of understanding how educational experience affects the behavior of firm owners and microenterprise financial lenders (Honig, 1993a). Interviews were also conducted with managers, loan officers, and nonformal trainers who were implementing credit and educational programs specifically aimed at supporting microenterprise. Although space limitations prohibit a thorough discussion of this research, a few highlights might be insightful.

Five financial organizations were studied, and all were found to have made significant efforts to complement credit distribution with some type of formal training program (four of the institutions conducted mandatory programs "in house"). These formal programs varied in length between organizations, ranging from two hour-and-a-half sessions to an indeterminate sequence typically consisting of twenty or more two-hour sessions spread over an eight-week period. Training programs mandated by lending agencies typically focused on financial issues such as simplified accounting and costing. These training courses were thought to be critical to the sustainability of the institutions because they were said to affect the overall default rates of microenterprise loans.

The research findings showed that these organizations are only subjectively aware of their target audience and have no specific systems in place to evaluate the success of educational intervention. There was no systematic study regarding the utilization of the concepts promoted nor were there mechanisms with which to evaluate the pedagogical techniques employed. When management was queried as to how effective their training programs were, responses typical of the one that follows were received: "That is something we have not really done. . . . We are remiss, in that we have never actually done a survey, or study, or have data to support (a particular training program or technique)."

It was found that the quality and consistency of the training sessions varied widely within organizations, as different individuals conducted the programs. There was virtually no formal monitoring or evaluation procedures. None of the trainers were professional teachers. They had little if any instruction regarding even the most basic pedagogical techniques. Had they not had a captive audience, it is unlikely that anyone would have been present at all.

The results of these training programs were dismal. Although there were extensive efforts to enforce compliance in the use of simplified accounting procedures by microenterprise support agencies, there was little if any bookkeeping or accounting conducted. Despite the fact that many microentrepreneurs had successfully completed courses ranging from two to twenty days, there was insufficient interest in applying what they had learned. Interviews with the firm owners indicated that they understood the material but were too busy to make use of it. They also frequently cited suspicion of the authorities regarding possible taxation.

Microentrepreneurs seemed to have a very diverse range of opinions regarding the utility of additional training. Most felt they already had the necessary qualifications and training. A little less than half the microentrepreneurs believed that they could benefit from additional educational programs, and only if they were relevant to their specific business and filled an identified "knowledge gap," such as technical or marketing problems.

Recommendations

Despite the relatively scant availability of empirical data on schooling and the informal sector in Africa, there exists a sufficient body of knowledge to inform educational policy decisions. Clearly there is a need for more collaboration between educators and the informal sector, particularly considering that projected microenterprise growth rates are twice that of the agricultural and modern sectors. Studies have shown that there is a considerable demand on the part of microentrepreneurs to learn specific aspects of their business. The World Bank found that over 50 percent of their sample had specific training wishes with an emphasis on technical skills, followed by a combination of technical and nontechnical skills (Birks & Fluitman, 1992). What is lacking, as seems to be reflected in the research literature, is a broader range of educational opportunities. For example, despite their low unit costs, correspondence and radio education have barely penetrated the informal sector. Programs that utilize the local expertise of micro-entrepreneurs are also markedly absent. As a result, preferences for more formal and structured alternatives are typically expressed.

It is probably a mistake to assume that as the overall levels of literacy and numeracy increase, vocational education in Africa will become more efficient and viable. First, African microentrepreneurs have identified skill development as their highest-priority item, while the gap between applied technology and what is taught in traditional vocational schools continues to widen. Second, as the Jamaican situation with its reasonably literate and numerate population illustrates, the promotion of subjects that are not of central concern to the microentrepreneurs themselves is largely ineffective.

Appropriate skill enhancement training that can be directly transferred to the workplace is of the utmost importance. We know that in the past, African vocational curricula have been largely designed by expatriate professionals. A central issue is to provide a curriculum based on local needs, which utilizes local technology to advance the range and effectiveness of microenterprise. The first step in accomplishing this goal is to recruit experienced microentrepreneurs as educators and disseminators of improved methods and technologies.

Unless microentrepreneurs see a practical return, they will not voluntarily invest their time in training. In Jamaica, the practice of using credit as an incentive only served to force microentrepreneurs through the motions. The techniques were not put into practice. Perhaps the best method of insuring local participation is by utilizing a community development model, configured as a bottom-up, rather than a top-down, organization. Linkages between curriculum and the kind of work typical of the local informal sector would be very direct. Incentives could be established with long-term returns to the microentrepreneurs themselves. For instance, local cooperatives can be organized to provide rotating credit and savings and to purchase raw materials in bulk. Local or regional experts can be identified to demonstrate new or improved techniques, perhaps utilizing a mobile delivery system (trade schools on wheels).

Considering the importance of traditional apprenticeship in the African informal sector, there is good cause to invest in programs that train the "master" in pedagogical techniques. Incentives will be a necessary and important component of such a program, as the microentrepreneurs may not perceive such training as a direct benefit, viewing the opportunity costs as too high. For example, governments can provide trained graduate apprentices with a license. They might also provide an apprenticeship placement service for connecting certified trainers with fee-paying apprentices.

It is also important to take a large-scale perspective in developing an efficient educational program for the informal sector. The government of Korea, for example, utilized a number of techniques to encourage efficient vocational education. For instance, to encourage low-status vocational education, the government provided scholarships, exempted graduates scoring above 50 percent on the national skills licensing examination from military service, and permitted the top 10 percent of secondary school graduates to enter college (Middleton & Demsky, 1989, p. 41). Korea implemented a national system for accreditation of postsecondary junior colleges to enforce standards on public and private schools. Korea also developed multifunctional agencies and support units for curriculum development and certification, including the Korean National Vocational Training Management agency and the Korean Institute for Research in Vocational Training.

Perhaps the most important consideration regarding vocational education and the informal sector is the necessity to weigh the overall costs and benefits. Monitoring and evaluation criteria should be in place at the very outset of the project, as this has been a major weakness of vocational education in sub-Saharan Africa (Psacharopoulos & Woodhall, 1985). Monitoring and evaluation should also consider secondary costs and benefits, such as technological and ecological effects, as well as intangible costs and benefits, such as job creation (Gittinger, 1982).

Many microentrepreneurs operate on the margin, often working twelve-hour days all week. For them, the opportunity costs of any traditional educational intervention are prohibitive. Hence, the World Bank found that a significant percentage (18 percent) preferred having a specialist visit their firm. Two possible alternatives to expensive site visits include correspondence and radio programs. Although these alternatives were not the preferred mode of training for African microentrepreneurs, this may be due to a general unfamiliarity with the approach. For example, it was found that many of the Jamaican microentrepreneurs had completed correspondence courses, particularly in the more technical fields such as radio and television repair. Correspondence schools, including radio programming, seem to perform well in both Korea and the Dominican Republic. The effectiveness might be even greater in sub-Saharan Africa considering overall equity issues (Psacharopoulos & Woodhall, 1985).

One final suggestion is to develop educational institutions that are not only community based but also derive curricula as a result of some type of market orientation or feedback. For example, auto repair students could apply their knowledge toward the repair and maintenance of the school's and faculty's vehicles, or competitive government contracts could be awarded for the production of a limited range of products and technologies taught at the school. This would promote a closer relationship between the work and school worlds, ensuring that practical and relevant skills are being taught, as well as subsidizing the overall costs of the institution itself.

The demands placed on African educational institutions by the expansion of the informal sector are likely to surge in the next decade, as self-employment becomes an increasingly necessary and popular component of the labor market. With careful and measured educational intervention, African governments can promote favorable social, economic, and technological outcomes for this rapidly growing component of the economy.

Notes

1. More highly educated individuals are somewhat atypical, representing a minority of informal participation.
2. Previously, the attempt to introduce agricultural work to the school environment in a number of African countries did little to stem the tide of urban migration (Tanzania, Kenya, Rwanda, Upper Volta, Benin, Uganda, and Botswana all tried this).
3. "In the majority of cases (labor requirements) were forecast from admittedly inadequate data, . . . not from global forecasts, but from enterprise surveys" (Middleton & Demsky, 1989, pp. 26–27).
4. Independent variables included parents' background, amount spent on teachers, and verbal and math aptitudes.
5. These findings were summarized as follows: "One year after 'O' levels, students with greater exposure to IE possess no advantage over others in finding employment. Hardly anyone is self-employed after one year. For those who do not stay on in school, the search for employment is so difficult that most remain unemployed after one year. Among those who find employment, most former IE students do not obtain jobs that seem to relate to IE in terms of skill requirements" (Lauglo, 1986).
6. As defined by the World Bank, a few African countries, such as Zimbabwe, Botswana, and Cote D'Ivoire are designated lower-middle-income countries.

References

Altback, P.G. (1982). *Comparative education.* New York: Macmillan.

Benavot, A. (1983). The rise and demise of vocational education. *Sociology of Education,* 56, 63–76.

Benavot, A. (1986). *Education and economic development in the modern world.* Doctoral dissertation, Stanford University, Stanford, CA.

Birks, S., & Fluitman, F. (1992). *A study of microentrepreneurial skill acquisition in Sub-Saharan Africa.* Washington, D.C.: World Bank.

Birks, S., Fluitman, F., Oudin, X., Salome, B., & Sinclair, C. *Skill acquisition and work in micro-enterprises: Recent evidence from West Africa.* (AFTED Technical Note No. 4). Washington DC: Education and Training Division, Technical Department, Africa Region.

Bock, J., & Papagiannis, G. (Eds.). (1983). *Non-formal education and national development.* New York: Praeger.

Carnoy, M. (1980). Segmented labor markets. In Carnoy et al., *Education, work and employment* (Vol. 2). Paris: Unesco-IIE.

Coles, E.K. (1982). *Maverick of the education family.* Oxford: Pergamon Press.

Coombs, P.H. (1968). *The world educational crisis: A systems analysis.* New York: Oxford University Press.

De Soto, H. (1989). *The other path.* New York: Harper and Row.

Fluitman, F. (Ed.), (1989). *Training and work in the informal sector.* Geneva: ILO.

Gittinger, J.P. (1982). *Economic analysis of agricultural projects.* Baltimore: Johns Hopkins University Press.

Gordon, R. (1982). *Segmented work, divided workers.* Cambridge: Cambridge University Press.

Gumbo, S.D. (1986, 7–9 May). Vocationalising curriculum in Zimbabwe: An evaluation perspective Vocationalizing Education Conference, Department of International and Comparative Education, University of London Institute of Education.

Haan, H. (1989). *Urban informal sector information, needs and methods.* Geneva: International Labor Organization.

Harbison, F.H. (1973). *Human resources as the wealth of nations.* Oxford: Oxford University Press.

Herschbach, D. (1989). Training and the urban informal sector: Some issues and approaches. In F. Fluitman (Ed.), *Training and work in the informal sector* (pp. 87–103). Geneva: International Labor Organization.

Honig, B. (1993a, 28–30 June). *Organizational structure and characteristics of demand in the Jamaican micro-enterprise credit market.* Paper presented at the request of the Office of the Prime Minister, Macro Policy Conference, Kingston, Jamaica.

Honig, B. (1993b, 15 September). *Segmentation in the Jamaican informal sector: The relationship between education, technology, and mobility.* Unpublished paper.

Hultin, M. (1987). *Vocational education in developing countries.* (Education Division Documents No. 34). Stockholm: SIDA.

Hultin, M. (1985, March). *Skill development for self reliance.* (Education Division Documents No. 25). Stockholm: SIDA.

Jauglo, L., & Narman, A. (1986, 7–9 May). *Diversified secondary education in Kenya: The status of practical subjects and their uses after school.* Vocationalizing Education Conference, Department of International and Comparative Education, University of London Institute of Education.

King, K. (1977). *The African artisan.* London: Heinemann.

Krueger, A.O. (1978, September). Factor endowments and per capita income differences among countries. *Economic Journal,* 641–659.

Kweka, A. (1987, May). *Adult education in a village in Tanzania.* (Education Division Documents No. 36). Stockholm: SIDA.

Lauglo, J. (1986, 7–9 May). *Practical subjects in Kenyan academic secondary schools.*

Vocationalizing Education Conference, Department of International and Comparative Education, University of London Institute of Education.

McLaughlin, S.D. (1979). *The wayside mechanic: An analysis of skill acquisition in Ghana.* Amherst: Center for International Education, University of Massachusetts.

Middleton, J., & Demsky, T. (1988, July). *World Bank investment in vocational education and training.* (Working Paper Series No. 24). Washington, DC: Population and Human Resources Department, The World Bank.

Middleton, J., & Demsky,T. (1989). *Vocational education and training: A review of World Bank investment.* (World Bank Discussion Papers No. 51). Washington, DC: The World Bank.

Narman, A. (1988, September). *Practical subjects in Kenyan academic secondary schools.* (Education Division Documents No. 39). Stockholm: SIDA.

Peattie, L. (1987). An idea in good currency and how it grew: The informal sector. *World Development, 15*(7), 851–860.

Psacharopoulos, G. (1986). *Curriculum diversification, cognitive achievement and economic performance: Evidence from Columbia and Tanzania.* Vocationalizing Education Conference, Department of International and Comparative Education, University of London Institute of Education.

Psacharopoulos, G., & Loxley, W. (1985). *Diversified secondary education and development.* Baltimore: Johns Hopkins University Press.

Psacharopoulos, G., & Woodhall, M. (1985). *Education for development.* New York: Oxford University Press.

Ravenhill, J. (1986). *Africa in economic crisis.* New York: Columbia University Press.

Republic of Kenya. (1983). *Code of law.* Nairobi, Kenya: Republic of Kenya.

Seymour, J.M. (1974). The rural school as an acculturating institution: The Iban of Malaysia. *Human Organization, 33,* 277–290.

Simkins, T. (1976). *Non-formal education and development.* (University of Manchester, Monograph 8). Manchester: University of Manchester.

Taylor, A., Rouse, L., Vanderveken, M., & Gabre-Maskal, H. (1987, 11 August). *Education and skill training for informal and rural employment in Cote D'Ivoire: A subsector study.* Washington, DC: The World Bank.

Trouve, J. (1984). Development of rural industries in French speaking Africa: A critical review. In S. Chuta & M. Sethuraman (Eds.), *Rural small-scale industries and employment in Africa and Asia.* Geneva: ILO.

United Nations. (1970, 1980, 1987). *UNESCO Statistical Yearbooks.* Paris: Author.

The World Bank. (1988). *Education in sub-Saharan Africa: Policies for adjustment, revitalization, and expansion.* Washington, DC: Author. Pp. 120–132.

The World Bank. (1992.) *1992 evaluation results.* Philadelphia: Author.

Wright, C.A.H. (1986, 7–9 May). Curriculum diversification re-examined—a case study of Sierra Leone. Vocationalizing Education Conference, Department of International and Comparative Education, University of London Institute of Education.

Section 2

Curriculum

Curriculum is a complex area that has been defined in many ways (Jackson, 1992). It is both overt and implicit. This section examines the six major issues and future concerns through the lens of teaching of four major disciplines in the curricula of sub-Saharan Africa: science, mathematics, citizenship, and literature. Each of these is found throughout much of the region and each is prominent in curricula worldwide.

The chapters in this section focus on curriculum and also on the instructional methodologies used to deliver it. These chapters deal with a common question: To what extent should the disciplinary curriculum and the methodologies used to teach it be Africanized? A related question is: What constitutes Africanization?

There are concerns regarding whether Africanization is defined as meaning nationalization with little consideration of relevant information relating to other African nations. Since sub-Saharan Africa is so diverse, not every relevant set of information from each African society can be taught. So, decisions must be made regarding selection of information. For example, in science, students should study the species of plant life found in their country. They should also study the diversity of plant species throughout Africa and the world. The relative proportions of the curriculum devoted to African species must be determined. Some instances have been identified where a national curriculum studies local examples in depth but then moves on to examples from Europe and mostly ignores examples from elsewhere in Africa or in the world. Osayimwense Osa considers similar instances in terms of literature studies in Chapter 7.

These are questions that are argued elsewhere in the world. In the United States there has been strong disagreement in the 1990s on interpretations of history, for example, and on which literature should be included in the curriculum from the worldwide choices available. As Africans debate these questions, they may develop a framework for the debate that informs others.

Africanization of the instructional methodology utilized to deliver the curriculum is a closely related issue considered by the authors of this section's chapters. Among the questions being asked are the following: Does it mean heavy utilization of traditional instructional methods? Since the nations of this region are striving to increase their levels of development and to compete successfully in the international sphere, do they have to adapt methodologies that are used in the developed nations? If such methodologies are adapted, how is the adaptation accomplished? How much are the methodologies adapted? How can teachers and the citizenry be encouraged to accept and use them? Tradition dominates instructional methodology in much of the world. Research studies in the United States consistently report heavy dependence on the use of lecture and the reading of textbooks and answering of questions on that reading by students (Sunal & Haas, 1993). Questions of appropriate instructional methodology are considered in many countries.

Both the curriculum and the methodologies used to teach it must deal with the prior knowledge, misconceptions, and expectations students bring to school. There is some research, particularly in science (Chapter 4) and in mathematics (Chapter 5) education relating to these areas among students in sub-Saharan Africa. The research has found some strengths deriving from culture and language. For example, the traditional spherical housing found in many parts of the region helps students acquire concepts of spherical geometry more easily than their peers in North America (see Chapter 5). African languages construct meaning for concepts related to heat differently than do European languages. As a result, students bring to the African classroom appropriate prior knowledge of heat (see Chapter 4). African teachers do not have to help their students eliminate many basic misconceptions about heat resulting from language, as do European teachers. Much more research is necessary to identify the range and depth of prior knowledge, misconceptions, and expectations African students bring to school. The research that has been done and is underway enriches the world's knowledge base in education. It helps make more evident the need to explore the strengths different cultures have in building students' conceptions and the misconceptions that are also engendered.

Science Education in Sub-Saharan Africa

Science education in sub-Saharan Africa is not a single or unified development. While there is similarity in the cultural and environmental forces affecting societies across Africa, the responses to those forces differ. Formal science education has a long history in the region that continues today. Informal science education always has been a part of African cultures. Chapter 4 focuses on formal science education in the region, but also gives some review of traditional informal science education.

Chapter 4 discusses all six of the major issues and future concerns that form the focus of this book. It groups its discussion into areas that heavily impact African science education. These are: language transitions and cultural metaphors, gender issues, environmental education, the impact of science and technology on society, preservice and inservice education, and classroom teaching. Narrative reviews and interviews with African science educators are used to identify patterns and trends across regions within a country and throughout sub-Saharan Africa.

Science education in the region has close ties with scientific research, much of which is done outside the region. Because of the expense of scientific research, much of it cannot be supported by African economies. This is a problem in all developing nations. However, some research relating to agriculture, traditional medicine, the history of science (for example, archaeoastronomy), nutrition, and the environment is being carried out in Africa.

Science education in the region must bring the forefront of research to students, yet it must not overlook indigenous science. Decisions have to be made regarding the level of technology supportable by the economy whether it be in educational technology or in hospital operating rooms. For example, should the typical 1950s operating room in the United States be the model for most of the region, since it has less reliance on high-technology equipment that is difficult and expensive to maintain? Or, can jumps be made directly to some level of high-technology use, skipping over developments that occurred in the 1970s and 1980s? Science educators throughout the region must help prepare students to contribute to the decision making. Indigenous science has a long history. Questions being asked in relation to indigenous science in the curriculum include the following: How can indigenous science best be incorporated into the classroom? How will it inform modern science? To what extent will it become a part of modern science? The wealth and diversity of indigenous science knowledge in the region fosters the debate on such questions in Africa. Solutions developed in the region should be of interest to science educators elsewhere.

Mathematics Education in Sub-Saharan Africa

As with science education, mathematics education is not a single entity across sub-Saharan Africa. Yet, many of the forces shaping it across the region are similar, although each country's response is unique. The similarities allow the authors of Chapter 5 to identify patterns and trends as they address the six major issues and future concerns. These are of importance to educators worldwide, since they suggest how mathematics education might best serve wide ranges of populations.

Mathematics and mathematics education have a long history in sub-Saharan Africa. However, until very recently formal mathematics education took its curriculum from Europe, as structured by colonial powers. The long history of mathematics education in the region is now recognized. The dearth of examples relevant to local culture and the absence of teaching materials derived from the local culture in colonial curricula are evident. Africans have begun to develop mathematics curricula that utilize local applications and materials. Throughout the developing world educators are attempting to "localize" the examples and materials used to teach mathematics. Strategies and ideas developed in Africa may be transferable elsewhere or may suggest avenues for local development in other regions.

Research on the development of mathematical concepts in the region has found strengths fostered by local language and culture. These findings are influencing the African curricula being developed. Yet, standardized testing drives much of the curricula and instruction as it does elsewhere in the world. These concerns exist in all nations. As Africans strive for a high quality of mathematics education, they may be able to offer suggestions to others in both developed and developing nations, regarding the utilization of local strengths in the mathematics curricula and the diminishment of the role of standardized tests in curricula and instruction.

Chapter 5 discusses the specific case of mathematics education in Zimbabwe. It examines the difficulties of the search to develop an authentic, deep, and well-understood mathematics literacy in sub-Saharan Africa. Both the search and the difficulties exist throughout the region and the world.

Citizenship Education: Defining a Nation

Nation building and national citizenship are of importance in much of sub-Saharan Africa as nations struggle to establish a national identity transcending ethnic, religious, or regional loyalties. Many of the region's nations were structured by colonial powers who paid little attention to the cultures within a region, often putting together pieces of different groups in one country and separating a single group over what are now two or more countries.

All nations deal with diversity of cultures within their borders. The diversity is a great challenge in sub-Saharan Africa, because the borders are so recently established and were imposed upon the populace by colonial powers. One means of dealing with the problems engendered is through citizenship education, usually using social studies as its vehicle. Citizenship education is considered the main goal of education in many nations (Sunal & Haas, 1993). Schools carry out a systematic teaching program aimed at producing well informed, democratically active citizens. Chapter 6 discusses citizenship education, considering all the six major issues and future concerns. As it does so, it looks carefully at Africanization of the curriculum, instructional strategies, and preservice and inservice education, parallels with the chapters on science and mathematics education.

This chapter examines the specific case of Nigeria, whose philosophy stresses that education should be geared toward self-realization, better human relationships, effective citizenship, national consciousness, and progress. Patterns and trends are identified as this nation tries to find a means of developing citizenship among a widely diverse populace speaking many languages and holding differing traditional religious, social, and political perspectives.

While African nations are stressing citizenship education as a part of nation building, they also must develop conceptions of the role of the nation and its citizens in an interdependent world. In their search for a common national identity and allegiance, Africans experience extreme versions of the difficulties faced to a lesser extent in all other nations. Keeping the whole together when the parts have very different identities is a consistent problem everywhere, and one that educators work with on a continuing basis as frictions between groups cause dissension. In the extremity of their difficulties the very diversity that fuels those difficulties also fuels efforts to address them. These efforts must be innovative if they are to meet the challenges before them.

Establishing an understanding in the citizenry of their partnership with others in an interdependent world is another challenge faced by all nations. Educators are challenged worldwide to work toward such an understanding. As African nations try to build a sense of world citizenship among the populace, they often do so before a sense of national citizenship is fully established. Innovative ideas growing out of the existing diversity may offer possible solutions to this problem.

Using Indigenous Literatures in Sub-Saharan African Schools

Perhaps even more than in science, mathematics, and citizenship education, literature education reflects the problems facing all disciplines in sub-Saharan Africa. There is a rich and deep diversity of oral and, more recently, written literature for students to study. At the same time, there are traditions that continue from the colonial period and have a narrow focus on the literature of the colonizer. The very form of the indigenous literature, more oral than written, results in additional concerns: oral literature may be written down, but then it loses some of its unique and important qualities. Chapter 7 discusses these problems, addressing all of the major issues and future concerns identified in the introductory overview.

Traditional literature in the region is tribally based and passed on within the group from storyteller to storyteller. Chapter 7 considers the development of oral and written literature and of what is conceptualized in modern terms as "African" literature. It considers questions such as the following: In modern terms, is there an indigenous literature in the region? Or, are there indigenous literatures? Once a story is told in a language other than the one in which it was originally told, does it lose too much of its linguistic and cultural qualities? Should students be exposed to much of their own tribal literature before exposure to other tribal literatures? Questions relating to balance between local, regional, and worldwide literatures in the curriculum have many parallels to the concerns expressed in the chapters on science, mathematics, and citizenship education. There are other parallels as well with these chapters.

Chapter 7 also examines issues related to the use of adolescent and young adult, rather than adult, literature with students. It considers the context, characters, and message in literature, and which literature is best understood and appreciated by students. These issues are related to the use of indigenous literature in African curricula.

The issues in sub-Saharan literature education appear elsewhere in the world. All literature originally had its basis in storytelling within a small group of people, the equivalent of a tribe. Modern literature often speaks to a larger audience, yet has strong cultural ties, although the group to which it is tied may be very large. There is an awareness that the education of many adults familiarized them with only a small and narrow portion of the world's literature. There is debate over the positive and negative aspects of that education. There is debate over how much that educational perspective should and must change. These questions are even more complex and deep in sub-Saharan Africa than in most other regions of the world. As with the issues facing the other major disciplines discussed in this book, African solutions are likely to be innovative, because they emanate from such diversity and because existing ideas have not provided the solutions needed. Because of the creativity that is needed to address these issues, other regions of the world may have an opportunity to examine new ideas, applying those that show promise in their region.

The chapters in Section 2 use the lens of disciplinary content for examining education in sub-Saharan Africa. Each chapter considers the six major issues and future concerns through that lens.

Patterns and trends are found within the diversity that characterizes the region.

References

Jackson, P. (1992). Conceptions of curriculum and curriculum specialists. *Handbook of research on curriculum* (pp. 3–40). New York: Macmillan.

Sunal, C., & Haas, M. (1993). *Social studies for the elementary and middle school student*. Ft. Worth: Harcourt Brace Jovanovich.

Chapter Four
Science Education in Sub-Saharan Africa

Dennis W. Sunal, R. Lynn Jones, and Peter Okebukola

The status of science education in sub-Saharan Africa cannot be described in a brief chapter, nor should it be viewed as a single or unified development. While some of the cultural and environmental forces creating change are similar across countries and various ethnic groups, the response to these forces in developing the educational discipline of science education has been unique in time, purpose, content, and organization. Formal science education in sub-Saharan Africa began at least as early as the fourteenth century with Arabic schools and continues throughout the regions in primary and secondary schools and at universities today. This chapter will focus on the formal school science education in sub-Saharan Africa.

There is a long tradition of informal science education in sub-Saharan Africa developed through local community education. Informal science education has influenced the formal system of education and provides a large segment of the population with a basic science education throughout sub-Saharan Africa today. Informal science education in sub-Saharan Africa is associated with a wide range of occupations including those of tradesmen, farmers, fishermen, and local cottage industries. These occupations involve concepts in the science and art of smelting and alloying techniques for working with metals, woodcarving and wood working, dyeing and weaving textiles and reeds, selecting and using medicinal plants, glass making, pottery making, charcoal production, astronomy and astrology, weather and planting seasons, irrigation, erosion control, multicropping, burning practices to provide fertilizer for the next crop, architectural styles and building materials, materials for use as fuels, well construction, boat building, navigation, fishing, herding, nomadic pastoralists' movements based on changes in food resources, control of disease, and using tools of communication. The process of informal science education today involves oral transmission, apprenticeships, experts in the community, roadside signs, leaflets, pamphlets and books, market trade fairs, and television.

The teaching of formal school science and preparation of science teachers in sub-Saharan Africa is diverse and varies locally, regionally, and by country. Efforts at change in science education range from local projects involving science equipment in a particular school to large-scale projects attempting to increase the capacity of a developing country in the area of inservice teacher education. Science education in many developing countries is the area in greatest need for quality improvement, both because of historic underdevelopment and the perceived importance science education has for national development aspirations (de Feiter, Vonk, & van den Akker, 1995a).

With such diversity in culture, time, and space the approach taken in this chapter was to describe science education in sub-Saharan Africa, beginning with an overview of the status of science education, and then to develop an in-depth review of critical issues affecting the field. The status of science education includes the following areas: student population and teaching, the science curriculum, and standardized testing. The critical issues are grouped in terms of the following research areas:

1. language transitions and cultural metaphors
   a. language factors and science learning
   b. science education research in Africa and Western culture
2. gender issues in science
3. environmental education
4. the impact of science and technology
5. preservice and inservice education
6. African classroom teaching

The procedure used to examine science education in sub-Saharan African involved sampling specific research efforts through narrative reviews and interviews with African science educators in order to identify patterns and trends across regions within a country and throughout sub-Saharan Africa. These patterns and trends are discussed along with the critical issues facing science education in sub-Saharan Africa.

Status of Science Education in Sub-Saharan Africa
Student Population and Teaching

Science teaching practice, curriculum, and the school context as intended through official policy are very different from those practices actually implemented and used in African schools. Beginning with independence, aspects of the nature and character of schooling and science education as a part of the process in sub-Saharan African countries has changed. Countries became aware of the importance of science education as a means for development as evidenced by numerous conferences, reports, and symposia over the past forty years. Declarations such as the Lagos Plan (1980) and the African Priority Program for Economic Recovery (1986) stressed development based on self-reliance in science and technology applications (Hassan, 1993). Without an adequate science education program, economic development cannot be achieved (OAU, 1981).

In most nations the policy of mass education and universal primary education developed in the past three decades created huge growth in enrollments. Due to the economic constraints of the 1970s and 1980s, dwindling resources for education became common. Since the late 1970s, the economic downturn resulted in decreasing spending on social services. This has had strong consequences for education. It has resulted in a general decline in enrollments and deterioration of the quality of education (Pendaeli, Ogunniyi, & Mosothwane, 1993). In addition, to meet International Monetary Fund conditions requiring cutting the number of civil servants, many countries have cut back on large numbers of their teachers.

Unemployment among qualified science teachers was at a high level, creating morale problems. Money was unavailable for school construction and repair, education of new teachers, inservice education of experienced teachers, and science equipment and textbooks for students, even though the school population exploded. In many countries teaching salaries decreased and teaching became the lowest-paid profession. In those communities where schools were built, these newly established schools were relatively disorganized and usually lacked complete facilities and a stable teaching force. These conditions led to instability in school organization and, along with the poor social and health infrastructure, influenced instability in the teaching force and low teacher morale (Fuller & Heynemann, 1989).

Teaching conditions in schools deteriorated, while at the same time many more students had to be accommodated. For students, these developments created poor basic science preparation due to many unqualified and underprepared teachers (Cantrell, Kouwenhoven, Mokoena, & Thijs, 1993). In a study of science teacher stress Okebukola and Jegede (1990) used the Science Teacher Stress Inventory with 206 science teachers in Nigeria. They found the greatest stress centered on the lack of equipment and materials for teaching science, followed by coping with teaching difficult, abstract concepts, inability to complete the syllabus before the external examination date, having to teach subjects for which one was not trained and having to cope with changes in program and science curricula. The researchers concluded that the stressors lowered on-the-job performance and reduced the quality of teaching in schools.

In a national survey of basic education carried out in Nigeria in 1992 deficiencies affecting student learning and literacy were noted. These included curricular deficiencies and inadequate facilities. Some schools were without buildings, 12 percent had no chairs, and 80 percent lacked science materials. Economic constraints for parents included the costs of books, uniforms, and lunches. Health issues led to poor attendance. Among these were common illnesses—diarrhea, measles, and malaria. Sociocultural constraints due to religious beliefs also had an impact (Okebukola, 1995).

Dropout, nonattendance, and repetition of a year's courses are common phenomena in many African countries. One exception is Botswana. Girls are in the majority in areas of Botswana. In Nigeria, girls are the majority of students in schools in the southern portion of the country, and boys are in the majority in the upper northern portion (Okebukola, 1995). While somewhat higher in the recent past, enrollment in primary school is down to 61 percent. Wastage, or dropping out of school, in primary school is 17 percent for the lower grades, but much higher for the upper grades. Students consider the completion of primary school as having no advantage for obtaining a job, and parents consider children completing primary school to be less suited to local community life. Wastage in junior secondary schools is about 20 percent but diminishes in senior secondary schools. Secondary schools enroll less than 30 percent of the total adolescent population. Nigeria aims at having 50 percent of school age children literate by the year 2000. However, the actual accomplishment of this aim is expected to occur between 2020 and 2050 (Okebukola, 1995).

Participation in science subjects is often low because most students and teachers regard science as difficult and avoid it. Scores on national examinations are also low. This is true for rural regions in most of sub-Saharan Africa, with the exception of South Africa, where many rural schools outperform urban schools. Even with high passes on examinations, the actual understanding and appreciation of science is usually questionable. The usefulness of what students have learned for future careers is generally inadequate. A large proportion of science teachers lack adequate qualifications or background. Advances have been made in the past decade; however, because of large growth in enrollment, many more teachers are needed. For those teachers qualified to teach science, many are qualified only to teach in the junior secondary level, but they teach in senior secondary schools. In Botswana, Lesotho, Swaziland, and Namibia as well as most other cultures, many qualified science teachers are new and have very limited experience (de Feiter, Vonk, & van den Akker, 1995b). Professionalization of the teaching force through inservice development is lacking (de Feiter, 1993).

Science Curriculum

School curricula in sub-Saharan Africa are mandated and implemented on a national basis. In many countries the science curriculum is derived from European models and/or utilizes European textbooks. At the senior secondary level few locally developed curricular materials are available. At the junior secondary level more innovation has taken place in school organization, which has led to a far greater amount of locally and nationally prepared materials for the teaching of science. Adjustments made to curricula tend to follow developments in the British, French, and Dutch educational systems, rather than needs mandated by the local society and developments in sub-Saharan African countries. Science curriculum development during the late 1960s and 1970s in anglophone African countries was influenced by developments in the United Kingdom, principally involving the Nuffield Foundation's secondary science textbooks. These textbooks put a strong emphasis on laboratory work and the methods of scientists in solving problems, with a goal of teaching students to become scientists. During the 1980s European textbooks changed, with new emphasis on issues in science and society, and the goal of providing science for all students. The same trends were noted in sub-Saharan African text materials (Ware, 1992). In many countries these materials are the only ones available in the market and in bookshops. In general, they are older editions.

The change in aims for schools create additional problems for teacher training and the science curriculum. Senior secondary schools in the past prepared students for university work. Universal primary education and the shift in emphasis to science for all students in secondary schools changed the nature of the intended curriculum. No longer was the sole aim of secondary education to have an academic orientation. Some sub-Saharan African countries are implementing a vocational emphasis in the schools and in the science curriculum provided to the students. For example, in Nigeria the junior secondary school curriculum has undergone development for more than a decade. The students are tracked into different courses of study. At present, these include tracks in grammar or academic studies (for higher education), teacher training, technical training, and vocational/commercial studies. The core curriculum in the junior secondary school includes science, mathematics, social studies, Nigerian languages, and foreign languages. The technical curriculum includes agricultural science, technology, local arts and crafts, and business studies. Rural and urban schools focus on different aspects of the technical curriculum. Urban schools will generally focus on business studies, while rural schools focus on agricultural science and local arts and crafts (Farouk, 1995). However, due to the lack of training, school facilities, and resources, as well as potentially difficult health conditions, the science curriculum as implemented in classrooms in many regions in sub-Saharan Africa does not reflect the intended official curriculum or examinations. Typically, few choices in science subjects are available, limiting the relevancy of the science curriculum. Often, instructional practice further limits relevancy and scientific literacy, because of its heavy use of lecture and memorization. Many times the language of the school is foreign. Little attention is paid to the home language of the students.

Another aspect of change involves introducing comprehensive education plans. It is generally found in sub-Saharan Africa that implementation takes a different form from what was originally intended. The professionals who are the target of the change are generally not provided with adequate information about the system of changes they are expected to implement. Meaningful involvement of all those who have a role in developing changes in policy, curricula, or pedagogy is important. Participants need to own the decisions and fully embrace the policy and its decisions. Otherwise, they are going through a process they do not understand and for which they have no conviction (Nyirenda, 1995).

Standardized Testing

National examinations are given at critical points in the school curriculum, typically at the end of primary school, junior secondary, and high school. Their purpose is to determine entrance to the next level of education. Each higher level has greatly fewer openings for students, so the national exams provide a selection mechanism for schools. The West African examinations (WAEC, West African Examination Council), for example, were originally modeled after the GCSE in Britain. The same examination pattern can be found in most sub-Saharan African countries. Since European examinations were designed for an economy and society different in many ways, numerous problems with students passing science sections have been reported with examinations. Some of the differences include lack of school facilities and equipment, lack of adequately trained teachers, and an ill-defined curriculum in terms of specific purpose and relevance. The economy of most sub-Saharan African countries provides primary school graduates with few jobs in view of their minimal-level skills. Most economies have not developed enough even to absorb most of the secondary school graduates who have higher science skills (Banya, 1995). The science curriculum and examination is not relevant to the needs of the majority of the students, those who do not attend university.

Although this description gives a general picture of the status of science teaching and learning in sub-Saharan African classrooms, there are variations in conditions between countries and within a country. There is a lack of systematic information on many regions.

Further research into the status of science teaching in sub-Saharan African schools is needed.

Research on Language Transitions and Cultural Metaphors

Transplantation of science curricula from one country to another has not had a successful history. Sub-Saharan African countries need to look for their own solutions to their particular educational problems, taking note of experiences, methods, and trends in other countries (Gray, 1989). There is an urgent need for current nationally developed criteria in science education at all levels. These criteria should not necessarily follow the example of European nations, where the complete learning context for science education for a foreign society is tied up in the aims, goals, administrative processes, assessment systems, teaching methods, and practical content of different syllabuses (Gray, 1989). If a rationale for the modernization of school science is attempted, then it must conform to the scholastic and social needs of Africa (Gray, 1989).

There should be a common ground for science education bearing in mind cultural, economic, and political differences between sub-Saharan African countries and the regions within them. Mohamed Khan, the Deputy Secretary of the Commonwealth Science Council of Lusaka, Zambia, believes that for science to be regarded as an integral part of each culture, it should be taught in the mother tongue. Khan also believes that scientific organizations in every country should institute adequate mechanisms to communicate with their own public by publishing brochures, reports, and so forth, both in the local language and in English (Gray, 1989).

Language Factors and Science Learning

The nature of the language and learning difficulties that South African Standard 3 children experience when they change from their mother tongue (Setswana) to English as a medium for instruction were studied by Macdonald (1990). The study was part of the Threshold Project work in 1987, focusing on a section of the South African Standard 3 general science syllabus on plant structure, growth, and reproduction. The empirical results obtained on the Setswana and English tests revealed the following. First, the students already knew a great deal in their mother tongue about the topic of plants before they began instruction. Second, after being taught in the conventional way in English, they were able to demonstrate no real learning gains in English. Third, after being taught in the conventional way in Setswana, they were able to demonstrate large factual gains in Setswana. Fourth, after being taught in the new "transitional way" in English, they were able to demonstrate some learning gains in English. The transitional way was a teacher-centered inquiry approach. The study did not provide a clear indication of whether long-term intervention would result in satisfactory levels of performance with the children. The study showed a significant positive change in performance, but not a large practical change as found with instruction in Setswana. The significant variable in using the transitional way in English was the use of science process skills. This indicated that students were able to deal with many of the science process skills that were appropriate in the English-based curriculum.

Harris (1981) suggested that the presence of misconceptions about heat among Westerners is a semantic problem. Western languages, such as English, use words for heat that convey the wrong idea because of their historical antecedents, causing students to think calorically rather than understanding heat as energy. Hewson and Hamlyn (1983) conducted a study of the role played by cultural metaphors in the conception of the physical phenomenon of heat in the Sotho and Tswana peoples in Southern Africa. The metaphor involving heat in these cultures refers to a concept of ritual impurity. The concept relates to the belief that on occasion a person's blood may become hot or cold for a period of time. Coolness implies health and social harmony. Hotness implies sickness and social disharmony. This metaphor involving heat is used frequently in everyday life.

In Western culture, the metaphor of heat refers to caloric conceptions. The caloric view of heat is an eighteenth-century European view of hot and cold. Heat was believed to be a fluid that flowed into and out of things when they became hot or cold. Heating an object meant filling spaces between atoms with caloric. This could be measured to determine the amount of caloric present. These scientific terms for heat are still used in European languages today; for example, heat flow, calorie, and heat capacity, even though the kinetic theory of heat energy is now prevalent. These caloric conceptions have been found in a number of studies to be barriers to learning, or alternative conceptions that inhibit the learning of modern scientific conceptions of heat energy. Sotho and Tswana students were not found to be inhibited in their learning of the modern concept of heat energy. They did not have to unlearn the outdated concept of caloric heat as rooted in the English language. It was concluded that for these students learning science in their everyday language, combined with their intuitive notions of heat, had an adequate basis on which to develop the modern concept. The notion of agitated blood is not so distant from that of energy associated with the movement of particles in a substance that learning may be slightly enhanced because of the cultural metaphor throughout the language. The results of this study suggested that consideration should be taken of linguistic factors in designing curricula and teaching science in the classroom.

Hewson and Hamlyn (1985), in a second study, examined cultural metaphors pertaining to heat as understood by the Sotho group in Southern Africa. Their research was an attempt to establish whether cultural metaphors are still subscribed to by Sotho people who have undergone extensive societal change. These changes include acculturation to a Western way of life, moving from a rural area to a life in towns or cities, exposure to Western schooling, and becoming conversant in a European language, namely English. As in the previous study, this one investigated the effect of heat metaphors on people's understanding of the physical phenomenon of heat and on their ability to learn the orthodox scientific view concerning heat. Two multiracial schools were involved in the study. School One was predominantly Sotho in a semirural area in Bophuthatswana; the other, School Two, was a predominantly English-speaking European school in the suburbs of Johannesburg. All students ($n = 10$) interviewed spoke English well. Six semischooled adult workers from Johannesburg (ages 20–40 years) and four unschooled women workers (ages 35–45 years) also were included in the interviews. Caloric conceptions were identified by four subjects in the total group. These subjects were a high school student from School Two, two students from School One, and one male semischooled worker. The student from School Two and the adult had Westernized cultural backgrounds. The researchers could not explain the responses of the students from School One using the study's hypotheses. Hewson and Hamlyn's research suggests that Sotho students do not have to learn and unlearn outdated notions of caloric heat deeply rooted in Western thinking before being able to acquire the kinetic view of heat. They further suggest that for these students their everyday metaphorical language, combined with their intuitive "prekinetic" notions of heat, provides adequate ideas upon which to construct the scientific conceptions.

According to Hewson and Hamlyn (1985) meaningful learning involves an active construction of knowledge by the learner. The growth of knowledge is influenced by the first language of the learner and, in particular, by the metaphors embodied therein. Metaphorical concepts are as essential to scientific language as they are to everyday language. Students, with the help of the teacher, need to be aware of metaphors and to recognize areas where metaphors conflict or overlap in order to reconcile everyday knowledge with scientific knowledge.

Science in sub-Saharan Africa is largely a product of Western culture (Ogunniyi, 1988). Throughout the region there is a great drive to import Western science and technology (Ogunniyi, 1985). The problems of learning science faced by Western and non-Western students are fundamentally the same. For both, the problem concerns conceptual change from existing knowledge accumulated from previous experiences to orthodox scientific knowledge, which is formal knowledge concerning natural phenomena. Hewson (1986) investigated the conceptions in a particular science concept area of a group of forty high school students. These students came from a non-Western culture, the Qwa Qwa area in South Africa. They used little modern technology. Their home language is non-Western. They have been exposed to certain orthodox conceptions in science in schools modeled on the Western system of education. The schools visited for Hewson's study were among the best in the area, but were relatively poor. The students were presented with a scientific task related to sinking and floating objects and then asked to explain the results of the task. Relatively few students answered in terms of the orthodox scientific definition of density and many of them answered in terms of alternative conceptions that were not the accepted scientific view of mass, volume, density, and force. These alternative conceptions represent barriers to learning in a typical science classroom. The alternative conceptions identified seemed to reflect the students' everyday experiences as well as the structure of their home language.

Science Education Research in Africa and Western Culture

The impact of science and technology in developing countries has tended to bear on two opposing directions. Western science and technology is being sought virtually without limits but there is local opposition to certain aspects of Western lifestyles, attitudes, and values (Urevbu, 1991). The movements in two opposing directions lead to the questions: Is the impact of science and technology on everyday-life situations to be viewed only in terms of Western attitudes, lifestyles, and values? Are indigenous cultures and value systems of developing countries to disappear in this transfer of science and technology? What should be the science-related educational concerns of developing countries? One major concern of developing countries worldwide, as it pertains to the impact of science and technology, has been what they consider to be their excessive dependence on the advanced industrialized countries for their development, and what appears to be an inevitable perpetuation of that dependence (Urevbu, 1991).

A case study in an African setting examined inservice teacher education and the transfer of knowledge (Rogan & Macdonald, 1985). The case study was based on the Science Education Project (SEP), conceived in 1975 with the aim of improving the quality of science education in some of the least-privileged schools (i.e. black) in South Africa. One main impression of the authors was that instructional methodology identified as important from reviews of studies undertaken in the United States was also important in the SEP experience. On the other hand, the setting of the innovation in the context of a developing country gave rise to additional methodologies that did not always appear to receive emphasis in developed countries.

Ogunniyi (1984, 1986) examined the nature of science curriculum in sub-Saharan Africa and its effect on student learning. He proposed that most science curricula in sub-Saharan Africa are modeled on those in the West and do not reflect the cultural background of the learner. The content of school science does not make a clear distinction between the traditional ways of viewing the world and that of science. Some differences include: people rather than things are the basis for African cosmology; the concepts of causality, chance, and probability are based on a different logic from that of science; and Africans do not have an attitude of externality to the world and do not see themselves as separate from the world in which they find themselves.

Using a science curriculum design to take into account the alternative conceptions as expressed in the African worldview, Ogunniyi (1984, 1986) investigated its impact on student learning. The following conclusions were suggested in regard to the adaptation of Western science to traditional African culture. First, the traditional worldview of the literate and the nonliterate people living in a so-called traditional society—in this case Nigeria—is not totally devoid of scientifically valid views of the universe. Second, the influence of traditional cosmology among urban and rural dwellers may not be as powerful as is generally believed. Third, the two systems of thought are not necessarily mutually exclusive of each other. It is possible to hold a scientific as well as a traditional view of the world, perhaps in the same way in which certain scientists in the West hold the scientific and the Christian worldview. While the two systems may not always be in conflict with each other, to the majority of students involved in the study, each system serves some useful purpose, but neither is adequate for coping with all experiences. Fourth, the sex, religion, ethnic group, or level of education of the people does not have any significant influence on their traditional worldview. Fifth, the scientific worldview may not be able to completely displace the people's traditional world outlook, even after a thorough exposure to the former. Sixth, an exposure to a well-organized history and philosophy of science that emphasizes a scientific worldview does enhance the peoples' orientation toward the view.

Based on earlier work, Ogunniyi (1988) concluded that it is not yet clear whether or not adapting science curricula will resolve all possible conflicts between the two systems of thought. What is evident from earlier studies is that people's traditional worldview can be enlarged to accommodate the scientific point of view. In spite of the significant differences between viewpoints, the traditional worldview of the subjects remained essentially the same following instruction. In sub-Saharan Africa, Western education has not been used to promote integration between the Western and African cultures, but to replace existing ideas (Ogunniyi, 1988). If the scientific view is to be part of formal education it should be geared toward adapting traditional views to include the more scientific one. Science curricula should not present modern science from a superior vantage point, but as a way to cope better with everyday life experiences. The individual in a traditional society should be made aware of the benefits and limitations of science and be exposed to the similarities and differences between the traditional and scientific worldviews. This should be done so that the student can use the understandings gained through science instruction to make appropriate decisions in daily life based on cultural beliefs and values.

Gender Issues in Science

Sub-Saharan African girls generally attend school less often and drop out of school earlier than do boys (Harding & Apea, 1990). In Kenya, for example, a higher proportion of girls than boys drop out of primary school, 26 percent as opposed to 7 percent, and a higher proportion of girls fail to qualify for the Certificate of Primary Education. The high level of wastage and the dropout rate of girls can be attributed to a cultural and educational system that discriminates against girls (Eshiwani, 1985). Most primary schools in Kenya are coeducational, but most secondary schools are not. This gives rise to inequities, because there are more government secondary schools for boys than for girls. In 1985, 36 percent of total enrollments in government secondary schools were girls. More than half the girls in secondary school that year went to Harambee, or private schools. These have fewer facilities, many offering no science, and more poorly motivated teachers with lower qualifications than have government schools (Eshiwani, 1985; Kinyanjui, 1988). Recent Nigerian data indicate a gender-related change occurring in school enrollment in some parts of the nation. More girls than boys are attending primary school in parts of southen Nigeria (Okebukola, 1995).

Tanzania is attempting to equip girls' schools with more adequate science teaching, but girls' schools with comparable facilities to boys' schools are fewer in number. For example, while twenty-one boys' schools offer physics as an advanced-level subject, only four girls' schools do so (Harding & Apea, 1990).

An awareness of gender biases in science, technology, and mathematics education in Africa was the focus of a regional workshop held in Ghana in 1987. The workshop was designed to identify stereotyped attitudes that prevent women from entering science and technology. It was recommended that women scientists and technologists should serve as role models to girls to challenge the stereotyped beliefs of teachers and parents (Harding & Apea, 1990). To meet this recommendation, women scientists were selected and interviewed. Tapes of the interviews were used to create profiles to be used in the publication of a resource guide and a script used by local radio stations. Finally, a resource book profiling over forty African female scientists and technologists was created by Harding and Apea (1990). The women were presented as role models to help challenge gender biases preventing African girls from entering scientific fields. This resource book is an example of the type of material that is being produced in accordance with the recommendations of the Nairobi Forward-Looking Strategies program and document. The strategies in this document state that the advancement of women is a precondition for establishing a humane and progressive society. One recommendation of the Forward-Looking Strategies stressed the importance of including examples and discussions of the contributions women have made to the economy in curricula at all educational levels. Teaching materials should demonstrate equality of the sexes and reflect positive, dynamic, and participatory images of women (Harding & Apea, 1990).

A study was conducted by Woodhouse and Ndongko (1993) involving ten Camerounian women to find out how they had managed to become scientists or science educators. The women identified four factors important to their success: (1) support from at least one family member, (2) a sense of collegiality with other girls in high school science, (3) a growing sense of determination on their part to do well in science, and (4) a gradual acceptance by lecturers and male students once they were accepted to university studies in science. The women reported that they were not given the opportunity to handle scientific equipment and to engage in the experimental process during laboratories. Emphasis was placed on memorization of dictated material for the purpose of passing examinations. Prevented from understanding science as a cultural and historical artifact by its presentation in school as a finished product, neither to be questioned nor critically examined, these women found it difficult to fathom the importance of science or its relevance to their own lives. The African women did not see these effects as discrimination. Only two of the ten women interviewed for the Cameroonian study believed that they had been discriminated against as women, either as high school students or at any point in their career. Of the two women who believed that they had been victims of discrimination based on gender, one had recognized discrimination as having taken place with regard to the sexual harassment by male teachers of female students in high school science, and the other for the refusal of social institutions to grant maternity leave to women.

Environmental Education

As population growth surges in the continent, the African environment suffers degradation on a large scale. Environmental science becomes a necessary part of the curriculum if a balance is to be struck between population needs and environmental stability. Concerns have been expressed for nearly three decades regarding the insufficient education sub-Saharan African students were receiving in environmental science. A number of writers have investigated the position of environmental education in South Africa (Clayton, 1979; Hurry, 1978; Millar, 1980; Nightingale, 1977). A study was conducted to assess the situation in secondary schools under the control of the Transvaal Education Department (Hurry, 1980). The assessment was based on a review of: (1) secondary school syllabi for biology and geography (aims, objectives, course content), (2) teacher training with special reference to preservice and inservice environmental education, (3) relevant resources (including fieldwork venues and teaching aids), with regard to both suitability and availability, and (4) contributions made by both governmental and nongovernmental administrative, advisory, and supplementary organizations.

Within the South African context the following six points seem to have attracted the most attention: (1) there appears to be a lack of suitable, broad-based aims and objectives relating to environmental education, (2) schools and other educational institutions appear to lack suitable facilities for conducting outdoor environmental education programs, (3) there appears to be a lack of suitable resource materials for either teacher or pupil, (4) teacher training programs do not equip teachers for meaningful environmental education, (5) school subjects are not taught holistically. It is therefore difficult to understand and gain insight into environmental matters, (6) teacher-initiated environmental education programs are not given sufficient support by the education departments.

Hurry (1980) concluded that while the Transvaal Education Department was making a contribution toward the development of environmental education in its secondary schools, there were a number of areas in which improvements could be made. One was to establish a clear definition of environmental education as it relates to science teaching in the schools. A second was to include identifying strengths and weaknesses in the biology and geography courses of study with reference to their contribution to environmental education. A third was the extent and value of assistance given to teachers and that the materials provided for classroom use must be increased.

A National Policy for Environmental Education in South Africa was proposed, highlighting the urgent need for inservice teacher training (Ballantyne & Tooth-Aston, 1989). The National Policy incorporates fundamental principles of environmental education established by the international community (Ballantyne & Tooth-Aston, 1989). Accordingly, the underpinning principles were that environmental education in South Africa should: (1) consider the environment in its totality, (2) be a continuous lifelong process, (3) be interdisciplinary in its approach, (4) encourage active participation in learners, (5) examine major environmental issues, and (6) stress individual responsibility toward the environment. Of major importance was the policy decision that environmental principles are to be taught across the school curriculum, rather than environmental education being promoted as an independent subject. Environmental education was described as a teaching approach leading to the development of students with environmentally sensitive attitudes, values, and behavior. The teacher was viewed as a key player in ensuring that environmental education goals are achieved in the schools (Ballantyne & Oelofse, 1989; Hurry, 1982; Maher, 1986; O'Donoghue & Taylor, 1988; Sterling, 1987).

In 1984, the development of science education in Botswana brought about a series of revisions of the old syllabi based on the

BOLESWA (Botswana, Lesotho, and Swaziland) integrated science (Ogunniyi, 1995). The revision exercise was undertaken by the Curriculum Development and Evaluation Unit in consultation with the Departments of Primary and Secondary Education, members of the National Subject Panels, and the Junior Secondary Education Improvement Program (JSIP). The primary science program included twelve themes, one of which was "care of the environment." The Junior Secondary science program also named "environmental awareness" as one of its twelve integrated themes.

The Impact of Science and Technology

How do science and technology affect society? How do social values effect technological change? What is the impact of science and technology on education and economics in a modern society? These questions were addressed by Mesthene (1970). He saw technology not only as a tool, but as an intellectual tool that defined the organization of knowledge for the achievement of practical purposes, in the sense that the effects of technology impact on society and everyday life. The basic survival, potential development, and ultimate fate of a people depends to a large extent on their access to material resources, on their ability to utilize these for food production and trade, and on their understanding of the consequences of their interactions with these resources. Survival and development are dependent on the possession and use of science and technology. Developments in science and technology have become in recent years important elements in world politics, with widespread international economic and sociocultural ramifications (Urevbu, 1991).

The myth exists that indigenous technological development did not exist in traditional sub-Saharan African societies. However, research studies have documented precolonial indigenous technology in Africa in many areas including, for example, manufacturing, agriculture, food processing, civil engineering, transportation, mining, and communication. For instance, Nwokike (1986) documented mining-extracting and metal-working technologies in iron, brass, bronze, and gold. In the 1850s, Kano, Nigeria, rivaled Manchester, England, in textile production. Many contributions by sub-Saharan Africans to the knowledge base of science can be found (Alic, 1986; Ezeabasili, 1977; Forje, 1989; Van Sertima, 1984). With the beginning of colonial rule indigenous technology declined in most of sub-Saharan Africa. The manufacture of many local products was banned. The importing of European goods replaced local manufacture. These events stopped the expansion of indigenous technology and led to its severe decline. The transfer of technology changed not only the indigenous technology of Africa, but was a strong force in changing economic, educational, and social systems. African scientists think that modern science and technology are highly influenced by Western views and therefore advocate the denigration of African history and customs (Ogunniyi, 1988).

Science education in sub-Saharan Africa must address these issues by building a new paradigm for science and technology education from a multicultural perspective. Science and technology exist in all cultures. These concepts and issues must be taught and explored at all levels of education. Most science curricula in sub-Saharan Africa are modeled on those in the West and do not reflect the cultural background of the learner and, thus, do not model careers and occupations available to graduates from the schools. Ogunniyi (1988) describes differences in the way Western and sub-Saharan African science might work. In investigating problems with malaria a Western scientist searches for a causative agent. An African scientist tries to determine why some individuals and not others are afflicted with malaria. They both are attempting to prevent malaria in the future. Western science education is more concerned with inanimate objects; African science education stresses the importance of people. As a part of the needed change in science education for sub-Saharan African schools the integration of a multicultural perspective, especially including contributions of African scientists, should be developed. Murfin (1994) suggests a number of techniques for integration of scientists and changes in teacher education and science textbooks to meet this problem.

Jones and Hughes provide examples of a curriculum that integrates science and culture for sub-Saharan Africa. Science is taught through events in everyday life. Some of the topics include house construction and building materials, energy converters, natural dyes, and plants and their role in medicine (1982a, 1982b),

Harding and Apea (1990) reported recommendations made by an expert group organized by the Commonwealth Science Council.

Fourteen areas of research crucial for development were identified. Some of the major areas were agriculture, energy resources, biological diversity and genetic resources, mineral and water resources, and remote sensing. In a number of these areas women form the backbone of the workers and have the most experience. So, women must be brought into decision making relating to the technology through appropriate science education at all levels.

In their comments on science management and organization, the expert group recommended that nations popularize science both for their public administrators and for the public. It also suggested the publication of appropriate local and regional materials that make science both entertaining and educational, while still relating it to pressing economic issues (Harding & Apea, 1990). Early technology education should include hands-on materials, working models, and the use of indigenous materials related to real science problems in the local setting.

Although computers are used to facilitate learning in schools in the developed world, they have not made an appreciable inroad into the teaching–learning process in most sub-Saharan African countries. The cost of purchase, maintenance, and supplying constant electricity are major inhibiting factors to the adoption of high technology in classrooms (Jegede, Okebukola, & Ajewole, 1990).

Contrary to expectations, the use of technology in schools may not always provide the expected results. Jegede, Okebukola, & Ajewole (1990) investigated the attitude and achievement of students using the computer for learning biological concepts in a community environment dominated by indigenous technology. Achievement and affective data were collected from sixty-four students enrolled for a three-month Nigerian Joint Matriculation Examination in Biology. The subjects were divided into three groups. One group of ten used the computer on an individual basis. Another group of thirty worked in ten three-member cooperative learning teams. The third group of twenty-four did not use the computer. The computer-assisted group was not better than the control group in science achievement, contrary to expectations. The attitude measures showed large differences favoring students using the computer. The study supports the idea that the computer has the capability of exciting students in an indigenous technology-dominated environment. Also surprising was the finding that girls in cooperative groups recorded significantly higher posttest attitude and achievement scores than did those who worked alone. Traditional practice does not utilize cooperative groups. The use of technology is increasing but may not bring about expected significant gains in achievement when compared to traditional methods in regular use in these settings.

Preservice and Inservice Science Education

In order to develop the needed scientific and technological resources, sub-Saharan African countries have committed a substantial amount of their economy to science education through expanding higher education institutions and inservice training programs to increase the number of science teachers. Despite these efforts there is a shortage of qualified science teachers, a lack of adequate science teaching facilities and equipment, generally poor teaching methods, and a weak communications network for facilitating inservice training (Ogunniyi, 1995). In a survey done in 1992 in Botswana, 41 percent of physics teachers and 57 percent of chemistry teachers had no teaching qualifications. There were no teachers with majors in interdisciplinary science at the senior secondary school level or integrated science at the junior secondary school level, even though these subjects were offered and taught. Also, 75 percent of secondary school teachers in science were expatriates. A considerable number of expatriate teachers have no professional teaching qualifications and teach mainly through the lecture method. Their proficiency in English varies widely. They are brought directly into the school system without any specific orientation (Prophet & Rowell, 1993). In Ciskei, South African science teachers in secondary schools are young and underqualified. Fifty percent had not passed physical science at the high school level and about 50 percent were trained as primary school teachers. Science teachers typically spent 99 percent of the lessons in talking. Errors in information were common. Excessive emphasis was placed on factual recall by students (Rogan & Macdonald, 1985).

In 1976, the Science Education Project (SEP) was initiated in South Africa with a four-year research and development phase in the Ciskei, Xhosa-speaking rural area of South Africa. One of the functions of SEP was to help teachers cope with the performance of laboratory work by pupils and improve the quality of science education in some of the least-privileged (i.e., black) schools in South Africa. The SEP was mainly designed to introduce laboratory work into science lessons and provide opportunities for the pupils to do experimental work themselves. SEP focused on the junior secondary segment of the school system; Standards 6, 7, and 8, which are the eighth, ninth, and tenth years of a twelve-year system. Teachers using SEP materials attempted to move away from predominantly teacher-dominated lessons toward ones in which pupils played a more active role, interacting with the materials, with their peers, and with their teachers.

A study was conducted by Rogan and Macdonald (1980) to analyze and compare the teaching behavior of teachers who had been trained to use new (SEP) material with the teaching behavior of teachers using traditional approaches and who had received no training by SEP staff. The Science Teaching Observation Schedule (STOS) was used in this study (Eggleston, Galton, & Jones, 1975). The STOS consisted of five sets of transactions that are mutually exclusive of each other, grouped into two sections; teacher actions and pupil actions. The subjects were junior secondary school science teachers in the Ciskei grades 8 through 10. The trial group of teachers ($n = 9$) had received little or no SEP training and did not use any of the SEP materials. The control group of teachers ($n = 9$) had attended all of the SEP training and were given teaching materials. Most teachers were under thirty years old and had taught for less than five years. Class size varied from less than thirty pupils to over seventy, with a mean between forty-five and fifty. Most schools had between 250 and 400 pupils, ranging in age from eleven to twenty-five in the junior secondary schools, with the majority being between fourteen and eighteen. During the third quarter of the school year teachers were observed three times.

The results of the study showed that instructional changes had occurred. The results were used to convince educational authorities and sponsors that the use of the SEP package did lead to instructional changes. SEP teachers offered students more opportunity to do laboratory work in their science lessons and used a wider variety of questions with their students. Other evaluation studies showed that students using SEP materials had improved performance (Gray, 1982; Gray & Macrae, 1982; Rogan, 1980a, 1980b;)

and attitudes (Curry, 1986; Macdonald, 1979, 1980; Macdonald et al., 1985).

Although students' scores rose significantly under the new method of instruction, SEP students still did poorly on the national examination. This was considered to be the result of an array of problems including the science textbook and curriculum, the science facilities, the home life necessities of students, and economic and political realities in society. The syllabus was lengthy and too difficult for the students to understand. Schools lacked instructional resources and science laboratory facilities. It was difficult to carry out appropriate instruction with classes between thirty and seventy students. Many families of the students had very low incomes and few modern amenities such as electricity and running water. Parents had a high rate of illiteracy and there was extreme rural isolation. Finally, the rules and regulations needed to run an apartheid society, restrictions on the freedom of speech and movement, and the consequent tensions within youth and the educational system led to unstable school classrooms and large absenteeism. Similar results, problems in low science achievement, were found in a study done in Nigeria and in rural regions of other countries. These studies provide support for science teacher education to broaden its approach beyond teaching technique only, to produce effective teachers for schools with extreme conditions (Sunal, 1984, 1985a, 1985b, 1991).

It was not possible for SEP to tackle most of these problems, so a way to operate relevantly and effectively had to be sought. For these reasons, SEP efforts tried to concentrate not only on materials, but also on teachers themselves and all aspects of teacher growth. Three points became important in attending to teacher growth. The teacher was seen as being part of the context, the teacher was the link between the pupil's world in the classroom and the rest of the context, and, finally, the teacher must have some control of the immediate context. As SEP evolved, the attention to staff development led teachers to take more responsibility inside and outside of the classroom (Rogan & Macdonald, 1980).

An adequate supply of qualified science teachers is a major problem facing the government of Botswana. The teacher–student ratio is greater than thirty-five students per teacher. The recent establishment of two colleges of education for the training of junior secondary school teachers has had a positive impact on the supply of science teachers at the junior secondary school level. However, at the senior secondary school level there has been an acute shortage of science teachers. Ogunniyi (1995) reports that 434 science teachers, 17 percent of the total demand for teachers, were needed for the junior secondary schools, but only 100 were produced at the two colleges of education in the 1992/93 academic year. At the senior secondary school level 206 science teachers were needed, but only thirty were produced at the University of Botswana in the 1992/93 session. Science teacher education programs throughout sub-Saharan Africa face significant challenges for the present and the future.

African Classroom Teaching

Many sub-Saharan countries over the past two decades have put a greater share of the national budget into primary and secondary schools as compared to higher education. This has occurred partially because large numbers of students do very poorly in their first year at the universities, as well as on the school-leaving examination. As in the case for South African schools, these students had participated in a science curriculum and yet were not able to perform in the science-related disciplines. The quality of implementation of the curriculum in the classroom is a factor in their poor performance (Mehl & Lochhead, 1987).

Studies of science teaching in Nigerian secondary schools identified some factors influencing poor results in later science courses (Ogunniyi, 1982, 1984). Using the assessment instrument Science Interaction Categories (SIC), Ogunniyi found that a typical lesson consisted of verbal exposition by the teacher with students listening and copying out notes. Teachers spent about 10 percent of their lessons demonstrating the manipulation of the apparatus and students spent from 5 percent to 12 percent of their time on activities usually associated with formal laboratory experiments.

A number of studies have described conditions in science teaching within specific locales in Nigeria. They report the lack of resources, underpreparedness of teachers, and disinterest of students in studying curriculum designed for a foreign Western culture (Bashir, 1982; Duniya, 1983; Idris, 1983; Mohammed, 1984; Mu'azu, 1984; Nna, 1981).

A study by Okebukola and Ogunniyi (1986) recognized that in countries with a high student–teacher ratio and limited resources, teachers tend to use verbal rather than nonverbal student-oriented teaching modes. In an observation study in Nigeria, Ogunniyi (1983) found that students in the laboratory rarely ask questions of their teachers and usually only when they require procedural information. Buseri (1987) reported on a study of questioning habits in Nigerian secondary schools finding that, in twelve lessons, 490 questions were asked by teachers and 44 by pupils. The low incidence of student questioning was attributed in part to the failure of the Nigerian culture to encourage young pupils to ask questions freely.

A study carried out in South Africa a few months after teachers first started working with SEP found that pupils were not asking questions (Curry, 1986). Later, in another study, after using SEP materials for at least two years pupils had started to ask questions, indicating that teachers and pupils can become accustomed to some pupil input in the classroom.

Schools in sub-Saharan Africa have very limited financial resources so facilities such as school laboratories and libraries are poorly equipped (Hewson & Hamlyn, 1985). This problem is particularly severe in South African black schools, since they have received a less-than-equal share of the educational budget (Macdonald & Rogan, 1988). Teachers are motivated, but are often inadequately trained in their subject areas, particularly in science. The teacher qualifications are low; 10–20 percent of the teachers are still teaching with only high school–level training. Due to the lack of training, teachers use a "catechism" style of teaching in which rote learning is prevalent (Hewson & Hamlyn, 1985).

A case study of the SEP found that to the casual observer, the most striking feature of a SEP classroom was that pupils could be found doing laboratory work and talking to each other (Rogan & Macdonald, 1985). In contrast, pupils in other schools never handled apparatus nor rarely saw any. Science lessons consisted mostly of reading the textbook, sometimes in unison, or listening to the teacher, followed by recitation. Laboratory work in SEP schools involved use of a specially designed kit with accompanying worksheets. Teacher guides were provided to help integrate the use of the kit and worksheets with the schedule derived from the textbook in use at the school. The SEP worksheets provided both the science problem and the procedure and were open-ended.

People not involved in the innovation judged the effectiveness of SEP almost exclusively on examination results. However, SEP teachers were trained to spend a significant amount of time in laboratory work. SEP did not provide any special examination-preparation courses or techniques. The 1979 examinations written in the Ciskei contained multiple-choice questions, as well as some longer questions. An analysis of the Standard 6 (Grade 12) results showed that the SEP pupils did significantly better on twenty-two of the fifty multiple-choice questions, as opposed to six out of fifty for non-SEP pupils. The means for the fifty questions were 29.14 and 22.74, respectively. The Standard 7 (Grade 13) results showed even greater differences. SEP pupils performed significantly better on thirty-one of the fifty questions, as opposed to one out of fifty for non-SEP pupils. The respective means were 30.23 and 19.36 (Rogan & Macdonald, 1985). The SEP pupils and teachers felt that they had improved their examination results because they had a better understanding of science and had remembered topics that had been covered in the laboratory work.

The West African Examination Council's (WAEC) policy and its impact on teaching chemistry in Nigerian secondary schools was studied by Alao and Gallagher (1988). The Nigerian government provides a standardized school certificate for those graduating from secondary schools nationwide and passing regional West African (WAEC) examinations in required and elected subjects. Scores on WAEC examinations determine admission to higher education and selection for available positions in public service departments.

A scientific attitude toward problem solving has long been a national objective of Nigerian secondary education (Fafunwa, 1971). This involves acquisition of skills in problem solving and reflective thinking, development of technical and vocational skills, and an understanding of the natural and humanmade environment.

A study was carried out in Ibadan, Nigeria, of teachers' class-planning notes as a way of determining the objectives actually implemented in Nigerian chemistry classrooms (Alao & Gallagher, 1988). Data analyzed showed that teachers focused on content, concepts, and principles of chemistry, rather than on the broader range of objectives of chemistry education, such as interest and logical thinking. The results demonstrated the role of examinations was very important in communicating the objectives of chemistry education to teachers. Teachers were able to skip significant parts of information contained in textbooks and syllabi, since there was no accountability for doing so in the examinations (Alao & Gallagher, 1988). Most of the chemistry teachers in the Ibadan area used the WAEC Guide Chemistry Syllabus to plan their chemistry lessons. About 82 percent of the sample thought the WAEC syllabus a good teaching guide. About half of the chemistry teachers surveyed were found to be underqualified. In addition, student interviews indicated a lack of educational resources including laboratory facilities and equipment, large class sizes, and the use of lecture as the major vehicle of instruction. These factors reduced the ability of the system to deliver quality chemistry education. The researchers concluded that the WAEC Chemistry Syllabus must serve as a guide for development of the regional examinations in chemistry, by organizations preparing educational materials including textbooks, and in science teacher education (Alao & Gallagher, 1988).

To investigate how examination policy influences the teaching of chemistry in Nigerian schools Alao and Gallagher (1988) studied a single school in depth. They used interviews, content analysis of documents, questionnaires, and field notes. Policy and practice existed as two rather separate entities, with policy having a limited influence on practice. One of the teachers, for example, decided not to use the recommended textbook because it had so many pages. Another teacher did not use any book to prepare lessons because he had a bachelor's degree in chemistry and had years of experience in teaching, so there was no need to use a textbook to teach ordinary (O-level) chemistry. Laboratory work, interviews, and observation showed that many of the students could not set up the apparatus in a way to obtain accurate values. At this school, as in many other Nigerian schools, the classroom conditions led to an inability to effectively implement WAEC's policy. As an alternative to the WAEC guidelines, many teachers taught students to memorize facts that would help them pass the chemistry examinations (Alao & Gallagher, 1988). Although a syllabus existed, 71 percent of the teachers surveyed said they were free to choose instructional content. Well-quali-

fied teachers displayed the attitude that the use of the text and syllabus is a sign of weakness. So, some of the best-qualified teachers
subverted the expected WAEC content in their teaching.

This study demonstrates that teachers without adequate resources and supervision selected content and methodology inappropriate for the attainment of the intended objectives of secondary
school chemistry. The focus was on the conceptual content of chemistry while laboratory work, higher-order reasoning, and positive
attitudes toward chemistry were ignored.

Classroom science teaching faces many difficulties. The nations
of sub-Saharan Africa are attempting to provide guidelines and leadership for their teachers. Syllabi have been developed and inservice
and preservice training established. Textbooks and indigenous materials have been created for use in classrooms. Much progress has
been made in recent decades. The difficulties will continue, but the
impetus for change exists.

Science Education in Sub-Saharan Africa: Implications

The short-term potential for change in the status of science education in sub-Saharan Africa is limited due to economic and political
realities. While in many countries a significant portion of the national budget (5–40 percent) is targeted for education, this amount
of money represents a small total expenditure in comparison with
more-developed nations in the world. However, change in specific
components of the science-teaching process and in science-teacher
education is probable. The identification of the need for an African
science curriculum meeting the needs of African students and society is a strong movement throughout sub-Saharan Africa. Although
some of the research strategies have been borrowed from more-developed nations, the results do identify critical indigenous needs.
Gradual change in the content of science syllabi, narrative, and structure of textbooks, and explanation by teachers in the classroom,
should be guided by research on cultural and linguistic factors. Additional attention must also be given to science research in sub-Saharan African and in other non-Western cultures if a scientific view
is to be an objective of education. This view should be geared toward adapting traditional views to a scientific one (Ogunniyi, 1988).
Science curricula should not present modern science as superior,

but as a better way to cope with everyday life experiences. Students should be made aware of the benefits and limitations of science. They should examine the similarities and differences between traditional and scientific worldviews in the context of their daily lives. To do this, the science course of study and textbooks should reflect both the current and the emerging needs of the culture. This would require the development of multiple science syllabi with different emphases. One emphasis is relevance. Although the content of science is universal, the topics must relate to the culture and economy of the area. Topics relating to modern farming, ecological balance, control of disease, production of food and drinkable water, and the development of all-weather roads are more relevant to the sub-Saharan African classroom than are such topics as nuclear energy and laser technology (Ogunniyi, 1986).

Although women are an important part of the workforce, science education has traditionally excluded them. The great majority of individuals working in science and technology-related fields today are men. The recognition that girls need to be introduced to science at a very early age and be encouraged to participate in science throughout their school years has occurred. What remains to be done is to implement strategies involving women in all phases of secondary and higher science education.

In all sub-Saharan African countries the condition of the environment is a critical issue for economic and social well-being. Unless all students are provided with the understanding and skills for dealing with local environmental problems, little can be done through political processes. Environmental education is a key science concept that needs to be woven through the curriculum. Another significant force in all sub-Saharan African countries is the impact of science and technology in all phases of everyday life. The presence of constant electricity and pure water are two basic survival aspects of this force. The myth that indigenous technological development does not exist in traditional sub-Saharan African societies must be dealt with in the school science curriculum. A new view of science and technology education from a multicultural perspective must be part of the new organization of science curricula.

There can be no change in student achievement unless resources and reforms are made part of science teacher education and of the classroom instructional process. Teachers are the key to positive change in student learning. New science curricula require teachers who are capable of using instructional procedures that support the new emphasis. Educational needs have grown beyond the competence and know-how of many of the present teachers. It is essential that teacher inservice education become a primary aspect in any future curriculum development activity. Courses presently available for teacher preparation at African universities should be replaced with courses related to the science relevant to the science subjects to be taught in primary and secondary schools. This refers to the develpment of a scienctific literacy in teachers that is relevant to the level of higher education. Efforts spent on preservice and inservice teachers have begun and are effective. These efforts must be extended throughout all the countries in sub-Saharan Africa.

Science education in sub-Saharan Africa is engaged in an enterprise found in all the world's regions, melding modern science with local culture so that it may enhance life in the local setting and national development. The limitations placed on science education are severe in sub-Saharan Africa and will continue into the foreseeable future. Nevertheless, the enterprise is moving forward and has made significant gains that inform other regions of the world as they engage in the same task.

References

Alao, D.A., & Gallagher, J.J. (1988, April). *Influences of examination policies on chemistry teaching practices in Nigerian high schools: An ethnographic study.* Paper presented at the annual meeting of the National Association for Research in Science Teaching, Lake of the Ozarks, MO.

Alic, M. (1986). *Hypatia's heritage: A history of women in science from antiquity to the late nineteenth century.* London: The Women's Press Ltd.

Ballantyne R.R., & Oelofse, C.G. (1989). Implementing environmental education policy in South African schools. *The South African Journal of Education, 9*(1), 16–25.

Ballantyne, R.R., & Tooth-Aston, P.J. (1989). In-service environmental teacher training in an apartheid education system. *Environmental Education and Information, 8*(1), 1–9.

Banya, K. (March, 1997). *The role of universities in the south after the Jomtien conference.* Paper presented at the annual meeting of the American Educational Research Association, Chicago, IL.

Bashir, D. (1982). *Problems and prospects of science secondary schools in Gongola State.* Bachelor's thesis, Bayero University, Kano, Nigeria.

Buseri, J.C. (1987). The influence of culture on pupils' questioning habits in Nigerian secondary schools. *International Journal of Science Education, 9*(5), 579–584.

Cantrell, M., Kouwenhoven, W., Mokoena, T., & Thijs, G., (1993). *Bridging school and university: The pre-entry science course at the University of Botswana.* Amsterdam: VU University Press.

Clayton, J.F. (1979). *Outdoor education in the United States of America, Canada, and Britain.* Unpublished master's thesis, University of South Africa.

Curry, N.O. (1986). *Implementation and evaluation of the Science Education Project in Transkei.* Unpublished master's thesis, Western Australia Institute of Technology.

Davidson, B. (1965). The African personality. In C. Legum (Ed.), *Africa: A handbook* (pp. 98–112). London: Anthony Blond Ltd.

de Feiter, L. (1993, 1 January). *The role of inservice teacher training projects in building a science teacher profession in some South African countries.* Paper presented at the international conference, Science Education in Developing Countries: From Theory to Practice. Jerusalem, Israel.

de Feiter, L., Vonk, H., & van den Akker, J. (1995a, 1 April). *Towards more effective science teacher development in some southern African countries.* Paper presented at the annual meeting of the American Educational Research Association, San Francisco, CA.

de Feiter, L., Vonk, H., & van den Akker, J. (1995b). *Towards more effective science teacher development.* Amsterdam: VU University Press.

Duniya, J. (1983). *A survey of the major problems of teaching integrated science in some selected post primary institutions in Kachia LGA of Kaduna state.* Bachelor's thesis, Bayero University, Kano, Nigeria.

Eggleston, J.F., Galton, M.J., & Jones, M.E. (1975). *A science teaching observation schedule.* London: Macmillan Education.

Eshiwani, G.E. (1985). Women's access to higher education in Kenya: A study of opportunities and attainment in science and mathematics education in women and development in Africa. *Journal of Eastern Africa Research and Development, 15,* 37–49.

Ezeabasili, N. (1977). *African science: Myth or reality.* New York: Vantage Press.

Fafunwa, B.A. (1971). Some guiding principles of education in Africa. *West African Journal of Education, 16*(1), 5–7.

Farouk, M.K. (1995). *Rhetoric and reality in curriculum development: The implementation of the junior secondary school curriculum in Nigeria.* Paper presented at the annual meeting of the American Educational Research Association, San Francisco, CA.

Forje, J.W. (1989). *Science and technology in Africa.* Northern Ireland: The Universities Press (Belfast) Ltd.

Fuller, B., & Heynemann, S.P. (1989). Third world school quality: Current collapse, future potential. *Educational Researcher, 18*(2), 12–19.

Gray, B.V. (1982). *Implementation strategies and the junior certificate examination results: An analysis of junior certificate physical science results in product schools in KwaZulu.* (SEP Evaluation Report 1–5009, p. 13). Pretoria, South Africa: Human Sciences Research Council.

Gray, B.V. (1989). *A preliminary investigation into modular physical science for standards 9 and 10.* (Report No. 0–328). Pretoria, South Africa: Human Sciences Research Council.

Gray, B.V., & Macrae, H. (1982). *Report on 1981 examination results for standard 6 and standard 7 in schools in the KwaMashu, Umlazi North, Umlazi South, Umbumbulu circuits.* (SEP Evaluation Report 1–5008, p. 25). Pretoria, South Africa: Human Sciences Research Council.

Harding, J., & Apea, E. (1990). *Women too in science and technology in Africa: A resource book for counseling girls and young women.* London: Commonwealth Secretariat.

Harris, W.F. (1981). Heat in undergraduate education, or isn't it time we abandoned theory of caloric. *International Journal of Mechanical Engineering, 9*(4), 317–321.

Hassan, M.A.H. (1993). *Science and technology for socio-economic development of Africa.* Presidential forum. Gabarone, Botswana: Government of Botswana.

Hewson, M.G. (1986). The acquisition of scientific knowledge: Analysis and representation of student conceptions concerning density. *Science Education, 70*(2), 159–170.

Hewson, M.G., & Hamlyn, D. (1983). *The influence of intellectual environment on conceptions of heat.* Paper presented at the annual meeting of the American Educational Research Association, Montreal, Canada. (ERIC Document Reproduction Service No. ED 231 655)

Hewson, M.G., & Hamlyn, D. (1985). Cultural metaphors: Some implications for science education. *Anthropology and Education Quarterly, 16,* 31–46.

Hurry, L.B. (1978). *Is conservation awareness one of the aims of formal education in South Africa? An assessment with special regard to geography and biology teaching.* Johannesburg: Wildlife Society of Southern Africa.

Hurry, L.B. (1980). *Environmental education in Transvaal secondary schools and its relation to the teaching of biology and geography.* Pretoria, South Africa: University of South Africa.(ERIC Document Reproduction Service No. ED 234 992)

Hurry, L.B. (1982). *Directions in environmental education and their implications for the training of primary school teachers in the Transvaal: Towards a synthesis.* Unpublished doctoral thesis, UNISA, Pretoria.

Idris, A. (1983). *Interest survey in physics and chemistry in forms 3 and 4 at Rumfa College Kano.* Bachelor's thesis, Bayero University, Kano, Nigeria.

Jegede, O.J., Okebukola, P.A., & Ajewole, G. (1990). *Attitude and achievement of students in an environment dominated by indigenous technology to the use of the computer for learning biological concepts.* Blosser, P.E. & S.L. Helgeson (Eds.). Abstract of presented papers at the National Association for Research in Science Teaching Annual Conference Proceedings, Atlanta, GA.

Jones, N., & Hughes, W. (1982a). *Third world science: Housing.* Bangor, UK: University College of North Wales. (ERIC Document Reproduction Service No. ED 235 040)

Jones, N., & Hughes, W. (1982b). *Third world science: Plants and medicines.* Bangor, UK: University College of North Wales. (ERIC Document Reproduction Service No. ED 235 044)

Kann, U., & Nganunu, M. (Eds.). (1992). *Science provision in academic secondary education.* Project for the International Institute for Educational Planning (IIEP). Paris: UNESCO.

Kingsley, C. (1989). *A guide to case management for at-risk youth.* Waltham, MA: Center for Human Resources.

Kinyanjui, K. (1988). *Secondary school education for girls in Kenya: The need for a more science-based curriculum to enhance women's greater participation in development.* (I.D.S. Working Paper No. 459). Nairobi, Kenya: Ministry of Education.

Macdonald, M.A. (1979). *Attitudes of Ciskei teachers towards science and science classes.* (SEP Evaluation Report 1–3006, p. 32). Pretoria, South Africa: Human Sciences Research Council.

Macdonald, M.A. (1980). *The response to Ciskei pupils to the Science Education Project.* (SEP Evaluation Report 1–3012, p. 84). Pretoria, South Africa: Human Sciences Research Council.

Macdonald, M.A. (1990). *Standard three general science research 1987–1988: A final report of the Threshold Project.* (Report No. SOLING–21). Pretoria, South Africa: Human Sciences Research Council. (ERIC Document Reproduction Service No. ED 352 253)

Macdonald, M.A., Gilmour, J.D., & Moodie, P. (1985). Teacher reaction to innovation: A case study in a South African setting. *Journal of Education for Teaching, 11*(3), 245–263.

Macdonald, M.A., & Rogan, J.M. (1988). Innovation in South African science education. Part 1: Science teaching observed. *Science Education, 72*(2), 225–236.

Macdonald, M.A., & Rogan, J.M. (1990). Innovation in South African science education. Part 2: Factors influencing the introduction of instructional change. *Science Education, 74*(1), 119–132.

Maher, M. (1986). Environmental education: What are we fighting for? *Geographical Education, 5*(2), 24–25.

Mehl, M.C., & Lochhead, J. (1987). *Teaching thinking in subject-specific contexts to disadvantaged South African communities.* Paper presented at the International Conference on Thinking, Honolulu, HI.

Mesthene, E.G. (1970). *Technological change: Its impact on man and society.* Cambridge, MA: Harvard University Press.

Millar, J.C. (1980). *The objectives of outdoor education.* Unpublished paper read at a conference on outdoor education. Pretoria, South Africa: UNISA.

Mohammed, S. (1984). *Adjustment to schooling: A case study of students in science secondary schools in Kano state.* Bachelor's thesis, Bayero University, Kano, Nigeria.

Mu'azu, D. (1984). *Cultural attitudes towards science in Kano state.* Bachelor's thesis, Bayero University, Kano, Nigeria.

Murfin, B. (1994). African science, African and African-American scientists and the school science curriculum. *School Science and Mathematics, 94*(2), 96–103.

Nightingale, C.S. (1977). *An analysis of the education potential of sites in the Cape Peninsular for secondary school field-work in environmental studies.* Unpublished master's thesis, University of Cape Town, South Africa.

Nna, B.A. (1981). *Factors affecting science achievement in Niger state secondary schools.* Bachelor's thesis, Bayero University, Kano, Nigeria.

Nwokike, E.I. (1986). *The place of indigenous iron technology in the development of the AWKA economy, 1980–1960.* Master's thesis, University of Benin, Nigeria.

Nyirenda, S. (1995). *From ministry of education and culture to ministry of dedication and torture: A top-down approach to the implementation of secondary school improvement policy in Malawi.* Paper presented at the annual meeting of the American Educational Research Association, San Francisco, CA.

OAU. (1981). *Lagos plan for action for the economic development of Africa: 1980–2000.* Lagos, Nigeria: Author.

O'Donoghue, R., & Taylor, J. (1988). Towards participant-centered resource development for environmental education. *South African Journal of Environmental Education, 7,* 3–5.

Ogawa, M. (1986). Toward a new rationale of science education in a non-Western society. *European Journal of Science Education, 8*(2), 113–119.

Ogunniyi, M.B. (1982). An analysis of prospective science teachers' understanding of the nature of science. *Journal of Research in Science Teaching, 19*(1), 25–32.

Ogunniyi, M.B. (1983). Relative effects of a history/philosophy of science course on student teachers' performance on two models of science. *Research in Science and Technological Education, 1*(2), 193–198.

Ogunniyi, M.B. (1984). Are the gods dead? Testing for the relative influence of supernatural forces among Yoruba youths. (Working Paper No. 2). Submitted to International Development Research Center (IDRC), Ottawa, Canada.

Ogunniyi, M.B. (1985). Problems of science education relative to the nature of scientific concepts and generalizations in developing countries. In F.M. Ukoli (Ed.), *What Science? The Problems of Teaching and Research in Science in Nigeria* (pp. 103–115). Nigeria: Heinemann Educational Books Ltd and Ibadan University Press.

Ogunniyi, M.B. (1986). Two decades of science education in Africa. *Science Education, 70*(2), 111–122.

Ogunniyi, M.B. (1988). Adapting Western science to traditional African culture. *International Journal of Science Education, 10*(1), 1–9.

Ogunniyi, M.B. (1995). The development of science education in Botswana. *Science Education, 79*(1), 95–109.

Okebukola, P.A. (1995). *National survey of basic education in Nigeria.* Paper presented at the annual meeting of the American Educational Research Association, San Francisco, CA.

Okebukola, P.A., & Jegede, O.J. (1990). *Survey of factors that stress science teachers and an examination of coping strategies.* Lagos, Nigeria: University of Lagos. (ERIC Document Reproduction Service No. ED 335 235)

Okebukola, P.A., & Ogunniyi, M.B. (1986). Effects of teachers' verbal exposition on students' level of class participation and achievement in biology. *Science Education, 70*(1), 45–51.

Pendaeli, J., Ogunniyi, M.B., & Mosothwane, M. (1993). *Strategies for the improvement of performance in science and mathematics at all levels in the educational system of Botswana.* Report of a policy study prepared for the National Commission on Education. Gabarone, Botswana: National Commission on Education.

Prophet, R., & Rowell, P.M. (1993). Coping and control: Science teaching strategies in Botswana. *Quantitative Studies in Education, 63* (3), 197–209.

Research and Development Forum for Science-Led Development in Africa (RANDFORUM). (1993). *Science and technology for the socio-economic development of Africa.* Nairobi: RANDFORUM Press.

Rogan, J.M. (1980a). *The std. 6 General Science examination results for 1979 in the Alice and Middledrift circuits.* (SEP Evaluation Report 1–1701, p. 15). Pretoria, South Africa: Ministry of Education.

Rogan, J.M. (1980b). *The std. 7 General Science examination results for 1979 in the Alice and Middledrift circuits.* (SEP Evaluation Report 1–3009, p. 33). Pretoria, South Africa: Ministry of Education.

Rogan, J.M., & Macdonald, M.A. (1980). *Reasoning ability and secondary school science: Problem areas and possible solutions.* (SEP Evaluation Report 1–1103, p. 50). Pretoria, South Africa: Ministry of Education.

Rogan, J.M., & Macdonald, M.A. (1985). The in-service teacher education component of an innovation: A case study in an African setting. *Journal of Curriculum Studies, 17*(1), 63–85.

Sterling, S.R. (1987). Provision for environmental Education in rural areas. *AREE, 1,* 12–13.

Sunal, D.W. (1984, November). *Factors affecting science achievement in rural settings—A Nigerian case study.* Paper presented at the annual meeting of the School Science and Mathematics Association, Roanoke, VA.

Sunal, D.W. (1985a, October). *Teaching science in rural schools: Research problems and prospects.* Keynote research paper presented at the annual meeting of the Rural and Small Schools Association, Manhattan, KS.

Sunal, D.W. (1985b, April). *Science teaching in Africa—Nigerian school practices and facilities.* Paper presented at the annual meeting of the National Science Teachers Association, Cincinnati, OH.

Sunal, D.W. (1991). Rural science teaching; What affects achievement? *School Science and Mathematics, 91*(5), 202–210.

Urevbu, A.O. (1991). Impact of science and technology on everyday life: An African prospective. *Impact of Science on Society, 41*(1), 69–79.

Van Sertima, I. (1984). *Blacks in science: Ancient and modern.* New Brunswick, NJ: Transaction Books.

Ware, S.A. (1992). *Secondary school science in developing countries: Status and issues.* (Background Paper Series No. PHREE/92/53). Washington, DC: World Bank.

Woodhouse, H., & Ndongko, T.M. (1993). Women and science education in Cameroun: Some critical reflections. *Interchange, 24*(1), 131–158.

Chapter Five
Mathematics Education in Sub-Saharan Africa
Concerns and Glimmers of Hope

Gail Jaji and Lazarus M. Jaji

Mathematics education in sub-Saharan Africa cannot be viewed as a single entity. Each culture and country possesses its own unique characteristics. While some of the forces shaping mathematics education are similar across the continent and among the various countries and cultures, each country's response to those forces has been unique. At the same time, because the forces have been similar, there are similarities among certain elements within the systems. These allow one to describe a general picture of mathematics education as it has developed and presently exists in most of the countries of sub-Saharan Africa. This chapter will present a brief overview of the present state of mathematics education in sub-Saharan Africa. It will then discuss in depth some of the critical issues affecting mathematics education, using a case study of Zimbabwe to examine these issues within the African setting.

In describing mathematics education as it has developed and presently exists in most of the countries of sub-Saharan Africa, the chapter will examine the common historical context and the present status as regards student population and teaching, the mathematics curriculum, and standardized testing. It will also look at some of the common issues within the area of mathematics education facing the mathematics education community in the sub-Saharan context. These issues include: language factors, gender issues, the impact of technology, preservice and inservice education, and classroom teaching.

Status of Mathematics Education in Sub-Saharan Africa
Historical Context
"In most formerly colonized countries, post-independence education did not succeed in appeasing the hunger for knowledge of its

people's masses" (Gerdes, 1988, p. 137). Because of the lack of economic resources and an exploding student population, post-independence situations produced overcrowded classrooms, a shortage of qualified teachers, and a lack of teaching materials. These, in turn, contributed toward low levels of attainment. Looking specifically at mathematics education, we see this tendency reinforced by a hasty curriculum transplantation from the highly industrialized nations to third world countries (Gerdes, 1988).

In discussing mathematics education in Sub-Saharan Africa, it is first necessary to examine the background of that education within the context of development in the countries concerned. All the countries involved have a colonial legacy of one form or another. The educational system inherited at the time of independence was largely a system devised by the colonizing power. In countries colonized by Britain, the type of system handed down was largely one devised for the education of the "British gentleman." Many colonists aspired to become members of the gentry, and therefore they imported into Africa the system devised for educating gentlemen for the purpose of educating their own children along the same lines as found back home in Britain. Many people among the colonized citizens also sought this type of education as a means of upward mobility. The education system was not devised for the purpose of educating a man who could help his nation develop, but for the purpose of educating the "gentleman" who had inherited wealth. At the time this took place, education in Britain was largely only for boys. It was only later that girls were allowed to enter the system and found it not wholly designed to fit their needs. As Bell, Costello, and Kuchemann (1983) point out:

It is not so long since mathematical education in England consisted, for the lower classes, of training to calculate accurately with large and complicated numbers, weights, measures and money, and, for the upper classes, of the rote learning of Euclid's books. This practice has been subject to continuous change and now we need to ask again, for this generation, what kind of knowledge of mathematics is appropriate for a general education. (p. 11)

Thus, the emphasis within the system was on acquiring a body of knowledge and not on the processes of the development of that knowledge. Unequal access to educational opportunities was common in most African countries prior to independence, and this lack of access certainly was a problem to be reckoned with once independence was achieved. (This is also true of other colonial powers in sub-Saharan Africa like Portugal, France, Germany, and the Netherlands.) This problem, however, often tended to overshadow, and thus caused to be overlooked, the problem of the discrepancy between the content of the curriculum and the environment of the learner.

Bell, Costello, and Kuchemann (1983) quote Peel (as quoted in Servais & Varga, 1971), who describes mathematics as "the study of the properties of the operations by which man orders, organizes and controls his environment" (p. 13), noting that while the operations which concern mathematicians are abstracted from reality, we cannot forget that "both the origin and the application of these operations are in the physical environment" (Bell, Costello, & Kuchemann, 1983, p. 13). Thus, the countries of Sub-Saharan Africa have a common legacy and a common problem. Habte (in Chikombah, Johnston, Schneller, & Schwille, 1988) writes, "The systems of education inherited by the African nations at the time of independence were not adequate to meet the needs of self-governance and rapid economic growth and development" (p. 3).

Student Population and Teaching

At independence, in most of the nations of sub-Saharan Africa the push was for educating the masses through the provision of universal primary education. Whereas prior to independence education had been for the privileged few, it now became available to the vast majority. This, of course, created huge growth in enrollments. In order to accommodate that growth, teachers had to be produced in large numbers in a relatively short period of time. Since prior to independence education had been reserved for the few, those who became teachers were often very intelligent and often went beyond their limited training and academic background in the quality of their teaching. However, when it became necessary to mass-produce teachers, this was no longer the case, and quality of teaching declined. This problem was further exacerbated by often using shortened training periods in order to produce quickly the needed teachers. In many of the countries, economic downturns had further serious consequences for the teaching of mathematics. Governments were forced to cut back on social services, which led to decreased ability to provide schools for a growing population. Additionally, in many of the countries efforts to meet International Monetary Fund conditions require cutting back the civil service, resulting in large numbers of teachers losing their positions. Taken together, these problems become a "vicious circle" in the sphere of education where the need is growing while the ability to meet that need is diminishing.

One result is that children are no longer in school. For many children attending schools, particularly in rural areas, there are often inadequate and dilapidated buildings. It is not uncommon to find rural children learning mathematics under a tree, and even when they are in classrooms they may have no chairs or benches to sit on and no desks to write on. They frequently have no books. This is not to say that there are no good facilities to be found. Even within the same country a poor, dilapidated school may be found not far from a very well equipped school (most often an urban private school) with all the latest facilities, plenty of books, even computers. But, for the vast majority, the lack of adequate facilities is the rule, not the exception.

Mathematics Curriculum

The curriculum in mathematics as found in the schools came largely from outside sub-Saharan Africa. In most of the countries the colonizing power had already established a curriculum that remained in place after independence. While the curriculum in other subject areas often changed emphasis immediately after independence, this tended not to be the case in mathematics. One reason for this is that mathematics was often viewed to be culture free. It is only recently that researchers and other educators have become aware of the importance of culture in mathematics. Even the materials used in the classrooms have tended to be from outside the culture of the students. Many of the countries have attempted to develop their own curriculum and textbooks at the primary level, but these have usually continued to be written in the language of colonization (partially due to the diversity of languages within single countries). These books often took little notice of the local culture and were frequently watered-down versions of books used elsewhere. The books were shortened, not simplified, for economic rather than educational reasons: a shorter book was a cheaper book. At the secondary level the use of imported books persisted for a longer period, but recently has given way to local materials. However, these have often been written by outsiders, and while some attempt was made to modify the content to suit the local culture, little was done to look at the local mathematics itself.

Standardized Testing

Standardized testing has tended to drive the curriculum at all levels. Many of the countries have few places for students at the secondary level, and therefore give national tests to determine who may or may not proceed to the secondary level. Even where enough places exist, the testing continues at this level for a variety of purposes, including placement and keeping teachers to certain standards. These tests tend to emphasize knowledge-level thinking, mainly computation. This, in turn, tends to encourage teachers to emphasize a mechanical rather than a problem-solving approach to mathematics.

At the secondary level many countries continued to use outside testing bodies for a limited period following independence, but have gradually moved to the use of their own examining bodies. These examining bodies have been structured after the examining bodies of the colonizing powers. Again, the exams drive the curriculum at the secondary level and continue to emphasize the more mechanical levels of understanding mathematics, rather than the higher levels of thinking. As a result, most students have only a mechanical understanding, and are unable to use their mathematics for development purposes.

Issues in Mathematics Education

A number of issues of concern in mathematics education across sub-Saharan Africa are also receiving attention elsewhere in the world. These include the problem of the language of instruction, gender issues (the unequal representation and achievement of girls), technological issues (the difficulty of making use of technological advances in countries that lack even the resources to provide adequate textbooks), the issues of preservice and inservice education, and the related issues of classroom teaching.

Language Issues

Language seems to play an essential role in the development of higher-order concepts in mathematics. According to Bell et al. (1983), "Both Piaget and Vygotsky provide some evidence that the development of linguistic structure in some cases precedes the appreciation of the corresponding logical relationship" (p. 275). Grammar precedes logic. Bell et al. go on to state:

Vygotsky, in an experimental study of concept formation, has probed more deeply into the dependence of the understanding of concepts on the language which describes them. It is fairly obvious that children themselves do not make the separation between linguistic form and meaning: the identification of the linguistic forms as non-arbitrary attributes of the objects they describe is seen by Vygotsky as characterizing "primitive linguistic consciousness." (p. 275)

Vygotsky (in Bell et al., 1983) concludes that concept and language are not only linked, but that concept formation depends on linguistic development. This view seems to have fairly general acceptance. The National Council of Teachers of Mathematics (1989), in the *Curriculum and Evaluation Standards,* makes communication one of the strands throughout the entire school program.

With language being so important to the learning of mathematics, one must consider the problem of bilingualism, the predominant pattern in schools throughout sub-Saharan Africa. In most African countries children learn a European language (usually English, French, Portuguese, or Afrikaans). Some researchers such as Macnamara, Morrison, and McIntyre (Bell et al., 1983) have found that bilingualism seems to hamper a child's progress in problem solving, but not in mechanical arithmetic. Other findings suggest that perhaps in situations where bilingualism is the case, it can be used to advantageous effect by expressing the mathematical ideas in several forms, thus enhancing mathematical abstraction by linguistic variability. However, this second finding, it seems, would only be the case when both languages are well known both to the child and to the teacher.

Brodie (1989) describes the situation of learning mathematics in a second language in South Africa. Many of the conditions that pertain are very similar to the situation in most of the other African countries. Brodie points out that it is commonly accepted that a bilingual person has achieved a certain level of proficiency in both languages, but that this is not true for many children in so-called bilingual education programs. She points out that while many of the programs are highly successful, others seem to produce a markedly different result. In general, children from dominant language groups such as English or French (dominant meaning, in this case, spoken by a majority of people in an economically powerful nation), attain a high level of bilingualism, whereas children from minority language groups tend to exhibit a low level of competence in both languages, and thus a lower level of academic achievement.

This lower level of academic achievement has been particularly devastating in mathematics. Children the world over seem to have had greater difficulty learning mathematics than other subject areas. But the difficulty is seen particularly clearly in the African context, where the learning of the language of mathematics is compounded by having to learn that language through the medium of a second, not particularly well-mastered language. This tends to lead to the learning of mathematics as a mechanical process rather than as a way of thinking.

Gender Issues

There has been widespread concern over the underrepresentation of girls in fields making use of mathematics, and also in the achievement of girls in mathematics throughout the world. It is far more acute within the African context. Girls, except in Botswana, have tended to be in the minority in African schools, particularly secondary schools. When having to determine which children will receive the meager amount available for education, families have traditionally educated their sons, in keeping with the cultural position of the sons. Often, within the society, girls have many chores to perform when they return home even if they do go to school, whereas boys often are excused from their traditional chores if they are in school. Girls do not have the time to do their school work and thus exhibit lower performance.

Recently, there have been a number of efforts aimed at increasing the participation of girls in the areas of mathematics and science. Additionally, studies have shown that girls benefit from single-sex schools. This is particularly true in mathematics and science. Efforts are underway to increase girls' understanding of mathematics through meaningful experiences in learning and using mathematics.

Technology Issues

The issue of technology is particularly important within the sub-Saharan African context. Economic downtrends have had devastating effects on the economies of African countries and have left them with little money to spend on education. It is difficult to provide computers and calculators for use in mathematics classes when there is not enough money even to provide textbooks for each student. But without the use of technology, African students will be increasingly disadvantaged within the world arena, where most students have ready access to calculators from preschool days and, increasingly, similar access to computers. Thus, for much of the rest of the world, computers and calculators are familiar tools used to learn mathematics within a problem-solving context. If African children continue to be denied such access, their learning of mathematics will be quite limited, and is likely to continue to emphasize mechanical procedures.

Preservice and Inservice Education

An adequate supply of teachers is a problem throughout the region. When it comes to teachers of mathematics, this problem is intensified. Students who study mathematics are more likely to find employment in the industrial sector of the country's economy and less likely to take one of the poorly paid positions in education. Countries such as Botswana and Zimbabwe have developed special programs for training science and mathematics teachers. Despite these efforts, they continue to have to rely on expatriate teachers to supply their mathematics and science classrooms.

One major problem faced by the expatriate teacher is the lack of knowledge of both the culture and the local language. Often, the language of instruction may not even be the language of the teacher, which makes instruction even more difficult. Additionally, the expatriate teacher is often untrained for the teaching profession. Take, for example, the use of Peace Corps teachers. These individuals usually receive a brief, two-month crash course that includes local culture, local language, and methods of teaching. There is no way that any of the areas can be adequately covered. This is not to say that they are not providing a very needed service, but only to point out the difficulties faced by both teacher and student within this context.

In attempting to provide for an adequate supply of local teachers, countries have had to establish training programs that not only provide training in teaching methods, but also upgrade knowledge of mathematics itself. When a student comes out of the secondary school, even if he or she has studied mathematics, the knowledge is likely to be inadequate because of the other difficulties encountered, such as lack of technology, language, poor teaching, lack of materials, and so forth. The programs that do exist are well developed, but also suffer from a lack of adequate staff.

When it comes to inservice education, the major programs that exist, which are few, do not begin to meet the needs of the practicing teachers. Some teachers are very much in need of help within the subject or area they teach. Added to this is the need to change from a mechanical approach to a more hands-on, higher-level-thinking approach. To make such a transition requires a great deal of attention and time. An example of a working inservice program is given in the case study of Zimbabwe below.

Classroom Teaching

As already discussed, classroom teaching throughout the region tends to emphasize the mechanical processes rather than the process of thinking mathematically. Today it is commonly recognized that children need to construct knowledge for themselves, particularly in an area such as mathematics. Many teachers in Africa lack the depth of knowledge of the subject of mathematics to be able to teach in this manner, since they themselves were taught in such a way that they possess only a mechanical understanding. Those involved in teacher training usually have limited additional training. They do not have an adequate grasp of the constructivist approach and are unable to develop such an approach among teachers. While some high-quality teacher education exists, there are many difficulties.

The teacher is faced with large classes, often forty or fifty students or more. The classrooms lack textbooks, adequate desks, chairs,

writing materials, and even usable chalkboards. All of these deficiencies contribute to lower achievement on the part of students of
mathematics in sub-Saharan Africa.

Mathematics Education in Zimbabwe

Mathematics education in Zimbabwe embodies the difficulties of
the search to develop an authentic, deep, and well-understood mathematics literacy in sub-Saharan Africa. Zimbabwe became independent in 1980, nearly twenty years later than the majority of African
nations. Like other nations, Zimbabwe faced problems such as unequal educational participation and low transitional rates from one
educational level to the next (Mungazi, in L. Jaji, 1988). This resulted in a pyramid-like enrollment shape that was extremely narrow at the top and very wide at the base. However, unlike other
nations of Africa, Zimbabwe had an impressive number of university graduates ready to take up higher-level posts in government at
independence time (1980). Still, at the time of independence, Zimbabwe faced enormous needs for expanded educational opportunity
and the development of the workforce. In the five-year period immediately following independence, primary education enrollment
alone expanded 150 percent, from 820, 000 to more than 2 million
according to Habte (in Chikombah, Johnston, Schneller, & Schwille,
1988).

Independence brought genuine change in the political system,
which in turn resulted in rapid quantitative expansion in both the
primary and the secondary school systems. Every child was to have
the opportunity to go to school (whereas previously only 12 percent
of school-age black children were afforded the opportunity to gain a
secondary education). The curriculum, however, remained highly
influenced by the British system. Educators in Great Britain had
little understanding of the Zimbabwean child, his or her environment, or his or her teacher. The educational system was highly elitist
(L. Jaji, 1988), while the society at large was aspiring to be egalitar-
ian. When the mathematics curriculum was transplanted, the perspective was also copied; thus, primary mathematics became viewed
as a stepping stone to secondary mathematics, which was seen merely
as preparation for university education. This viewpoint produced
and continues to foster a situation in which children in the schools

see mathematics as something foreign and useless to their lives (Gerdes, 1988). Thus, there has continued to be a need for the development of a genuinely Zimbabwean curriculum that is relevant to the needs of the Zimbawean society (Nyagura, in Chikombah, Johnston, Schneller, & Schwille, 1988).

The Present Position in Zimbabwe in School Mathematics

The mathematics curriculum of the primary school years (grades 1–7) has been under local control since before independence (grade 7 became the end of primary education in 1969; previously it had been grade 8). Since independence (1980) the syllabi have been produced by a syllabus panel composed of Ministry of Education (MOE) regional education officers, Curriculum Development Unit (CDU) officers, practicing teachers, representatives from the Schools Psychological Services Unit of MOE, the University of Zimbabwe, other government ministries, and commerce and industry (private sector). Panelists were urged to consult widely with the people they represent so as to make the exercise as democratic as possible (Vere, in Chikombah, Johnston, Schneller, & Schwille, 1988). Vere indicates:

The Primary Mathematics Syllabus panel met in late 1983 to decide whether changes were needed in the syllabus developed just before independence. Earlier these panelists had been given several months for consultations with the people they represented. Except for a few alterations, the syllabus was retained. The one major change was that there should be an emphasis on learning that relates mathematics to the environment and on solution of real-life problems (for example, investigative projects in local agriculture). (pp. 116–117)

The syllabus developed by the panel includes the following aims (*Primary School Mathematics Syllabus*, MOE, 1984), to help pupils to:

1. be permanently literate and numerate;
2. understand, use, and effectively communicate mathematical information;
3. acquire mathematical concepts and skills for use as tools in work, study, leisure, and everyday transactions;

4. develop sound mathematical skills that will enable them to interact more meaningfully and rewardingly with their environment;
5. develop a positive attitude toward mathematics as an exciting
   subject and to be aware of its creative aspect;
6. think and express themselves clearly and logically;
7. acquire attitudes of enquiry and experiment, cooperation, confidence, honesty, neatness, self-reliance, and perseverance
   through appropriately challenging mathematical and mathematically related tasks;
8. prepare for present and further studies in mathematics and
   related subjects;
9. grow intellectually. (p. v)

The syllabus itself is further divided by grade level and within grade
level by the following topics: number (whole and fractions), measure, shapes and lines (money, time, mass, length, area, capacity and
volume, rate, shapes, directions, angles, and lines), operations (addition and subtraction, multiplication and division), and relationships (ready reckoners, graphs). The objectives of the syllabus are
written in behavioral terms: for example, an objective from grade 1
is, "Can sort objects according to one or two criteria from length,
mass, color, texture (hard or soft, rough or smooth), thickness and
kind, and can distinguish between flat and rounded objects" (p. 3).
    It can be seen that the intended curriculum is not so different
from that of schools in the United States, particularly during the
period of time that the syllabus was produced (note that the syllabus
is dated 1984, before the National Council of Teachers of Mathematics in the United States produced their Curriculum and Evaluation Standards in 1989). The textbooks in use in the schools have
been produced to directly reflect the aims and objectives specified in
the syllabus. One series (Lawton & Jaji, 1978) produced by a member of the panel and one of the authors of this chapter more clearly
reflects the problem-solving, investigative approach advocated, but
all series clearly reflect the stated aims and objectives of the syllabus.
We have to look further than the intended curriculum to see the real
state of affairs in terms of mathematics education as it pertains to
Zimbabwe. The implemented curriculum is clearly not matched to
the intended curriculum. Jaji and Nyagura (1989) state,

It is of concern that items which involve greater conceptualization seem to be the ones where Zimbabwean students fare the worst and that Zimbabwean students only seem to hold their own on those which are of a rote nature. This suggests our teachers do a good job on drill and practice but need to do much more in developing understanding and problem solving skills. (pp. 155–156)

Shumba (1988) also found that teachers emphasize mechanics and the rote acquisition of skills without adequate conceptual frameworks. Thus, there is evidence that the implemented and attained curriculum in mathematics in Zimbabwean schools does not match the intended curriculum.

At the secondary school level there are three levels of syllabi: the junior certificate level, the ordinary level (O level), and the advanced level (A level). The junior certificate level covers the first two years of secondary education and is seen to be mainly a preparation for the O level. Prior to independence the junior certificate was a terminal point for black students, but with the attainment of independence (1980) most pupils now proceed to O level if they enter secondary level. The O level covers the next two years of secondary schooling and when completed it is roughly equivalent to completing high school in the United States (it is considered equivalent for purposes of entering most U.S. universities). The A-level certificate then covers the last two years of secondary education. Very few pupils are able to proceed to do A level, as entrance into A-level schools in Zimbabwe is highly selective; and A-level mathematics is even more selective. A level is equivalent to the first year or two of university in the United States—it is not like U.S. junior colleges, in that it is highly selective (A-level courses are given university course credit by most U.S. colleges). Note that, like British universities, the Universities in Zimbabwe are mainly three-year institutions, since students enter with A levels (the equivalent of one year of university-level work by U.S. standards).

At present, both the junior certificate and O-level syllabi are localized in Zimbabwe. These syllabi have been designed in Zimbabwe and are examined by Zimbabweans. The O-level syllabus examination is still monitored (i.e., samples of marked exams are sent to the United Kingdom) by the Cambridge Examinations Syndicate. The junior certificate was local even before independence, and the O-level syllabus became fully local in 1994. The A-level syllabus, however, remains under the control of the University of Cambridge Local Examinations Syndicate in Britain. The junior certificate is seen as mainly preparatory to the O-level syllabus and thus is highly tied to the content and methodology of the O-level syllabus. Likewise, to a great extent, the O-level syllabus is seen as preparatory to the A-level syllabus, and is thus tied to the A-level syllabus. This clearly leaves the control of the secondary syllabi by default in the control of outside forces rather than indigenous forces, as was intended when localizing the syllabi. Certain other intentions, such as saving foreign currency by examining locally, were better served.

Local control of the O-level syllabus was further eroded by the fact that the syllabus had to be acceptable to the University of Cambridge Local Examinations Syndicate. When the Zimbabwean mathematics syllabus panel met over a period of several years to work out the details of the mathematics syllabus, it eventually devised a two-tier syllabus called the core and extended syllabus, respectively. The core syllabus was intended to give a basic and solid education in secondary mathematics which included the usual algebraic, geometric, trigonometric, and arithmetic topics. These topics would extend only to the level needed for those who would enter the workforce in fields where mathematics was not the main underpinning, such as auto mechanics, building, or nursing, and so forth. The extended syllabus was intended for those who had special mathematical inclinations and whose intention was either to study mathematics at university or to take up areas where a strong mathematics background was necessary, such as the physical sciences, computer science, or engineering. All students were to study the core syllabus and then the few with mathematical inclinations would add the extended version. The core syllabus alone was not considered to be of O-level status (even though similar syllabi existed in Britain under the British Local Boards), and thus the local panel was forced into the position of accepting as a single syllabus the combination of the core and the extended. This, in fact, meant that all students would have to study and be examined on the syllabus that was designed and intended only for the elite few. If we look at the general introduction to the mathematics syllabus (University of Cambridge Local

Examinations Syndicate International Examinations [UCLESIE] and
Ministry of Education and Culture, Zimbabwe [MOEZ], 1994) we
begin to see the lack of coherence between intention and final outcome:

*Since 1980 when Zimbabwe came into being, there have been consider-
able institutional changes in response to national needs, goals and aspirations. In the field of Education, the government has democratized educational opportunities by making both primary and secondary education
available to almost all children of school-going age.*

*The long-term implications arising from this tremendous and rapid
expansion are that:*

   *a)   the majority of Zimbabwean pupils are unlikely to find places
        in institutions of higher training and learning. The GCE Or-
        dinary level Examinations will, therefore, be a terminal one
        for this majority before they go out to work:*
   *b)   education, particularly at secondary level, should prepare pupils
        for the world of work and at the same time provide opportuni-
        ties for admission to institutions of higher learning.*

*Arising out of the above it has been found necessary to initiate cur-
riculum change, as an on-going process, in order to:*

   *c)   incorporate within the education system values that are consis-
        tent with the social and political aspirations of Zimbabwe, e.g.
        the inculcation of a work ethic and the usefulness of productiv-
        ity, patriotism, co-operation and an understanding of Zimba-
        bwean regional and world history, culture, politics and ideology;*
   *d)   provide the many who are not likely to go on to higher learning
        institutions with an education which will be functionally use-
        ful in the world of work. The integration into the curriculum
        of the philosophy of Education with Production is aimed at
        helping pupils to relate knowledge and theory to their practical
        application in production within the Zimbabwean context;*
   *e)   incorporate social, scientific and technological content and con-
        cepts wherever possible across the curriculum so that this essen-
        tial knowledge is accessible to as many people as possible. (p. ii)*

The syllabus panel (UCLESIE & MOEZ, 1994) go further to specifically state the syllabus aims as being to enable pupils to:

> understand, interpret and communicate mathematical information in everyday life;
> acquire mathematical skills for use in their everyday lives and in national development;
> appreciate the crucial role of mathematics in national development and in the country's socialist ideology;
> acquire a firm mathematical foundation for further studies and/or vocational training;
> develop the ability to apply mathematics in other subjects;
> develop the ability to reason and present arguments logically;
> develop the ability to apply mathematical knowledge and techniques in a wide variety of situations, both familiar and unfamiliar;
> find joy and self-fulfillment in mathematics and related activities, and appreciate the beauty of mathematics;
> develop good habits such as thoroughness and neatness, and positive attitudes such as an enquiring spirit, open-mindedness, self-reliance, resourcefulness, critical and creative thinking, cooperation and persistence;
> appreciate the process of discovery and the historical development of mathematics as an integral part of human culture. (p. 2)

And further on the panel suggests:

> In this syllabus, teaching approaches in which mathematics is seen as a process and which build an interest and confidence in tackling problems both in familiar and unfamiliar contexts are recommended.
> It is suggested that:
> concepts be developed starting from concrete situations (in the immediate environment) and moving to abstract ones;
> principles be based on sound understanding of related concepts; and whenever possible, be learnt through activity based and/or guided discovery;
> skills be learnt only after relevant concepts and principles have been mastered;
> the human element in the process of mathematical discoveries be emphasized;

> *an effort be made to reinforce relevant skills taught in other subjects;
> pupils be taught to check and criticize their own and one
> another's work;*
>
> *group work be organized regularly;*
>
> *a deliberate attempt be made to teach problem-solving as a skill,
> with pupils being exposed to non-routine problem solving situations;*
>
> *pupils be taught to identify problems in their environment, put them
> in a mathematical form and solve them e.g. through project work. (p. 3)*

Topics considered include: numbers (concepts and operations on integers, fractions and percentages, factors and multiples, approximation and estimation, standard form, number bases, ratio, proportion, rates and scales); sets; consumer arithmetic; measures and mensuration; graphs and variation including coordinates, kinematics, variation (direct, inverse, and partial); functional graphs (solution of equations, gradients, area under a curve); algebraic concepts and techniques (symbolic expression, formulae, change of subject); algebraic manipulation (operations, factor, multiples, expansion); indices (laws of indices, squares/square roots, cubes/cube roots); equations (linear, simultaneous, quadratic, logarithms, inequalities—signs, linear inequalities, linear programming); geometric concepts and techniques (points line and angle—types of angle, parallel lines); bearings; polygons (triangles, quadrilaterals, n-sided polygons); parallel lines and area; circles; similarity and congruence; constructions (triangles, parallelograms, regular polygons, scale drawings, loci, symmetry); trigonometry (Pythagoras's theorem and trigonometrical ratios, area of a triangle); vectors and matrices (vectors in two dimensions, translation and notation, operations); position vectors; equal vectors; parallel vectors; matrices (dimension, operations, identity matrix, determinant, inverse matrix); transformations (translation, reflection, rotation and enlargement, stretch, shear); statistics (collection and classification, data representation, measure of central tendency, cumulative frequency); and probability (terms, experimental probability, theoretical probability, probability of single/combined events).

The aims and methodology of the intended syllabus clearly emphasized understanding, problem solving, and discovery. But Jaji (1990), in a survey of mathematics teachers concerning how they implement the methodological aspects of the curriculum, found that most teachers emphasize mechanical processes and that the predominant approach to teaching is chalkboard explanation rather than projects, group work, or discovery. She also found that many classrooms do not have enough textbooks for the pupils and that teachers spend large amounts of time on preparation, marking, and other classroom-related activities. In relationship to pupils she found that pupils spend a substantial amount of time on homework and most of their class time listening to lectures. It should be noted that while the study was conducted prior to the full introduction of the syllabus for examination, teachers were already being asked to implement it and at the time it was introduced for examination purposes, many teachers were unaware that it was a new syllabus.

If we look at the attained curriculum at the junior certificate level, only 12 percent of the candidates passed the mathematics examination, contrasted with 35 percent passing English, 28 percent passing Science, and 45 percent passing History (note that passing means scoring 50 percent or better, since the level of performance demanded is so high and the grading system is so strict that a score of 75 percent or better is awarded an A grade). It can clearly be seen that the pass rate in mathematics is considerably lower than these other subjects. Also note that at Grade 7, 58 percent of the pupils passed the mathematics examination, 76 percent passed English, and 74 percent passed the general paper. Here the mathematics pass rate, while still much lower than for other subjects, is not so far out of line with the overall pass rate (Secretary for Education and Culture, 1993). Again, the mismatch of the intended with the attained curriculum is clearly apparent.

Possible Causes for the Disparity between Intended and Attained Curricula

When there is such a clear disparity between the intended, implemented, and attained curricula it becomes necessary to look for the probable causes. In order to consider ways to rectify such a situation, the possible sources of the problem need to be known. Some indicators will be easily identifiable, whereas others may be so hidden as to defy any means of identification.

Whenever a curriculum does not quite fit a situation, we can be sure that there will be some kind of mismatch between the intended, implemented, and attained curriculum. This is clearly the case in Zimbabwe, where even though to a large extent Zimbabwe has assumed control over the syllabus and examination system up through O level (equivalent to 12th grade in the United States), that control has not produced a truly Zimbabwean curriculum for a number of reasons. First, there is the constant concern with standards. These standards are essentially Western, and specifically British. Even among those who are opposed to some lingering colonial dominance, mechanisms of the hidden or unconscious mindset clings to a belief that the curriculum must meet British standards, or at least what are perceived to be British standards, to be "good." This, in essence, means that the curriculum must remain as much like the imported British curriculum as possible and that changes that are made should be largely cosmetic. The implicit belief is that Western mathematics is better than African mathematics, or that there is little real mathematics in African culture. This belief is held by both educated and uneducated members of the society. There is a belief that to change significantly is to lower standards. Few can see that change is necessary to bring about meaningful development. There appears to be a deep-seated belief that what was inherited from the colonial power has intrinsic worth or value perhaps because it seemed to be the means of making the colonizer dominant for so long. Thus, while the nation may now have the power to change the curriculum to one which more nearly serves the needs of the developing nation, it is difficult to achieve the required change since it will certainly be met with resistance from the masses. And even among the curriculum developers themselves, the need for significant change may not be readily perceived. This is coupled with the fact that the A-level syllabus at present remains in the hands of the former colonizer.

The A level is the bridge between secondary and tertiary studies. It will be very difficult to change the curriculum significantly because of the lingering perception of each level being just a preparation for the next level. Some of the lower levels may be terminal points for the majority of students. However, most teachers and curriculum developers have difficulty finding a balance between these two endpoints, particularly in a subject as hierarchical in nature as mathematics. Hence, teachers usually succumb to accepting the preparatory demands, while neglecting the needs of the majority for whom that level will be terminal. Here economics perhaps plays a major role. Employment in the formal sector of the economy is seen by most to be desirable (this is particularly true of teachers). For these individuals to deny the child who might go on to further learning the chance to do so seems tantamount to condemning the child to being poor and to possibly having no employment, at least in the formal sector of the economy. That this scenario may not actually be the case does not occur to those who still cling to the idea of British-type education being the means to upward mobility.

Another cause might lie in the language of instruction. Brodie (1989) describes the situation in South Africa as it pertains to bilingual education, stating that the languages of the black children in South Africa are all languages which are not dominant world languages, as is also the case with the languages spoken at home by the majority of black children in Zimbabwe. The usual pattern in both countries is for the vernacular to be used during the first years of primary school (in Zimbabwe this is specifically limited to the first two years) and English in the later primary and secondary school, with the vernacular being studied as a separate subject. In Zimbabwe all children must also learn one of the two dominant vernacular languages (Shona or Ndebele), but if English is their mother tongue, they are never required to learn subjects such as mathematics in their second language (Shona or Ndebele) as are the children whose mother tongue is not English. Note that there are pragmatic reasons for education in English, such as lack of materials in the vernacular (the need for a common language of instruction in the face of cultural and linguistic diversity makes English a common language of instruction), and also the necessity for those aspiring to tertiary level to be able to read materials in English. Many have also suggested that the African languages are unsuitable for expressing mathematical and scientific ideas, as the required technological vocabulary does not exist. Certainly, this argument was discussed at some length in Zimbabwe during the 1980s, with the issue really not resolved. But it should be noted that experts like Fishman (in Brodie, 1989) point out that we are not "helplessly trapped by the language we speak" (p. 43). Brodie also quotes Streven's assertion that "there is overwhelming evidence that any language is potentially able to be developed so as to express all the communication needs of the people who speak it, including scientific discourse" (p. 43). And it should also be taken into account that there are some advantages besides the clear advantage of learning in one's mother tongue to using Shona or Ndebele (the two major local languages). These two languages are both place-value-embedded languages, and thus assist in the learning of place value. Place value is essential to the learning of the basic computational algorithms for addition, subtraction, multiplication, and division. Using Shona or Ndebele has a clear advantage over using English in this situation, because English is not place-value-embedded, and English-speaking children often have difficulty learning the meaning of place value. (Place-value-embedded means that the spoken word directly reveals the place value—for example, in Shona twelve is expressed as gumi ne mbiri meaning literally ten and two. Note in English the concept that twelve means ten and two is not apparent in the number's name and is thus not apparent to the learner.)

While the language we speak, therefore, does not bar us from any aspect of cognitive discovery or experience, it does make a difference in the structures and classifications that we impose upon our interpretations of those experiences. Brodie (1989) goes on to draw the relationship between language and cognition, pointing out that the language we speak influences our thought patterns. She points out that children in South Africa often are not very proficient in either language, and thus experience negative cognitive effects which lead to a lower level of attainment in mathematics. Note also that the African languages are quite different from English; the linguistic distance makes the task of learning English more difficult and also has implications for cultural effects as well. Brodie (1989) quotes Dawe:

Mathematical reasoning in the deductive sense is closely related to the ability to use language as a tool for thought. In the case of bilingual children this involves competence in both languages. It has been clearly shown that the ability of the child to make effective use of the cognitive functions of his first language is a good predictor of his ability to reason deductively in English as a second language. (p. 45)

Other problems related to the use of a second language include the close correlation between reading skills and mathematical problem-solving abilities and the specialized nature of mathematical language. Even a child using his or her first language experiences difficulty related to the reading of mathematics and the specialized nature of mathematical language. Therefore, how much more difficulty is faced by the child operating in a second language.

Jaji and Hodzi (unpublished and still in progress) found that children in Zimbabwe were hindered in problem solving when they had to operate in English, but that when allowed to express themselves in their home language, they became more proficient. In their study, teachers were instructed to allow children to express themselves in their home language and only later translate this into English.

Gerdes (1988) describes the work of Gay and Cole in their study of the mathematics learning difficulties of the Kpelle (Liberia). According to Gerdes, Gay and Cole found that there were no inherent difficulties, but that the contents of the curriculum made no sense from the point of view of Kpelle-culture. Additionally, the methods used in the classroom were primarily rote and discipline tended to be harsh. Yet, experiments on Kpelle illiterate adults showed that they performed better than North American adults when solving problems such as estimation of the number of cups of rice in a given container. Observation of schools in Zimbabwe tends to show similar situations. Gerdes quotes D'Ambrosio: "'learned' matheracy eliminates the so-called 'spontaneous' matheracy." He goes on to say, "The former, let us say, spontaneous abilities [are] downgraded, repressed and forgotten, while the learned ones [are not being] assimilated, either as a consequence of learning blockage, or of an early dropout . . ." (p. 138). Such experiences lead children to a sense of failure, a sense of not being able to do mathematics, and a dependency on the teacher. According to Gerdes, Gay and Cole became convinced of the necessity to investigate "indigenous mathematics" so that it could be used to build an effective bridge into the mathematics of the school. It should be noted here that this is very much in line with the thinking of making connections to the world of the child and allowing children to build their own mathematical ideas that is advocated in the United States by the National Council of Teachers of Mathematics.

Gerdes (1988) points out that as a consequence of colonialism, African mathematical traditions have become ignored and even despised. In Zimbabwe this disregard for the indigenous mathematical traditions has reached such an extent that it is difficult to find African children who know how to count in their mother tongue. Parents (even those who do not speak English) have come to regard knowing how to count in English as so important to success that they teach their children to count in English rather than in the mother tongue. Studies have suggested that when the language used for counting is not place-value-embedded it becomes more difficult to learn and understand place value.

Presmeg (1988) says:

For a mathematics curriculum for mutual understanding when diverse cultures come together, the following points appear to be of importance:

(1) *Children need the stability of their cultural heritage, especially during periods of rapid social change.*
(2) *The mathematics curriculum should incorporate elements of the cultural histories of all the people of the region.*
(3) *The mathematics curriculum should be experienced as "real" by all children, and should resonate, as far as possible, with diverse home cultures.*
(4) *The mathematics curriculum should be seen by pupils as relevant to their future lives. (p. 169)*

Certainly some attempt was made through the primary school texts to incorporate elements of the cultural histories of all the people; however, it clearly was not done in sufficient depth. To some extent, many of the curriculum developers believed that mathematics was a "culture-free subject." Bishop (1988) states, "Mathematics curricula though, have been slow to change, due primarily to a popular and widespread misconception. Up to five or so years ago, the conventional wisdom was that mathematics was 'culture-free' knowledge" (p. 179). That this is not the case is becoming increasingly apparent. Secondly, because of the long period of colonial domination, much of the mathematics culture of Zimbabwe has been frozen and hidden away. The search for this hidden element is only just beginning. This gives reason for hope, but it will take time to uncover the essentials of the indigenous mathematics culture of Zimbabwe, and in the meantime, many children continue to find mathematics somehow divorced from their lives. It must be borne in mind that while Zimbabwe is not multicultural in the same sense as the United States, as it does not have the same kind of multiplicity of cultures that the United States has, it is still a multicultural society with many children coming from diverse backgrounds. (There are several indigenous tribal groups with their own unique traditions, as well as several different European settler groups and several Asian settler groups and, of course, various mixes of these groups.)

Relevance of Culture in Enhancing Mathematics Education for All among Sub-Saharan African Students

Culture, as has already been pointed out, is the milieu in which the mathematics to be taught must be embedded if it is to be truly meaningful to the learner. We, therefore, now look specifically at ways to enhance the mathematics education of children in the classroom through better use of the Zimbabwean culture.

According to Singleton (as cited in Presmeg, 1988, p. 166), if culture is to be understood as encompassing patterns of meaning, reality, values, actions, and decision making that are shared by and within social collectives, then the teaching of mathematics must be relevant and accessible to all students in sub-Saharan Africa. The case for culture and its place in learning to count among Zimbabwean students, like other students in the region, is very significant. There is a need for specific studies in the indigenous culture which have mathematical content to be publicized so that those who develop the mathematics curriculum and those who teach mathematics feel confident about methods and activities which build upon the cultural attitudes that students already have by the time they enter their early formal education.

In Zimbabwe almost all boys who are brought up in a rural environment herd cattle from a very young age. While families with daughters only, and even those with sons and daughters, may send them to herd cattle, this, in general, has been a chore for boys. Even those who are raised in an urban environment, but have had an opportunity to visit the extended family in the rural environment, quickly learn to herd cattle when they go out to play with their friends. Girls, who might not necessarily herd cattle, have chores like gathering firewood. Girls play a game called "Nhodo" in holes dug in the ground; boys play its equivalent, called "tsoro." Both games involve the use of stones, some wild fruit seed, or other materials that may be readily available in the immediate environment. The advantage of these games and chores such as cattle herding is that they teach children to count at a very early (preschool) age. The children understand how to add, subtract, multiply, and divide as a result of these games. The awareness of the existence of these games is of relevance to the teacher and curriculum developer so that they build upon them as children enter formal schooling. The methods that incorporate this understanding are likely to win the confidence of the child and convince the child that mathematics is indeed a subject already familiar and within reach of everyone. Such a positive attitude would go a long way toward dispelling the gloomy myth that mathematics is too difficult a subject to be offered for all students, at least at elementary through secondary school level.

While herding cattle or fetching firewood or doing other chores, children learn cultural values, patterns with meanings that they can clearly explain, and get involved in activities that lead them to make meaningful decisions. All these patterns are said to be necessary in the learning of mathematics. Children learn more and more sophisticated patterns as they swim, run down slopes, and build toys that can fly. All of these are learned informally as play and game activity. In many cases children can describe vividly what they know after they have watched, played, put things together, or taken them apart. The putting together/building of most objects in Zimbabwe may be done during harvesting time when the remains of maize stalk (corn stalk) are split into all kinds of artifacts. All the examples cited are very strong elements with which to build a firm foundation for the teaching of mathematics. Any location in which the teacher finds herself or himself can be used to an advantage by identifying the games and activities as well as resources available that could be used to enhance the learning of mathematical concepts.

Shape plays a very important role in mathematics. Different shapes seem to abound from one culture to another. From a cultural viewpoint, every Zimbabwean child is familiar with round shapes (huts, wells, monkey apples, etc.). Round huts, to choose a specific example, fit easily into Western geometry. The huts are built with the use of a central pole that acts as a hypotenuse in Euclidean geometry. Certainly, there are other shapes out of which the Cartesian system and even calculus teaching could be developed. Familiarity with the traditional and cultural values of a people is a major asset for the curriculum developer and teacher who can thus be more effective in the teaching of mathematics at any level, making it an interesting and enjoyable subject.

Mathematics is the study of patterns. When one studies mathematics the study of patterns of shape and number should be paramount. Most cultures abound with patterns in shape and Zimbabwe is no exception. Patterns that these cultural values have taught people can be seen in the pottery and woven baskets of the Zimbabwean folk. The same could be said of other artifacts that abound in sub-Saharan Africa. These patterns offer materials for the effective design of a rich curriculum of mathematics education. An understanding that the curriculum means more than the syllabus is very important here, because only when the teacher encompasses the content, methods, and assessment procedures that accept and build upon the rich mathematics taught by the culture, whether formally or informally, will teachers be able to communicate mathematics effectively.

Signs of Progress in the Region
One of the most hopeful signs for progress toward a curriculum where the intended, implemented, and attained curricula are closely aligned is the emergence of work in the area of ethnomathematics. A number of researchers are beginning to publish in this area. Perhaps the most notable among these is Gerdes, who has done quite significant work in this area in Mozambique. Other researchers of note are Mtetwa in Zimbabwe and Mmari in Tanzania. In this vein we should not forget the contribution of Zaslavsky in her major work, *Africa Counts: Number and Pattern in African Culture*, (1973). Zaslavsky writes, "In Africa, too, physical environment, inherited cultural resources and the impact of external forces determined the nature and extent of mathematical development" (p. 16). She points out that mathematics is but one of the streams of the total culture of a people. Much more needs to be found out about the mathematical stream of the various cultures of the peoples of Africa. It is certainly

encouraging to see that researchers in this area are emerging and undertaking this vital task. It is to be hoped that curriculum developers will quickly incorporate this vital work into the materials used for teaching mathematics to the youth of the continent.

Turning to but a few of the examples of cultural effects available due to the work of Gerdes (1988), we begin to see the potential of the use of this material. One of the areas Gerdes suggests is to study alternative axiomatic constructions of Euclidean geometry. He points out that the peasant farmers of Mozambique use rectangles in their daily lives, and in order to build the rectangular bases of their homes they make use of a rectangular axiom. One way that they build is to take two sticks of equal length and combine them with two other sticks, also of equal length, but shorter than the first two. The sticks are then moved to form a closure in the shape of a quadrilateral. This shape can then be adjusted until the diagonals (which are measured with a rope) become equally long. This shape can then be drawn on the ground and the house built from there.

Another method that the peasants use to lay out the floor plan of their house is to start with two ropes of equal length tied together at their midpoints. Then sticks whose lengths are equal to the desired breadth of the house are laid down on the floor. At the ends of the sticks the ropes are secured, and then the ropes are stretched and secured at their endpoints, thus determining the four vertices of the house to be built. This leads to two alternative rectangle axioms: (1) an equidiagonal parallelogram is a rectangle, and (2) an equisemidiagonal quadrilateral is a rectangle. This is but one example of the mathematical knowledge available in the culture that can be tapped for teaching purposes and for purposes of contributing to cultural–mathematical confidence.

Similar knowledge exists in many areas of mathematics in both Mozambique and Zimbabwe and, for that matter, throughout sub-Saharan Africa. It just needs to be documented and tapped into for the purpose of mathematical instruction. Teachers need to be helped to be more aware of this type of cultural material and the need to tap into the culture in order to make mathematics more meaningful to children. For example, fishermen use fish traps made in the shape of a cone, pointed on one end and spherical at the other end to attract fish into the trap. The fish find it hard to escape once trapped. Other examples could also be cited, such as circular straw hats or rectangular and circular hand bags made out of fiber rope or other cultural materials. All these items are rich with mathematical concepts that lead to higher-level skills.

Boys who hunt mice and birds may use mathematical ideas such as using rectangular and triangular stones and slings to shoot birds at specific vertically opposite angles with the birds. Thus, teachers and curriculum developers could cite such familiar examples and many others to teach high-level mathematical skills. If documented, such information could enhance effective teaching of mathematics in the region.

Another type of event that is taking place in the region is the emergence of teacher development work which is leading to new approaches to the teaching of mathematics. Jaji and Hodzi (in progress) developed an action research project for teaching problem solving in mathematics and science in elementary schools aimed first at Zimbabwe, but developed with the view that it could be adapted for use in other African countries. The project was based upon the constructivist model (all knowledge is constructed by the learner for him/herself from his/her experiences with the environment). Thus, a major aim of the project was the development of activities that would encourage children to actively construct strong and accurate concepts within mathematics and science. Another aim of the project was the development of teachers who would have the skill to ask questions, create problem-solving situations, and make available appropriate materials for strong constructions to take place. A third aim of the project was that these teachers would not only acquire these new teaching skills for themselves, but would also be able to pass their newly acquired skills on to other teachers, both at their own schools and in other nearby schools. A sort of mushrooming effect was envisioned whereby, as teachers acquired the skills, they would pass them on to teachers at another school, thus keeping the program moving from one school to another. As the project developed, the acquisition of the teaching skills required took longer than at first anticipated. It took about three years for the teachers to acquire the skills and gain confidence in using them. It is hypothesized that this prolonged period was made necessary by the fact that moving from essentially rote teaching to the constructivist model is an extremely radical shift. Teachers were encouraged to develop and write materials for use by themselves and other teachers to help them gain a sense of ownership of the methodology and problems. Evidence available suggests that this is indeed the case. The project is not yet complete and is in a continuing state of flux, as is often the case with action research. The evidence thus far has been promising. There has been great interest from teachers not only within the project but also outside it. Many curriculum developers have taken an interest, and interest has also been expressed from administrators to extend the activities within the project to as many schools as possible.

These two examples of new directions give reason for hope in the improvement of a mathematical curriculum that more nearly meets the needs of the culture as it exists and changes, and also lays the groundwork for growth by supplying the main tool of development, problem solving. The second change provides specifically for improvement in the implementation of the curriculum, which we have seen has been one of the major sources of the discrepancy between the intended and attained curriculum. But it is necessary here to say that the intended curriculum must include the input from the culture if it is to become truly relevant and thus worthy of implementation.

Much progress has been made in mathematics education in Zimbabwe and in the whole of sub-Saharan Africa, but much more needs to be done. Researchers have only begun to scratch the surface of the vast amount of research that needs to be done to make the curriculum, the methodology, and the assessment of learning truly relevant to the needs of this vast and developing area of the world. The development of closer economic ties among these countries is most encouraging indeed. The case in point is the transformation of the then Southern African Development Countries Conference (SADCC) into Southern African Development Community (SADC) just before the birth of a post-Apartheid South Africa under President Mandela (1994). It is hoped that the SADC region will move toward the development of curriculum that is shared across the regional nations, thereby extending the cultural value and patterns already practiced among the various groups. This will enhance the teaching and development of a more exciting and relevant mathematics curriculum and textbooks for all among SADC's African students.

References

Bell, A.W., Costello, J., & Kuchemann, D. (1983). *A review of research in mathematical education: Part A: Research on learning and teaching.* Windsor, England: Nfer-Nelson.

Bishop, A.J. (1988). Mathematics education in its cultural context. *Educational Studies in Mathematics 19,* 179–191.

Brodie, K. (1989). Learning Mathematics in a Second Language. *Educational Review, 41*(1), 39–53.

Chikombah, C., Johnston, E., Schneller, A., & Schwille, J. (Eds.). (1988). *Education in the new Zimbabwe.* East Lansing, MI: Michigan State University, African Studies Center and Office for International Networks in Education and Development.

Gerdes, P. (1988). On culture, geometrical thinking and mathematics education. *Educational Studies in Mathematics, 19,* 137–162.

Jaji, G. (1990). The teacher as implementor of the curriculum in Zimbabwe secondary schools: The case of mathematics. *Zimbabwe Journal of Educational Research, 2*(1), 1–24.

Jaji, G., & Hodzi, R. (1993). *The effects on mathematics development of the use of pupils' home language.* Unpublished report to Rockefeller Foundation. New York: Rockefeller Foundation.

Jaji, G., & Nyagura, L. (1989, July). Attained mathematics curriculum in Zimbabwe primary schools. *Zimbabwe Journal of Educational Research, 1*(2), 147–160.

Jaji, L.M. (1988). *School improvement research and future educational policy efforts in Zimbabwe.* Unpublished doctoral dissertation, University of Illinois at Urbana-Champaign.

Lawton, O., & Jaji, G. (1978). *Let's do mathematics: Grade 2.* Harare, Zimbabwe: Longman.

Ministry of Education, Zimbabwe. (1984). *Primary school mathematics syllabus.* Harare, Zimbabwe: Curriculum Development Unit.

National Council of Teachers of Mathematics. (1989). *Curriculum and evaluation standards for school mathematics.* Reston, VA: Author.

Presmeg, N.C. (1988). School mathematics in culture-conflict situations. *Educational Studies in Mathematics, 19,* 163–177.

Secretary for Education and Culture. (1993). *Annual report of the Secretary for Education and Culture for the year ended 31st December, 1991.* Presented to the Parliament of Zimbabwe. Harare, Zimbabwe: Government Printer.

Servais, W., & Varga, T. (1971). *Teaching school mathematics.* Harmondsworth, UK: Penguin.

Shumba, S. (1988). *An investigation of teaching approaches and their relationship to pupil performance with specific focus on common fractions in sixth and seventh grade classes.* Unpublished master's thesis, Department of Curriculum Studies, University of Zimbabwe.

University of Cambridge, Local Examinations Syndicate International Examinations. In collaboration with The Ministry of Education and Culture, Zimbabwe. (1994). *General certificate of education for examination in November 1994: O Level Syllabuses for Candidates in Zimbabwe: Mathematics* (4008, 4028).

Zaslavsky, C. (1973). *Africa counts: Number and pattern in African culture.* Westport: Lawrence Hill.

Chapter Six
Citizenship Education in Sub-Saharan Africa
Defining a Nation

Mohammed Kabiru Farouk

Citizenship education in sub-Saharan Africa is an important issue as nations struggle to establish a national identity that transcends ethnic, religious, or regional loyalties. As diverse as the region is, each nation's response to the need for creating a viable program for the effective preparation of youth for citizenship in a modern democratic state is invariably different. However, the primary concern of all modern nation-states in Africa today is how to design educational programs that provide the knowledge, skills, values, and attitudes required in a citizenry in an ever-changing, politically unstable, economically uncertain, yet interdependent world. The issue is even more challenging for sub-Saharan African countries that were a by-product of European imperialist ambitions that resulted in divisions and conflicts among and between hitherto homogeneous groups. After gaining political independence, the challenge became that of establishing an educational system that reflected the needs, concerns, and aspirations of the new nations whose major goal was creating a sense of national identity and loyalty to ensure rapid economic and political development.

This chapter examines the status of citizenship education in sub-Saharan Africa and some of the issues that are germane to establishing viable programs for citizenship education. An in-depth study of citizenship education in Nigeria is then discussed. The issues addressed in the chapter are: Africanization of the curriculum, instructional strategies, teacher education, and implications.

Citizenship education has been declared as the main goal of education in various places and at various times. In the United States, citizenship education has been viewed as the most important goal of education (Beyer & French, 1965). In their study of civic education in ten nations, Torney and associates (1975) found that in each of the countries studied (Federal Republic of Germany, Finland, Iran, Ireland, Israel, Italy, the Netherlands, New Zealand, Sweden, and the United States), the schools carried out a systematic teaching program aimed at producing well-informed, democratically active citizens.

In Nigeria, education has been adopted as the most important vehicle for producing an effective citizenry. The philosophy of Nigerian education stresses that "education should be geared towards self-realization, better human relationships, . . . effective citizenship, national consciousness, as well as towards social, cultural, economic, political, scientific, and technological progress . . ." (Federal Republic of Nigeria, 1981, section 1, subsection 4). Based on this premise, the Nigerian National Policy on Education stresses, among other goals of education,

citizenship education as a basis for effective participation in, and contribution to the life of the society; character and moral training, and the development of sound attitudes; developing in the child the ability to adapt to his changing environment . . . (Federal Republic of Nigeria, 1981, section 3 and section 13, subsections c, d, and e)

Characteristics of a Citizenship Education Program

A holistic conception of citizenship education must not only encompass the acquisition of knowledge, skills, and attitudes necessary for competent participation in a democratic society, it must also foster in the individual a constructive desire and capability to improve and change the society. This has implications for the role of the other agents of political socialization; namely governmental institutions, the work place, mass media, voluntary organizations, and the primary groups—the family and peer group. This suggests that there has to be cooperation between the school and these other agents of political socialization if the aims of citizenship education are to be realized. This will be consistent with recent efforts to define the social studies as an "integration of experiences and knowledge concerning human relations for the purpose of citizenship education" (Engle & Ochoa, 1988, p. 69).

Although it is difficult to list the characteristics of a comprehensive citizenship education program, it is possible at least to delineate some fundamental features that such a program should have. Any citizenship education program should provide students with the knowledge that they need about the world they live in and make them informed about the social forces in which their lives are enmeshed. The National Council for the Social Studies (NCSS) Curriculum Guidelines (1979) indicate that subject matter for the social studies curriculum should be selected from such areas of knowledge as history—national and world history; geography—physical, cultural, economic, and worldwide relationships of all sorts; government—theories, systems, structures, and processes; economics—theories, systems, structures, and processes; law—civil, criminal, and constitutional; anthropology and sociology—cultures, social institutions, the individual, the group, the community, and the society; psychology—the individual in intergroup and interpersonal relationships; humanities—the literature, art, music, dance, and drama of cultures; and science—the effects of natural and physical science on human relationships.

However, social studies/citizenship education programs need to go beyond the conventional disciplines of the social sciences, history, the humanities, and science for their sources of content. They should reflect an understanding of the personal, social, and cultural experiences of students. The knowledge and information acquired should enable students to understand the reality of the world they live in and become competent at solving the personal and social problems encountered in a complex, changing democratic society.

Students also need to be provided with opportunities for acquiring and developing the skills necessary for competent participation in a democratic society. These skills can be grouped into three categories: skills for acquiring information, skills for organizing and using information, and interpersonal and social participation skills (Parker & Jarolimek, 1984).

Specific intellectual skills needed by a democratic citizen are: identifying and defining a problem; identifying relevant sources of information and analyzing these sources for reliability; being able to see a problem in its broadest possible context, including the value considerations involved; being able to build a scenario of likely consequences regarding any proposed solution to a problem; the ability to make reasoned judgements; empathy; being able to choose solutions that ensure progress toward resolving a problem; and being able to exercise political influence and political involvement (Engle & Ochoa, 1988).

The third component of a citizenship education program is fostering democratic beliefs and values. Every society has ways of shaping the behavior of young people consistent with the values of that society. Values are standards or criteria against which individual and group behavior is judged. Beliefs reflect commitment to those values. Through family life, community living, and school experiences, young citizens are expected to internalize a belief system that characterizes the behavior of people in the society. Such beliefs in a democratic society as freedoms, justice, equality, responsibility, diversity, rights, respect for the worth and dignity of the individual, openness to new ideas, opportunity for improvement, and the protection of minority rights and opinions should be fostered through a citizenship education program preparing students for living in a democratic environment.

Citizenship Education in Africa

With the attainment of independence in the late 1950s and early 1960s, many African nations sought ways to change the colonial education systems to make them more relevant to the needs and aspirations of the new nations. Since many of these new nations were arbitrarily created by Europeans without regard to historical and cultural ties, the issue of creating a citizenry whose loyalty is to the nation rather than to ethnic and regional entities was paramount. Education was seen as the most important vehicle for bringing about social and political change (Merryfield, 1986). Some of the major efforts to change the education system included the expansion of schooling, especially at the primary level, Africanization of the curriculum, and the development of vocational and technical education.

In their desire to produce loyal and effective citizens, the new nations of Africa agreed that the colonial history and geography curricula needed to be revised to emphasize citizenship education, national unity, interethnic and intercultural understanding, and new methods of teaching that emphasize problem solving, critical thinking, and inquiry. This new approach came to be known as social studies. Eleven African countries met in Mombasa, Kenya, and adopted social studies as the integration of history, geography, and the other social science disciplines. They identified four goals for the social studies that have continued to guide the social studies movement in Africa. These were: (1) to enable students to understand people's interaction with their cultural, social, and physical environments; (2) to help students appreciate their homes and heritages; (3) to develop skills and attitudes expected of citizens; and (4) to teach students to express their ideas in a variety of ways (Merryfield & Muyanda-Mutebi, 1991).

In an examination of social studies in Botswana, Barth (1989) pointed out that social studies has been accepted as the best subject for preparing students for citizenship and nation building. Social studies in Botswana is defined as "the practice of integrating the skills, attitudes, and knowledge from the social sciences and humanities to educate effective citizens for Botswana" (p. 58). Social studies curricula at all levels emphasize the integration of the social sciences and humanities with stress on the social, political, and economic development of the country.

In Kenya, social studies has also been accepted as citizenship education. However, the integrated approach to citizenship education that is practiced in countries such as Nigeria and Botswana is not evident in Kenya. A comparison of social studies curricula in Kenya, Malawi, and Nigeria by Merryfield (1986) showed that the curriculum in Kenya still emphasized the separate subjects of history, geography, and civics, although there was some degree of interdisciplinarity in some topics. Similarly in Malawi, history and geography were more emphasized than integrated social studies.

Citizenship Education in Nigeria

This chapter examines the status of citizenship education in Nigeria and the implications for other sub-Saharan African nations struggling to establish viable programs for preparing their young people for effective citizenship in a modern society that is increasingly interdependent on other nations and peoples of the world. Specifically, citizenship education was researched in selected Nigerian junior secondary schools (JSS) in terms of how teachers perceive the definitions, rationale, content, and instructional strategies that are appropriate for a comprehensive citizenship education program within the context of the evolving form of democracy in Nigeria.

The study reported in this chapter focused on examining Nigerian junior secondary school teachers' perceptions of the citizenship education program. Since schools are officially responsible for the formal education of citizens through the social studies curriculum, it is important to examine how teachers view the program. Before presenting the results of the study, it is pertinent to discuss briefly the development of citizenship education in Nigeria from the precolonial period to the present.

Citizenship Education in Traditional Nigerian Societies

Prior to European colonialism, modern Nigeria did not exist as a single political entity. There were several societies at varying levels of political, social, and economic development, with distinct cultures. The precolonial education system aimed at producing a functioning member of the society—family, community, ethnic group, or a larger political entity. Loyalty was to the immediate group to which a person belonged. Group welfare was more important than individual achievement. Social studies was an integral part of the education system. The aim of indigenous education was preparation for effective living in the society. Education was seen as a vital instrument for societal living, self-reliance, citizenship education, and community development. It was perceived as an important instrument for socializing the young into the community, making them aware of their immediate environment, and of how to adapt to it and function productively for the benefit of the whole community.

Indigenous education also aimed at inculcating in the people the skills, knowledge, values, and attitudes needed to enable them to effectively live or survive in their environment. Every member of the group was expected to learn and practice a trade or vocation for his or her own economic survival and for the progress of the group as well. It fostered cooperation, interdependence, and active participation in the life of the community for the improvement of the people's quality of life. Respect for elders and constituted authority was inculcated through the education system. It was also meant to inculcate in the people a sense of belonging and responsibility that would make them utilize their abilities positively and contribute meaningfully to the community's development. The transmission of cultural heritage from one generation to the other was an important objective of indigenous African education. Citizenship training encompassed several components ranging from local history, myths, proverbs, geography, vocational education, physical education, science and technological education, religious and moral education, and computation, to home economics education.

Citizenship Education during the Colonial Period

During the colonial period, social studies education included the separate subjects of history, geography, civics, and religion, which were taught from either the Christian or the Muslim perspective. Geography and history had very little local content: geography emphasized landforms in foreign lands, world capital cities, European production systems, and so forth, while history dealt essentially with the European imperial majesties, adventures, and wars. Civics emphasized citizen responsibilities and loyalty to the colonial overlords. In short, social studies education during the colonial period was clearly not intended for self-consciousness, national consciousness, or national development.

In 1958, the term "social studies" began to emerge in the curricula of some schools in the former Western Region. The social studies curriculum reform taking place in the United States during the post-Sputnik era influenced the development of social studies education in Nigeria. The Western Region government collaborated with Ohio University in 1958 in the Ohio Project. While the project lasted, social studies was taught in teacher training colleges in the Western region.

Citizenship Education in Post-Colonial Nigeria

During colonial rule in Nigeria, the school curriculum promoted character education in order to socialize the students as proper British subjects. The informal curriculum of fair play, allegiance to the school symbols and rituals, and the prefect system supplemented academic work in British history and geography. At independence in 1960, the schools were neither teaching responsible citizenship for a national political culture nor preparing youth to assume participatory roles in the new democracy. In the early to mid-1960s, social studies education expanded in the Western Region and was introduced in Northern Nigeria. The emphasis now was on an integrated approach to social studies with emphasis on innovative teaching strategies that promoted inquiry and decision making for responsible citizenship. The need to revamp the curriculum was even more obvious after the civil war (1966–1970). The war brought about disunity among various ethnic and regional groups in the country, thereby exacerbating the loyalty to primordial interests. The need to establish a new educational program that emphasized loyalty to the nation and respect for the democratic rights of individuals and groups to exist as fellow citizens of one nation was paramount in the various curriculum reform projects undertaken in the late 1960s and the 1970s.

In 1969, a national curriculum conference was held to overhaul the Nigerian education system. The importance of social studies was recognized by the conference participants. Changing the traditional history, geography, and civics courses into integrated social studies was felt to be more appropriate for a Nigerian society undergoing rapid change. In recommending a national social studies program at the primary and secondary levels, the conference noted the need for "effective citizenship, national consciousness, national unity, and national reconstruction" (Adaralagbe, 1972, p. 213). The recommendations of the National Curriculum Conference and subsequent seminars and workshops in the early 1970s led to the formulation of a new national education policy for Nigeria in 1977, which was revised in 1981. The philosophy of Nigerian education stresses the inculcation of effective citizenship (Federal Republic of Nigeria, 1981, subsections 1 and 2). No other school subject is more appropriate for the fostering of this philosophy than social studies. Therefore, Nigerians have accepted citizenship education for the social studies curriculum to help students understand and appreciate democracy, learn about their national heritage, and practice social responsibility.

As Ogundare (1991) points out, the goals and objectives of social studies education are essential for, and facilitate attitude formation of Nigerian youth through sociopolitical mobilization. He examined the goals, objectives, and strategies of the Mass Mobilization for Self-Reliance, Social Justice, and Economic Recovery (MAMSER) program that was initiated in 1987 by the Federal Government of

Nigeria and concluded that the objectives of social studies education were in agreement with those of MAMSER. Social studies indeed helps to inculcate in Nigerian youth the values and habits that will give rise to a self-reliant civic society.

The junior secondary school (JSS) citizenship education program is part of the social studies curriculum. In Nigeria, social studies is taught in the primary (grades 1–6) and the junior secondary school (grades 7–9) levels, and in primary teacher training colleges as an integrated subject. At the senior secondary level (grades 10–12), the separate subjects of history and the social sciences are offered.

At the JSS level, the social studies curriculum aims at making students aware of the problems of nations (including Nigeria) and global interdependence. Developing a positive attitude toward their citizenship, and the desire to make a positive contribution to a united Nigeria are important attitudinal objectives (Sunal & Farouk, 1986).

Citizenship Education in Nigerian Junior Secondary Schools: The Study

This study examined Nigerian junior secondary school social studies teachers' perceptions of the content and methods of the JSS citizenship education program. The specific research questions asked were:

1. Do teachers' perceptions of citizenship education in the JSS differ according to the type of training they received?
2. Do teachers who took social studies methods courses have different perceptions of citizenship education in the JSS?
3. Do teachers' perceptions of citizenship education in the JSS differ according to their ages?
4. Do more-experienced teachers have different perceptions of citizenship education in the JSS than less experienced teachers?
5. Do teachers with more years of social studies teaching experience have different perceptions of citizenship education in the JSS than those with less experience in social studies teaching?

The adoption of social studies and citizenship education as the most important vehicle for educating an effective citizenry cannot by itself ensure that the objectives of the program are achieved.

Investigating how teachers perceive the program helps in highlighting the success or effectiveness of the curriculum reform.

Very little research has been done on citizenship education in Nigeria (Adedoyin, 1983; Adeyemi, 1985; Barth & Norris, 1976; Orimoloye, 1983; Sunal, Gaba, & Osa, 1987). In a study investigating the various conceptions of social studies held by teachers, administrators, and students in Lagos State, Nigeria, Adedoyin (1983) found that social studies as citizenship education attracted favorable responses from all the respondents. However, there was no agreement on any one of the conceptions of social studies among the three groups of respondents: that is, social studies as citizenship education, economic studies, skill development, a discipline, and social science. Rather, the responses were eclectic.

The Barth/Shermis Social Studies Preference Scale (B/S SSPS) was administered to undergraduate social studies education majors at Ahmadu Bello University (ABU), Zaria, Nigeria, by Barth and Norris in 1976. The B/S SSPS is an instrument that measures how well respondents differentiate between the three social studies traditions of citizenship transmission, the social science approach, and reflective inquiry. It also clarified which of the three approaches the respondents prefer in their own teaching. Results showed that there was an ambiguity toward social studies among the respondents. Only 43 percent clearly chose one tradition and many students agreed with all possible positions.

In 1981, the same instrument was administered again to social studies education undergraduate majors at ABU. Results showed a significant change in awareness and identification of the nature of social studies. Over 73 percent of the students clearly chose one tradition, compared with 43 percent in 1975. Those who chose reflective inquiry content and methods increased from 20 percent and 2 percent, respectively, in 1975 to 70 percent and 41 percent (Merryfield, 1986).

Adeyemi (1985) studied the philosophic orientation of social studies teachers in Oyo State, Nigeria. The B/S SSPS was also used in this study. He concluded that teachers needed more training and better instructional materials in order to improve their understanding of social studies and subsequent classroom instruction. In 1987, he administered the same instrument at the Obafemi Awolowo

University (formerly University of Ife) at Ile-Ife, Oyo State, Nigeria. Eighty percent of the social studies education majors made clear choices as to their philosophic orientations. Over 36 percent favored reflective inquiry and 22 percent chose social science combined with reflective inquiry. He concluded that the choices of the students reflected the availability of knowledgeable instructors and attempts at complying with the provision in the National Policy on Education on the use of reflective inquiry techniques.

Orimoloye (1983) investigated the perspective of social studies teachers and educators on citizenship education in primary and secondary schools in Oyo State, Nigeria. A modified version of the B/S SSPS was used, but the social action and criticism model was added. Results indicated that teachers and other social studies educators were eclectic in their philosophy of citizenship education. Teachers leaned more toward citizenship transmission, whereas educators preferred reflective inquiry and social action and criticism. Secondary school teachers were found to be more favorably disposed to reflective inquiry and social action and criticism, whereas primary school teachers were more inclined toward citizenship transmission. Young and very old teachers were found to have less positive attitudes toward citizenship transmission. Less experienced teachers also had the same dispositions.

Sunal, Gaba, and Osa (1987) studied Nigerian social studies teachers' perceptions of the primary school citizenship education program. University undergraduates with social studies experience ($n = 147$) attending one northern and one southern university were administered the Citizenship Education Status Survey (CESS) instrument. Results showed that social studies teachers defined social studies mainly in relation to the content areas of history and the social sciences, rather than the citizenship education orientation as intended by the government and curriculum planners. The teachers agreed on the basic concepts necessary to democratic beliefs such as justice, equality, responsibility, and freedom. They did not, however, see diversity as a necessary concept of a citizenship education program preparing students for living in a pluralistic democratic society. Reading skills were ranked high among the skills the social studies teachers considered necessary in a primary school citizenship education program. However, decision-making skills were rated low, while social participation skills such as personal and group interaction and skills relating to peer relationships were well supported. Personal and group communication skills were also considered important. Strong support was found for the inclusion of a wide variety of values in the curriculum, though the freedom to pursue a way of life was not well supported. With regard to the characteristics of a citizenship education program that would foster the realization of the goals, values, skills, and concepts identified by teachers, community involvement was highly supported, whereas encouraging students to deal with critical issues received less support. Teachers also favored instructional and evaluation methodologies that emphasized rote memorization.

Strategies

Sample teachers responded to a survey instrument that measured their perceptions of citizenship education in the JSS. Sixty-two social studies teachers selected from twenty-one JSSs in ten local government areas (LGAs) of Kano State, Nigeria, were involved in this study. The teachers varied in terms of level of training, exposure to social studies methods courses, age, total years of teaching experience, and years of social studies teaching experience.

There was a big disparity in terms of level of training. There were sixteen graduate teachers in the sample. Four of the graduate teachers with BA and BS degrees were not professionals because they did not take professional teacher education courses. The majority of the teachers (62.9 percent) held the Nigerian Certificate in Education (NCE). Two teachers held the Diploma in Hausa, Arabic, and Islamic Studies, a three-year program producing NCE-equivalent secondary school teachers of the listed subjects. These two teachers did not take professional teacher education courses either. Five teachers held the Elementary Teachers' Grade Two Certificate. Although they were not officially qualified to teach at the JSS level by virtue of their training, they were, however, teaching in the JSS. In the analysis of data, the levels of training were combined into four categories in order to make the statistical analysis more powerful: Graduate Professional, Graduate Nonprofessional, NCE/Diploma, and Grade Two.

Eighty-nine percent of the sample teachers had majored in social studies, one of the social science disciplines, or a combination of the social sciences and/or other areas. Seventy-four percent indicated that they had double majors. Of the forty-six nondegreed teachers (Diploma and Grade Two holders), seven were not social studies/ social science majors.

More than half of the sample (63 percent) did not take social studies methods courses in their teacher education programs. All seven of the Diploma and Grade Two holders did not have exposure to social studies teaching methods in their career. Twelve of the thirty-nine NCE teachers said they took social studies methods courses, while eleven of the graduate teachers reported taking social studies methods courses in their undergraduate coursework. In total, twenty-three teachers had a social studies methods background while thirty-nine did not.

The ages of the sample teachers ranged from twenty to fifty years. Most of the teachers (53 percent) were between twenty-six and thirty years of age. Only 8 percent of the sample was thirty-six years or older. A total of fifty-two teachers had between one and six years of teaching experience. Three teachers had less than one year of teaching experience, while seven teachers had ten or more years of teaching experience.

Eighty-seven percent of the sample teachers had taught social studies for between one and six years. Teachers who had taught social studies for seven or more years and those with less than one year of social studies teaching experience each constituted only 7 percent of the sample.

Instrument

Data for this study were collected through a questionnaire. The questionnaire gathered demographic information about the teachers: name, school, Local Government Area (LGA), highest level of training, age, years of teaching experience, and professional preparation. The questionnaire incorporated the Citizenship Education Status Survey (CESS) developed by Cynthia Sunal and used in a previous study on Nigerian primary school teachers (Sunal et al., 1987). It focuses on six areas covering the essential parts of a citizenship education program. Its eighty-one questions use a five-point Likert-type scale ranging from "I strongly agree," worth one point to "I strongly disagree," worth five points. Section one of the questionnaire deals with the definitions of social studies and contains three questions focusing on citizenship education orientation and content-area orientation.

Section two (seven questions) concerns important areas of knowledge from which the goals for social studies can be selected. The third section (ten questions) deals with concepts that may be necessary to democratic beliefs and should be taught in public school social studies. Section four (eight questions) examines the skills that students should be taught if they are to put democratic beliefs into action. A fifth section with twelve questions deals with the characteristics that a social studies program should have if it is to achieve its goals in citizenship education. Section six has forty-one questions focusing on values and beliefs that should be taught in a citizenship education program.

A panel of ten social studies educators validated the questionnaire in the United States. Another panel of ten validated it in Nigeria. Interobserver agreement rates of 87 percent were obtained among the American and Nigerian panelists, respectively.

Procedure

The questionnaire was personally administered by the researcher. Instructions were given on how to complete the survey instrument. The researcher returned to the schools the following day to collect the completed surveys. All selected teachers completed the questionnaire on time with 100 percent rate of return. Only five teachers (Grade Two holders) asked for more explanations. Their problems stemmed from lower proficiency in the English language.

The variables: level of training, social studies methods, age, teaching experience, and social studies teaching experience were used to divide the sample teachers into groups in order to test for possible differences among them in terms of their perceptions of citizenship education in the JSS. To test for differences at the .05 level in the teachers' perceptions of citizenship education, the Multivariate Analysis of Variance (MANOVA) was used.

Nine groups of variables that corresponded to the questions on the CESS instrument were tested using the MANOVA. These clusters of variables included: definition and rationale of the social studies (three variables); sources of goals for the social studies (seven variables); concepts necessary for democratic beliefs (ten variables); skills for citizenship education (eight variables); program characteristics (seven variables); values taught in the JSS (forty variables): individual rights (nine variables); individual freedoms (eight variables); responsibilities (sixteen variables); and social conditions and responsibilities (seven variables). The five characteristics: level of training, social studies methods, age, teaching experience, and social studies teaching experience were used as the independent variables in calculating the MANOVA.

In order to do the statistical analysis of the data collected, null hypotheses derived from the research questions were formulated. They expected no significant difference in the perceptions of citizenship education in the JSS among teachers divided into groups based on: level of training, social studies methods, age, teaching experience, or social studies teaching experience.

Results

All sample teachers responded with a rating of 1 (strongly agree), 2 (agree), or 3 (somewhat agree) on sixty out of seventy-six questions on the CESS. Only thirteen questions were ever rated 4 (disagree), and only three questions received a rating of 5 (strongly disagree). This suggests that these teachers had a positive attitude toward and were supportive of most of the concepts, skills, and values incorporated into the JSS social studies curriculum.

No significance was found among teachers divided into groups based on their level of training, exposure to social studies methods, and age. To further examine the impact of training, the nine levels of training were reduced to four (Graduate Professional, Graduate Nonprofessional, NCE, and Diploma/Grade Two) in order to increase the power of the statistics. Still no significant difference was found.

A significant difference was found in the perceptions of the teachers regarding history, economics, and political science as important sources for selecting social studies goals. The differences among the teachers were, however, less important given that the teachers' opinions on all sources were similar. Their responses indicated strong agreement on most of the sources.

The various experience groups were significantly different.

Teachers with less than one year of teaching experience were significantly different from the other groups in their perceptions of the sources of goals for the social studies. They gave stronger support for sociological goals (intergroup relations and international relationships) than history and the social sciences as the most important sources from which social studies goals should be selected. This finding shows that first-year teachers have a broader view of social studies as incorporating global issues and cooperation and interdependence between and among groups and nations.

Teachers' perceptions of citizenship education in the JSS appeared to be influenced by the number of years they had taught social studies. Significant differences were found in teachers' perceptions of the sources of goals for the social studies values taught in the JSS: individual rights, individual freedoms, and individual responsibilities, and concepts necessary for democratic beliefs based on social studies teaching experience.

The sample teachers were significantly different on only twelve of the fifty variables tested. Teachers' perceptions of history, geography, economics, and political science as sources for social studies goals were significantly different. Sample teachers also differed significantly in their perceptions of liberty, dignity, and security as individual rights that should be taught in the JSS. They differed significantly also in their perceptions of freedom to pursue a way of life and freedom of inquiry as values that should be taught in the JSS. Significant differences were found in the teachers' perceptions of respect for human life and valuing criticism as the values of individual responsibilities that should be taught in the JSS. Finally, teachers also differed significantly in their perceptions of a conception of social studies based on the belief that students should be taught not to question important political beliefs.

First-year teachers tended to account for almost all of the significant differences. The only exception is on the variable "beliefs can be questioned," where the most experienced social studies teachers also accounted for some of the significant differences.

Teachers with less than one year of social studies teaching experience had a less favorable attitude toward history, geography, economics, and political science as important sources of goals for the social studies than all the other groups of teachers. This group of teachers strongly favored sociological goals, though they were not significantly different from the other groups in their perceptions of sociological goals. On the other hand, teachers who had taught social studies for four to six years gave the strongest support for history, geography, political science, and economics as the most important areas for selecting social studies goals. This difference has implications for teacher education.

These teachers also differed significantly in their perceptions of liberty, dignity, and security as individual rights that should be taught in the JSS. Teachers with less than one year of social studies teaching experience were found to be significantly different from the other groups of teachers on the variable "liberty" as a value that should be taught in the JSS. These first-year social studies teachers ranked liberty as a less important value than did the other teachers. The same group of teachers also gave significantly less support for "dignity." The least-experienced social studies teachers also rated "security" lower than those with four to six years and those with one to three years of social studies teaching experience. These findings show that new social studies teachers do not have as strong a feeling for the teaching of these values in the JSS as do the more experienced social studies teachers.

Perceptions of freedom to pursue a way of life and the freedom of inquiry as values that should be incorporated into the JSS curriculum also differed. Those teachers who had taught social studies for less than one year gave less support for "freedom to pursue a way of life" as a value that should be taught in the JSS. These first year social studies teachers gave weaker support for the variable "freedom of inquiry" also.

In terms of perceptions of the values of individual responsibilities, teachers with less than one year of social studies teaching experience differed significantly from those with one to three years and those with four to six years of social studies teaching experience, respectively, in their perceptions of respect for human life. As for valuing criticism, teachers with less than one year of social studies teaching experience had the least favorable attitude toward respect for human life and valuing criticism as values that a JSS citizenship education program should foster in youngsters.

These teachers were significantly different in their perceptions of questioning important political beliefs. However, the difference was found on only one out of ten statements under concepts necessary for democratic beliefs. Teachers generally agreed that all the concepts that are necessary for democratic beliefs should be incorporated into the JSS social studies curriculum.

Teachers with seven or more years of social studies teaching experience agreed with the idea of citizenship education based on the belief that students should be taught not to question important political beliefs, while those with one to three years of social studies teaching experience gave the least agreement for the statement. Statistically, the differences between the most-experienced social studies teachers and the group with one to three years is significant. Those who had taught social studies for less than one year also differed significantly from those who had one to three years and those with four to six years of social studies teaching experience. The least-experienced social studies teachers gave the strongest support for the idea that students should be taught not to question important political beliefs. Those with four to six years of social studies teaching experience gave less support for the idea.

Discussion and Implications

Social studies in Nigeria is officially seen as a subject that prepares students with the knowledge, skills, and attitudes for active citizenship in a democratic society. The teachers who were involved in this study generally had a positive attitude toward and were supportive of the rationale, concepts, skills, and values inherent in a JSS citizenship education program that prepares young people as active and informed participants in a democratic society.

Social studies in the JSS is officially conceived as an interdisciplinary subject, the central goal of which is citizenship-education. Teachers' strong leaning toward defining social studies in relation to the content areas appears to be antithetical to the official definition of social studies. The teachers endorsed the citizenship-education orientation, but they gave stronger support for the content-area orientation. The preference for content was further reflected in the teachers' perception that history and the social sciences are the most important areas of knowledge from which social studies goals should be selected.

The content preference evident in the teachers' perceptions of social studies may be a result of the system of professional teacher education and of the course work available at the various levels of teacher education institutions. Course work, especially at the university level, focuses on specific social science disciplines in which a student specializes rather than upon an integration of social studies. Teachers may not have a holistic view of social studies as integrating all the social science curricula toward helping students develop into effective citizens in a democratic society. Prior to the mid-1970s, social studies education was not part of the teacher education programs of most Nigerian universities. Since the early 1980s, more university departments and institutes of education and advanced teachers' colleges/colleges of education have expanded their social studies education programs, and new ones are being developed in more teacher education institutions (Farouk, 1994). Since most of the teachers had their training in the separate social sciences, it is likely that this influences their perception of the subject and how they teach it. Teachers are likely to teach in the same way or from the same perspectives as they were taught at the university or teachers' college (DuBey & Barth, 1980).

Teachers' perceptions of the definition of social studies may change due to waning emphasis on the West African School Certificate Examination, which tests the separate areas of history and the social sciences. Students now take a statewide JSS examination at the end of ninth grade. Integrated social studies is tested in this examination rather than the separate subjects.

There was a strong agreement among the teachers on the concepts that structure the belief system appropriate for the goals of a JSS citizenship education program. Strong support was given for all the concepts that are necessary for democratic beliefs.

When asked to identify the skills students should acquire to function as citizens, the teachers noted intellectual, decision-making, social participation, group interaction, and personal-social skills as those important to be included in the JSS social studies curriculum. Teachers gave less support for the teaching of skills in the use of reference books, perhaps because of the scarcity of reference materials in their schools. Public libraries can only be found in the urban areas and the local government area headquarters. Students and teachers have limited or no access to these facilities. The official curriculum strongly recommends the use of reference books in social studies teaching, but teachers are limited by the scarcity of materials and resources.

Values are an essential part of citizenship education. They are reflected in all aspects of the curriculum as well as in the selection of content. Teachers' support of values relating to individual rights, individual freedoms, individual responsibilities, and social conditions and responsibilities was examined. Strong support for the inclusion of all these values in the JSS social studies curriculum was found. This reflects a positive attitude on the part of the teachers toward democratic values. It probably also reflects the growing desire of Nigerians to accept and tolerate one another irrespective of religious, ethnic, linguistic, or socioeconomic background. Diversity is recognized and supported by the teachers. Social studies teachers strongly agreed with the role of the school in supporting the idea of unity in diversity. This is a healthy development for the operation of pluralistic democracy in Nigeria. Respect for the rights and values of others, valuing criticism, working for the common good, and respect for the due process of law were all strongly supported by the sample teachers. Social conditions and responsibilities were also strongly supported by the teachers.

This has implications for the practice of democracy in Nigeria. The country is now in a transition to civilian democratic rule after three unsuccessful attempts at democratic rule and a succession of military regimes.

The study also considered the characteristics of a citizenship education program that would foster the goals, concepts, skills, and values that the sample teachers identified. A comprehensive curriculum that encourages active community involvement was identified by the teachers. Such a program also promotes active student involvement and encourages students to deal with critical issues and the world as it is. This is probably a reflection of the teachers' awareness of the changes introduced into the new National Policy on Education relating to national education objectives at all levels and the new philosophy of Nigerian education (Federal Republic of Nigeria, 1981). Teachers' support for the use of instructional strategies and assessment procedures that discourage memorization and drill and practice was rather low, though results indicated agreement.

Nigerian society, like all societies, is in transition. Traditional customs and values are being transformed. It is likely the new society emerging will be democratic and will support a politically active citizenry. Schools can certainly play a significant role, as agents of socialization, in bringing about change in the society. The Federal Government of Nigeria has recently published thousands of copies of the 1989 Constitution of the Federal Republic of Nigeria under the Federal Government School Book Aid Programme and distributed them to all secondary schools in the nation for the purpose of citizenship education.

Moreover, Nigerian children, like children in many other societies, do actively contribute to their families more than do their Western counterparts. These experiences provide opportunities for the children to develop many concepts that are essential to social studies education. The school must enter into this active learning process and incorporate it into its culture.

Nigeria has made great strides in developing social studies education. As Merryfield and Muyanda-Mutebi (1991) pointed out, social studies is more developed in Nigeria than in other African countries. It is also more widely accepted. Several textbooks and other scholarly materials have been published and curriculum development is more advanced than in most sub-Saharan African nations. Other African nations that are trying to develop viable citizenship education programs may not have the advantages that Nigeria enjoys such as financial resources, trained personnel, and other resources needed for such programs. In developing citizenship education programs in African schools and elsewhere a careful study of the cultural, political, and economic realities of the nation as a basis for developing a program that is relevant to the needs of the people is needed. Teacher education programs should reflect the philosophy, goals, and objectives identified in the citizenship education program. Regular inservice workshops to make teachers aware of the rationale, content, and methods of the new program and to help them improve their instructional skills are needed for the effective implementation of a viable citizenship education program.

188   Section 2

References

Adaralagbe, A. (Ed.). (1972). *A philosophy for Nigerian education: Report of the national curriculum conference, 8–12 September, 1969.* Ibadan, Nigeria: Heinemann.

Adedoyin, F.A. (1983). Teachers', education administrators', and students' conceptions of social studies in Lagos, Nigeria. *Journal of Research in Curriculum, 1*(2), 51–65.

Adeyemi, M.B. (1985). *Secondary school teachers' perceptions of the instructional goals of social studies in Oyo State of Nigeria.* Unpublished doctoral dissertation, Indiana University.

Barth, J.L. (1986). A comparison of Nigerian and Egyptian university students' responses to the Barth/Shermis social studies preference scale. *African Social Studies Forum, 1*(1), 24–32.

Barth, J.L. (1989). Botswana social studies: Citizenship and nation building. *International Journal of Social Education, 4*(2), 53–59.

Barth, J.L., & Norris, W.R. (1976). A cross-cultural study of teacher candidates: Preferences for styles of learning social studies. *Indiana Social Studies Quarterly, 4*(2), 22–38.

Beyer, B.K., & French, H.P., Jr. (1965). Effective citizenship: A continuing challenge. *Social Education, 39,* 341.

DuBey, D.L., & Barth, J.L. (1980). *Social studies: The inquiry method approach.* Lagos, Nigeria: Thomas Nelson.

Engle, S.H., & Ochoa, A.S. (1988). *Education for democratic citizenship: Decision-making in the social studies.* New York: Teachers' College Press.

Farouk, M.K. (1994). Social studies teacher education in Nigeria: Implications. In C. Sunal (Ed.), *Teacher education in the Caribbean and Africa: Points of contact.* (Monograph No. 2). Tuscaloosa, AL: American Educational Research Association Special Interest Group: Research Focus on Education in the Caribbean and Africa.

Federal Republic of Nigeria. (1981). *National policy on education.* Lagos, Nigeria: Federal Ministry of Information.

Merryfield, M. (1986). *Social studies education and national development in selected African nations: Vols. 1 and 2: Nigeria, Malawi, and Kenya.* Unpublished doctoral dissertation, Indiana University.

Merryfield, M., & Muyanda-Mutebi, P. (1991). Research on social studies in Africa. In J.P. Shaver (Ed.), *Handbook of research on social studies teaching and learning* (pp. 621–623). New York: Macmillan.

National Council for the Social Studies (1979). Revision of the NCSS guidelines. *Social Education, 43*(4), 262.

Ogundare, S.F. (1991, October). How social studies educators see the essentiality of their discipline for social mobilization of youth in Nigeria. *Social Education, 55,* (10), 375–378.

Orimoloye, P.A. (1983). *Social studies educators' perspectives on citizenship education in primary and secondary schools in Oyo State, Nigeria.* Unpublished doctoral dissertation, Michigan State University.

Parker, W., & Jarolimek, J. (1984). *Citizenship and the critical role of the social studies.* (Bulletin No. 72). Washington, DC: National Council for the Social Studies.

Sunal, C.S., & Farouk, M.K. (1986, November). *Social studies in Nigeria: Adapting to the needs of a multiethnic population.* Paper presented at the Annual Meeting of the National Council for the Social Studies, New York.

Sunal, C.S., Gaba, B.B., & Osa, O. (1987). Citizenship education in the primary school: Perceptions of Nigerian teachers. *Theory and Research in Social Education, 15*(2), 115–131.

Torney, J., Oppenheim, A., & Furmen, R. (1975). *Civic education in ten countries: An empirical study.* New York: Wiley.

Chapter Seven
Using Indigenous Literatures in Sub-Saharan African Schools

Osayimwense Osa

Using indigenous literatures in sub-Saharan African schools requires a certain degree of stock-taking and self-analysis in terms of literature curriculum and instruction in a vibrant heterogeneous continent. Such an endeavor takes a look at literary education in ancient times, in precolonial Africa, in colonial times, in the present; examines its possible future direction; and has the potential to enrich African literature and multicultural literature studies.

Indigenous literatures in Africa's multitudinous tongues have existed from time immemorial on the African continent. But when colonialism became a fact on the continent, the use of indigenous literatures, especially in formal schools, was relegated to the background. Casting the indigenous as always and only outside or underneath the "mainstream" literary discourses of modern Africa ignores the actual mainstream, the cultural discourses of the majority, in most of Africa (Barber, 1995). In the past three decades following colonialism, the place of Africa's indigenous literatures in African education in terms of content and purpose is being recognized.

It is only natural that the history of indigenous literatures should be projected back into the period preceding the emergence of the nations which eventually came to make up Africa. There is no language called "African." Similarly, there is perhaps no one culture that cuts across the continent as we know it today.

The Berlin Conference both carved us up into islands and then, with the help of anthropologists and Africanists of other persuasions, glued the pieces together rather crudely into an artificial "homogeneity." One's first gripe, therefore, is that somehow someone came up with the label

"African" to characterize a whole host of activities and concepts, including "African" literature. (Kunene, 1992, p. 7)

The traditional storytellers and griots in Africa certainly did not call themselves "Africans." They identified themselves with the name of their indigenous ethnic group. That is, they called themselves sons and daughters of an ethnic group—*ovbi Edo* (an Edo person), *omo' Yoruba* (a Yoruba person), or the Igbos, the Zulus, the Gikuyus, and so forth. Today this attitude is detectible in Africans. For example, a Kikuyu person is likely to refer to himself or herself first as a Kikuyu rather than as a Kenyan. This is possibly a means of maintaining a primary identity while differentiating oneself from the other ethnic groups of Kenya.

The pattern is similar in every sub-Saharan African country. Truly, "African literature is still tribally based and derives its strength from tribal sources" (Jones, 1992, pp. 1–2).

Unlike the literatures of the various ethnic groups, "African" literature is a relatively new concept. It is a new concept not because there was no literature in Africa before the missionaries and other white people "brought it," but because those who performed it in their indigenous languages did not perceive what they were doing as an "African" activity (Kunene, 1992, p. 8).

With the European invasion and subsequent colonization of Africa came colonial education that had a very limited understanding of the indigenous literatures of the many ethnic groups on the continent. Latent in the African countries created by the colonial powers were potential forces for strife as reflected by the different ethnic groups. George M. Houser (1993) describes a grim picture of contemporary Africa as a result of such creations:

The litany of tragedy in many African countries is appalling. In Liberia, the civil war has left thousands dead and half the population of 2.8 million displaced. In Angola, 1.5 million have been uprooted by the civil war of the last eighteen years. In Somalia, internal conflict has blown apart one of Africa's most homogeneous peoples who share the same language and religion; 14,000 people were killed in the fighting around the capital, Mogadishu, in the three months from November 1991 to February 1992. In Mozambique, the terrorist attacks by

Renamo have resulted in a million refugees. In the Sudan, the war continues between the government in the north and the southerners. (p. 17)

The artificial creation of these countries paid no regard to differences or similarities among ethnic groups, but to territorial possessions. While the various ethnic groups continued with their respective indigenous literatures, they did not develop a spirit of national unity—a major factor behind the various political problems in African countries.

Inequities in Education

African countries did not inherit democratic traditions of governance. The colonialists were autocrats. They destroyed African traditions and institutions, and in their place put those in the image of their own institutions from Europe (UNESCO, 1987, p. 36). Like their autocracy, colonial education was an imposition as evidenced in its aim to make English people out of some Africans, and in its British literature offerings in schools; to make French people familiar with French literature out of some Africans; and to make Portuguese and Germans out of other Africans.

Literature instruction in colonial times was essentially instruction in the literature of the colonizers, succeeding mainly in making literature strange and remote from students and irrelevant to their needs. But there is a vast body of indigenous literatures in African indigenous tongues that predates written contemporary literatures in English, French, or Portuguese. The sheer volume of indigenous literature is a massive challenge to scholars, critics, translators, and readers (Halpe, 1992). The teacher has a crucial role to play in putting it in its proper place in African education and in its relationship with literature in English, French, and other European languages, especially in contemporary times when multicultural thinking is at its peak. A judicious use of indigenous African literatures in African schools could be a formidable force in bringing that lasting unity and peace of which Africa is in dire need.

A look at the literary education of the past in Africa is invaluable in planning and using indigenous literatures for a responsive and relevant education in sub-Saharan African schools.

One of the things which has been hindering a radical outlook in the
study of literature in Africa is the question of literary excellence that only
works of undisputed literary excellence should be offered. [In this case it
meant virtually, the study of a disputable "peak" of English literature.]
The question of literary excellence implies a value judgement as to what
is literary and what is excellence, and from whose point of view. For any
group it is better to study representative works which mirror their society
rather than to study a few isolated "classics," either of their own or a
foreign culture. (Ngugi wa Thiong'O, 1972, p. 149)

Certainly, the English literature classics have not always excited
a substantive number of African students, because the contents of
most of these novels deal mainly with the adult world whose complexity they are yet to understand. English literature classics such as
Jane Austen's *Persuasion,* Thomas Hardy's *Mayor of Casterbridge,* or
Chaucer's *Canterbury Tales* are recommended for students because
African education in many African nations was, and is still, strongly
British, French, or Portuguese. However, an early attempt to make
African education less British or less colonial and more African in
these countries is seen in the first realistic appraisal to be conducted
on the secondary school curriculum in Africa as a whole in Tananarive
in 1962 under the ageis of the United Nations Education Scientific
and Cultural Organization (UNESCO) (Fafunwa, 1974, p. 194).
According to Babs Fafunwa, "the Tananarive conference expressed
the yearnings of many educators when it stated":

The attainment of independence in Africa now makes it necessary to re-
examine a type of education which in many African countries was for-
merly designed to "assimilate" young Africans to the culture of the met-
ropolitan countries. Curriculum reform is a corollary of political
emancipation–cultural emancipation being the means by which the
"African personality" can be asserted. This calls for the rediscovery of the
African cultural heritage and the transmission of that culture to African
Adolescents in the secondary [high] schools. (UNESCO conference re-
port on The Adaptation of the General Secondary School Curriculum in
Africa Tananarive, July 1962, p. 5)

The theme of that Tananarive conference was reiterated and amplified later in Nigeria in 1969 with the National Curriculum Conference and in 1977 with the National Policy on Education—the need for a more relevant and culturally enriching curriculum. A study of the indigenous literatures of Africa certainly enhances relevance in literary education in Africa.

Indigenous Literature or Indigenous Literatures?

In a multilingual sub-Saharan Africa, indigenous literature is multifaceted. A literature can only be indigenous to the specific ethnic group from which it springs. For example, *An African Night's Entertainment*, which Cyprian Ekwensi published in English in 1962, is a popular folktale of the Hausa people. Ekwensi himself admitted hearing it from an old Hausa Mallam (scholar):

While I was writing "Ikolo the Wrestler," I was lucky enough to meet an aged Hausa Mallam who told me a single folktale of book length. Amused by the short tales which I was collecting, he asked me if I would care for one which would keep my readers awake all night. Thus was born my African Night's Entertainment, which is still to be published. But such chances are rare, and one cannot bank on them. (Ekwensi, 1950).

In its original tongue, Hausa, it is truly indigenous to the Hausa ethnic group. Earlier in 1934, *Jikin Magayi*, a Hausa pamphlet was published by Rupert East and J. Tafida Zaria. The similarities between *An African Night's Entertainment* and *Jikin Magayi* have been noted by Neil Skinner (1973). *An African Night's Entertainment* adds, omits, and modifies some areas of this traditional tale of the Hausa people, and Neil Skinner (1973) concludes:

An African Night's Entertainment . . . [has then] on the whole, weakened the tale through its omissions, while its anthropological additions have hardly added to the art. As for the extra items of descriptive detail where they are not cliche, these are probably improvements. This is the natural line of development that a writer should follow to turn oral into written art. But paraphrase is a retrograde step, justifiable only where the original is exceptionally difficult and it is desired to simplify its content for young students. (p. 164)

Many young African students, especially non-Hausas, have truly come to know this popular Hausa tale and its content through Ekwensi's rendition of it in English.

There are similarities and differences between *Jikin Magayi* and *An African Night's Entertainment*. But no one can categorically assert or prove that Ekwensi had *Jikin Magayi* by his side when he was writing *An African Night's Entertainment*. It is an oral tale of the people. Which individual can really claim sole ownership of it? As Hugh Keenan (1992) maintains, "literary works can be copyrighted; oral tales cannot. To treat oral tales as copyrightable reduces their universality and accessibility to any writer" (p. 82).

Whether narrated orally or in print, the story of *An African Night's Entertainment* in its core and essence is a traditional African tale that retains its spirit of oracy. It re-creates a typical African storytelling session and captures the true spirit and essence of an African tale that is intended to drive home a moral that is usually stated subtly or overtly at the end of the tale. For example, the moral at the end of *An African Night's Entertainment*—one cannot take it upon oneself to wreak vengeance—is the lesson learned from the multiple tragedy of Abu Bakir, who relentlessly seeks vengeance to settle his score with Mallam Shehu for stealing his sweetheart Zainobe; Zainobe herself; and Kyauta, the product of Shehu and Zainobe's marriage. All the characters are, in the final analysis, losers in *An African Night's Entertainment*. The thrust of the moral is for people to refrain from malice and to shun a revengeful spirit.

Can *Jikin Magayi* be regarded as indigenous literature simply because it is in Hausa? Is the indigenous nature of *An African Night's Entertainment* destroyed simply because it is published in English? The issue of indigenous African languages in expressing truly indigenous African literature is a perennial one. In 1963, Obi Wali contended that the true African literature has to be written in African languages. Twenty-five years later in 1985, Ngugi wa Thiong'O asserted that "an African writer should write in a language that will allow him to communicate effectively with peasants and workers in Africa—in other words he should write in an African language." Okot p'Bitek wrote in Acholi and translated later into English (for example, *Wer Per Lawino—Song of Lawino*); Mazisi Kunene writes in Zulu and translates later into English; Ngugi wa Thiong'O now writes in Gikuyu, his native tongue, and his works in Gikuyu are translated later into English for an international audience.

Ngugi's choice to write in Gikuyu undoubtedly brings him closer to his fellow Kikuyus and also adds to the utility of Gikuyu as a language that can be adapted to literary use to convey immediacy of experience, particularly for Gikuyu users in Kenya. Ngugi's experience when he created his play *Ngaahika Ndeenda* (*I Will Marry When I Want*) in his indigenous tongue, Gikuyu, is significant enough to warrant quoting this chunk of his recollection and reflection:

When we scripted the play in Gikuyu called Ngaahika Ndeenda *(or "I Will Marry When I Want"), something happened which was very interesting. The people in the village of course knew their language much better than we did; so they began to offer their comments on the script. They would say, "Oh, this image is wrong here, or that type of language is inappropriate there. An old man doesn't speak like this; if you want him to have dignity, he must use a different kind of speech. Oh my god, you are making him speak like a child! You university people, what kind of learning have you had?" In other words, our relationship with the community was changed. In fact, we became students in-so far as language was concerned.*

The final script of the play was really a community product (Ngugi wa Thiong O, 1985, p. 152).

Such activity or exercise in the above excerpt can enhance the Gikuyu language as a medium for indigenous literary expression. Ngugi has done a remarkable service to his indigenous tongue in using it to write. Truly, every language deserves its own written literature, and every writer who speaks that language should give something back to it. The quality of any literature depends on the quality of the minds that are engaged in its production (Isola, 1992, p. 25). In the March 22–28, 1993, issue of *West Africa*, the question of English language in African literature is a special focus.

Undoubtedly those who know and use the English language or other European languages are fewer than those who don't in Africa. Chris Dunton contends:

If a majority of the people are barred from full participation in the life of the state because they are not owners of English, isn't the primary task to discuss the way English acts as a debarring or inhibiting force in government, in education, in law and in commerce? In a situation where the remoteness and authoritarian nature of government is assisted by its recourse to a language hardly accessible to a majority of its people, and if children flunk school partly because they are required to do their schooling through the medium of a language hardly integral to their daily lives, surely the question "whether English is a suitable medium for African literature" is peripheral and luxurious? (1993, p. 457)

In Lesotho in 1992, native Sesotho speakers and educationally elite students who represent a tiny minority of Basotho entering the country's single university agreed with Chinua Achebe that they find it easier to express themselves in English than in Sesotho. Here lies a serious problem that needs to be addressed in Africa.

Actually, there is now a chilling trend that does not promise any growth or development of some African languages, but a weakening. Let me illustrate with one ethnic group—the Edos of Benin City, Nigeria. Today many Western-educated Edo couples, in their desire to immerse their children into the world of English for communication, often use the English language for communicating with their children. The result is that these adult couples do not creatively increase their command of their own indigenous tongue, and the children themselves are unintentionally subtly denied the use of their indigenous tongue. If the trend continues unchecked, a next generation of this ethnic group might neither speak, read, write, nor understand their mother tongue, nor use it imaginatively.

The most beautiful expressions in a language are found in its literature, and there is every likelihood that using its indigenous literature will help students know and appreciate the language more. No indigenous African tongue, whether it is one spoken by three people or one spoken by ten million people, should suffer neglect. They all need nutrients, and using indigenous literatures in African schools is a very major nutrient that will reduce the neglect. There should be a revival of instruction in all African indigenous literatures, using African languages alongside African literature in English or French or Portuguese. Without such effort, some African languages and their indigenous literatures stand the risk of disappearing within a few generations. Today, for example, the promotion of Setswana as a national language and the neglect of the minority languages in Botswana do not augur well for the growth of its minority indigenous languages and literatures.

While oral literature is vibrant, it must of necessity be put into print for permanence. But books are few, and printing technology is poor in Africa. In spite of this, indigenous literature is slowly becoming a part of the curriculum in the elementary schools, high schools, colleges, and universities.

The available literary works range from traditional tales of yesteryear, unpublished and published, through contemporary written literature. Traditional folktales by their nature are usually the first tales children hear at home and in the neighborhood, before entering the elementary school. For a smooth experience in literary education then, it seems logical that the folktales children hear at home should act as materials of introduction to literary studies. But from the vast body of African folktales in various countries, what proportion of these folktales should be selected for classroom use? This problem involves making decisions regarding the extent to which the curriculum should focus on indigenous African literature, and how heavy the focus should be on local literature. Africa's indigenous tongues, and English, French, German, and Portuguese, should be given equal strength in expressing African indigenous literatures.

The indigenous, vernacular literatures are the ones that can reach users of specific tongues and not Africans in general because all Africans do not understand the numerous tongues of their continent. However, the importance of these indigenous literatures cannot be overemphasized. John Press (1965) stated in the published proceedings of the first Commonwealth Literature Conference held in Leeds in 1964 that "The vernacular literatures of the Commonwealth are for millions of men and women the most effective means of embodying in words their intimate hopes and fears, and the values of their societies" (p. v). But to reach the wider population of African students as well as non-Africans, they must be translated into English, French, German, or Portuguese and put in print for wider dissemination within the continent and within the global community.

F.H. Dutton's translation of Thomas Mofolo's *Chaka* in 1931 brought this work to the attention of scholars in Europe, North America, and other parts of the world including Africa. Albert S. Gerard's studies, *Four African Literatures—Xhosa, Sotho, Zulu, Amharic* (1971) and *African Language Literatures: An Introduction to the Literary History of Sub-Saharan Africa* (1981) are incisive scholarly works on literatures expressed in some of Africa's indigenous tongues. Gerard is not an African, but he rightly asserts that "cogent critical comment on the works that have been written in their own languages" are essentially the territory of "African scholars." Why Gerard made such an assertion is obvious. It is the African scholars who know the subtleties and nuances of their own languages and bodily gestures that can make significant comment on the literatures in these languages.

The indigenous literatures of sub-Saharan Africa are those that originate in black Africa. They are expressed in Africa's numerous tongues and in English, French, German, or Portuguese, and their content and theme are solidly rooted in African culture. Because they are many and they are in various languages, it is more meaningful to call them indigenous African literatures.

A Once Bookless "Big School"

Although the whole machinery of book production in sub-Saharan Africa is poor, it should not put a damper on literary productivity in the continent. Today, as observed by Adolphe O. Amadi (1981), the Western tradition is pervasively the order of the day in African bookshops, libraries, educational institutions, and the mass media (p. 14). African educators need to reflect on this Western tradition and place it in proper perspective in the literary education of their young population. When Africans realize that they should not be absolutely dependent on printed materials, especially as far as their indigenous literatures are concerned, scarcity of books will no longer be seen as a disaster. In fact, such scarcity may be a stimulus for a revival and strengthening of their oral tradition, which seems to be dying. Perhaps it is worthwhile to know why printed material and books are scarce in Africa.

A major reason for the book famine in Africa is poor technology and weak economic growth. As Gretchen Walsh (1991) observes:

Little machinery is manufactured anywhere in Africa. Equipment must therefore be imported to manufacture paper, and to print and bind books. Once purchased, that machinery must be maintained; spare parts must be obtained for repair. Ink, glue and other products used in book production must, for the most part, be imported. Requests for each of these items, each time it is needed, must be submitted to some form of government review, and approval may take a long time in coming, or may be arbitrarily denied. (p. 12)

The process of importation due to bureaucratic red tape and the current economic slump in Africa is long, frustrating, not always successful. This may perhaps compel Africans to look inward, to their indigenous education heritage.

Illiteracy in Africa was not a problem prior to the advent of Europeans. The whole society was one big school. Education was carried out by means of socialization. Teaching and learning were done by one generation passing on its values, norms, culture, history, and religion to the next generation by word of mouth or by example. There were no school dropouts and no libraries. The whole society was the repository of information and knowledge, and parents were the transmitters or disseminators of that knowledge. The aged person was the symbol of wisdom and society's memory databank. In some societies there were people who were the traditional oral historians and storytellers. Whenever one of them died, it has been said, a whole library died with him (Cram, 1993, p. 14). The spirit of this "big school" can still be captured in today's African schools through a conscientious and dedicated attention to making indigenous literatures a solid part of the school curriculum.

Meaningful African literary education demands that indigenous literatures be entrenched in the curriculum at all levels of schooling, from elementary school through college and university.

Using Indigenous Literatures in Sub-Saharan African Elementary Schools: Curriculum and Instructional Methodology

In one's formative years, certain interesting readings as well as experiences lodge deep in one's memory. In the words of Ngugi wa

Thiong'O (1983), one of Africa's leading novelists, "there are certain images in literature, especially children's literature which live long in one's memory" (p. 71). For Ngugi, the encounter between Sinbad and the old man of the sea—their parasitic relationship in which Sinbad is host and the old man is the parasite still forms a reference point in his essays about the underdeveloped and developed worlds. As far as he is concerned, Sinbad is from the underdeveloped world, politely referred to as the developing or the third world. The old man could come from anywhere—Europe, America, or Japan. While there is political import to the image of Sinbad and the old man, it is important to stress how memorable the image is for Ngugi. In one's impressionistic years, then, good or quality literature is invaluable—it ignites and kindles imagination, and promotes and sustains reading zest.

In planning an intriguing approach to literature instruction in the sub-Saharan African elementary school, the teacher must emphasize children's participation especially in the performance of their traditional tales. Such participation is usually exciting, making children receptive to what is being taught. Presumably, elementary school children have heard and listened to the popular tales in their homes and in their local community. Telling and listening to stories and mutual sharing of yarns should be enhanced in the elementary school. Development of reading and writing skills can come later through good children's literature, an area of literary studies which has been neglected for too long in Africa. Until relatively recently, it has always been the existing lacuna filled with books meant for European and American children—books to which African children cannot readily relate. But this field cannot just be ignored. There is quite a vast mine of knowledge in this area for scholars to tap into. According to Zohar Shavit (1992):

Children's literature presents a range of provocative and, to our minds, highly productive questions concerning the history of culture and cultural mechanisms. One might even go so far as to say that no other sphere of cultural studies approximates quite such a vast scope of cultural issues as does children's literature.

Belonging simultaneously to the literary and the socio-educational systems, it is the only cultural field whose products purposefully address two antithetical audiences, catering to the needs and expectations of both. Children's literature evolved from the convergence of and interaction among several cultural fields or systems, of which the most prominent are the social, the educational, and the literary systems. (p. 2)

Against this background, a lot can be studied in sub-Saharan African culture through African children's literature. African children do not live in a vacuum. They interact with adults. In this interaction is seen the idiosyncrasies and values, of course, of the African adult world, their method of socialization, and their general concept of childhood. Nancy Schmidt (1981) contends that all individuals live in culturally defined worlds that influence the directions in which their imaginations develop . . . while literature does not mirror either culture or history it is deeply rooted in both (p. 194.). The sociocultural context of African children's reading was addressed above with attention drawn to the fact that quite a number of African children do not really read at home. Since there is no model reading adult for the child to emulate, it seems it is only the formal school backed by libraries that can improve African children's reading (Osa, 1986, p. 194). The development of a reading culture thrives on the availability of a plentiful and varied supply of literature from infancy into adolescence. In content and context books must be available that arrest and sustain the interest of the reader, so that he or she continues to ask for more (Kotei, 1978, p. 233).

As a stimulator of reading, which is at the heart of the education process, literature occupies a very special place in the language arts program. Besides stimulating reading zest, children's literature brings children in touch with themselves as human beings and brings them in touch with the outside world:

Literature goes beyond reading and language arts, cutting across all content areas and life experiences. Literature gives children the opportunity to travel to the corners of the earth, to explore the known and the unknown. Literature gives children insight into human nature and motivation. They discover that others have often experienced joys, sorrows, and fears similar to their own, and they gain perspectives on problem solving. Literature is an adventure, and those who work with children have the privilege and responsibility of guiding them on an unforgettable journey that will last forever. (Rothlein & Meinbach, 1991, p. vi)

However, before African children's imagination expands to embrace the outside world, they should be well grounded in their own indigenous literatures. Such grounding forms their base for a takeoff into other literatures.

Inclusion not Exclusion

In a world in which pride in identity is stressed, it is especially important that no children feel that their family's customs or beliefs or language are unworthy of recognition and respect (Sutherland & Hill, 1991, p. 13.) Similarly, especially in a multilingual continent like Africa, no child should feel that his or her indigenous tongue or tribal customs, beliefs, and practices are insignificant. It follows, therefore, that all the indigenous literatures of all sub-Saharan African communities should have a place in the elementary school curriculum. In fact, the use of indigenous literatures in African schools should reflect the African multiethnic heritage. In this onerous task, certain principles must be adhered to. A child must be introduced to literature through the stories of the local community, and the child's relevant prior knowledge should be considered a good foundation for schoolteachers to build on. Africa's children grow up listening to the prevailing stories of their communities, and this body of tales constitutes a part of African children's literature that has only recently begun to receive serious attention. Chinua Achebe (1981) notes the educational and cultural value of these indigenous tales:

Our responsibility as Nigerians [or as Africans] of this generation is to strive to realize the potential good and avoid the ill. Clearly, children are central in all this, for it is their legacy and patrimony that we are talking about. If Nigeria [or Africa] is to become a united and humane society in the future, her children [and all other African children] must now be brought up on common vocabulary for the heroic and the cowardly, the just and the unjust. Which means preserving and refurbishing the landscape of the imagination and the domain of stories, and not— as our leaders seem to think—a verbal bombardment of patriotic exhortation and daily recitations of the National pledge and anthem. (p. 192)

Moral Guidance

While stories are for entertainment, they are also seen as moral guides. Indigenous literatures in the African elementary school should be a continuation of young children's enjoyment of storytelling sessions in their homes. It is this enjoyment that piques their interest and whets their appetite for more. Descriptive details that can mar young children's interest in literature should be kept to a minimum. Short stories of adventure like Kola Onadipe's *Adventures of Souza* (1963), which deals with a village boy who goes hunting, joins a secret cult, and meets a magician are an edifying reading experience for elementary school children. Besides such actions that can sustain reading zest, morals in stories help to build good character in youngsters. In their ethical messages, these stories offer a cultural and intellectual service to sub-Saharan African children, and to the adults as well.

The simple tales are not predicated on any complex philosophical position. An understanding of the stories gives the youngsters a positive feeling of achievement. Such feeling is necessary for a good early foundation in literary education. The simple and transparent works stimulate children to read and learning to enjoy good books in childhood can be the start of a lifelong habit that brings knowledge and satisfaction.

Introductory Literature Curriculum

As mentioned in the introduction, sometimes the literature that is indigenous to one part of sub-Saharan Africa is not indigenous to another. All the various ethnic groups of sub-Saharan Africa have their traditional tales whose origins are unknown. In their original indigenous tongues, they are almost unknown by others. Therefore, it is educationally expedient for elementary school children to be introduced to literature through their own ethnic group's tales, in their indigenous tongues, and in a European language such as English—published or unpublished—before reading folktales from other groups. Such a procedure ensures some degree of rootedness in their culture before taking off to explore others.

African children's ability to project themselves into the African children's literature which they read validates the premise that literature emanates out of a people's historical and cultural experience. Undoubtedly, African children who have not seen snow will readily understand the meaning of "as white as sugar" and not the meaning of "as white as snow." While one image is familiar and concrete to them, the other is strange and abstract. At their level of development, it is the concrete that should be taught before the abstract. The pedagogical rationale for inclusion of this children's literature in the school curriculum of sub-Saharan African schools is that it makes literature meaningful to African children in their sociocultural environment. With such a foundation, they can look forward with excitement to reading literature other than theirs.

Folktales that African elementary school children in one area find intriguing can be used to introduce new literatures to other parts of Africa. Charles Mungoshi's *Tales from a Shona Childhood* (Zimbabwe, 1989), Thomas Decker's *Tales of the Forest* (Sierra-Leone, 1968), Kavetsa Adagala and Mukkabri Kabira (Eds.), *Kenya Oral Narratives* (Kenya, 1985), and Cyprian Ekwensi's *African Night's Entertainment* (Nigeria, 1962) will undoubtedly form interesting reading for youngsters. Instruction should be done first with a folktale from their particular community in their indigenous mother tongue and later in English. For example, Zimbabwean children first should be taught *Tales from a Shona Childhood* and Nigerian children first should be taught *An African Night's Entertainment* before receiving instruction in tales from other parts of Africa. In using folktales, it is worthwhile to perform them because, in essence, folktale sessions are performances. All the appropriate songs and bodily gestures should accompany the narrative of a folktale. Such a rendition brings the folktale to life. It is this action and vitality that are capable of hooking children into listening and reading, sharpening and increasing their imaginative powers, and whetting their appetite for more folk works. After a thorough grounding in their own indigenous folktales, both in the indigenous and in the European languages, instruction can then be given to them in the folktales in a European language translation from other parts of Africa; and later, in the folktales of other parts of the world—like reading about Paul Bunyan, a lumberjack in American folklore noted for his ability to perform superhuman feats.

The renewed interest in multicultural literature for children and young adults necessitates instruction in international folktales. Besides broadening the minds of sub-Saharan African children, an equal modicum of instruction of such nature is of relevance to Americans and other nationals. As Jeff House (1992) recently observed:

We don't teach mythology. Most of our students recognize mythology as a collection of Greek tales, supplemented by reference to King Arthur and, perhaps, American folk heroes like Paul Bunyan. That mythology is anything more than a group of long-dead stories does not occur to them.

The truth, of course, is that these tales are a small part of the world of myth, and myth making is very much alive, a multicultural expression of universal symbols and beliefs. An effective approach to mythology should illustrate the connection among international myths, folktales, and legends that continue to be told in current literature and media, including films, songs, television, and cultural icons. (p. 72)

Using indigenous literature in the sub-Saharan African elementary school should be primarily geared toward impressing on children that literature is an enjoyable experience, preparing them particularly for literature in the high school. It is *not* at the elementary school level that children should be told or taught that the African folktale is a living art that is constantly being created. This could be delayed until late high school or to the college and university level, because the children are not yet intellectually and emotionally mature enough to grapple with such ideas.

Using Indigenous Literatures in the African High School

Movement from the elementary school into the high school indicates students' progress in their general education and in their literary education as well. The teacher needs to know the interests and characteristics of adolescents in order to bring them and African indigenous literatures into meaningful interaction. Sub-Saharan African high school students need to learn to discriminate between well-crafted works and mediocre ones in the present overwhelming body of works meant for adolescents or young adults. The teacher's major goal is to guide the selection of books and to help adolescents read literature as human experience—not to teach a fixed number of books, a smattering of bibliographical data, or a miscellaneous collection of historical facts. Such information may support and extend but can never supplant the reader's perception

of experiences communicated by the author (Loban, Ryan, &
Squire, 1961, p. 436).

In the canon of literature one meets good novels, mediocre ones,
and worse, but it is the significant and well-written ones, irrespective of cultural milieu, that are worth the reading time of adolescents (Osa, 1983). Good literature is one of the few places left in
modern life where the uniqueness of the individual is celebrated,
while at the same time common threads that bind people together
are revealed (Donelson & Nilsen, 1980, p. 403). Research into the
fundamental uniformity or difference in adolescent development in
various societies, especially in literature, is rare but worthwhile. Indigenous literatures in the African high school should broaden teenagers' or young adults' minds as responsible citizens of a nation as
well as of the world, while concentrating on their interests and developmental tasks.

Curriculum

For sub-Saharan African high school students it is indigenous young
adult or adolescent literature that addresses their interests and characteristics. High school students can identify with the protagonists
of the junior novels who are in their age group. For example, the
heroine of Buchi Emecheta's *Bride Price,* thirteen-year-old Aku-nna,
is not really a strange character to the African student. Beyond even
African shores in the United States, the heroine of Bette Greene's
Summer of My German Soldier, Patty Bergen, is one with whom the
African young girl can identify. Buchi Emecheta's *Bride Price* (an
indigenous African novel) and Bette Greene's *Summer of My German Soldier* (An American youth novel) make good instructional
materials relating to adolescent girls' need for love, and to adults'
relationships with their young teenagers. Such novels from any culture are worthy of discussion and should be incorporated in the teaching of even indigenous African literatures in the high school. Early
adolescence is the age when the concept of positive multicultural
thinking should be inculcated in students. In this regard, the place
of the International Youth Library in Munich, founded in 1948,
and the new International Institute for Children's Literature in Osaka,
Japan, as centers of international children's literature should be taught.

Young adult literature could be used as a stepping stone to reading sophisticated literature in higher institutions—colleges of education, polytechnics, and universities. The philandering of Tade Eji in the youth novel, Agbo Areo's *Hopeful Lovers* (1977) may serve as a good introduction as well as a transition toward considering the philandering of Sergeant Troy in Thomas Hardy's *Far from the Madding Crowd.* Nurse Joe's "It's hard to tell good people from bad people until they begin to act," in Ekwensi's *Drummer Boy* (1960) is not very different from Duncan's "There is no art to find the mind's construction in the face," in Shakespeare's *Macbeth.* While one is easily understood by a young adolescent, the other is not. Simple, satisfying material rooted in African culture is usually a good prerequisite for enjoyment and understanding of a complex work. "Just as there must be a continuum from simple arithmetic to higher mathematics, so must there be a continuum in literary education" (Burton, 1980, pp. 18–19).

Besides providing some continuum in literary education, indigenous sub-Saharan African junior novels can be used to supplement intensive in-class study of literature. Classroom study of any piece of literature can be supplemented by reading junior novels. The brevity of the novel, its prose lucidity, and its embodiment of the African young adult's world draw students to reading rather than repel them from it. Once the students discover the rich experience in reading, their later reading of more sophisticated literary works is facilitated.

Instructional Preparation

A giant slice of students' motivation in reading can be enhanced through the guidance of the literature teacher. If literature teachers are to make use of the African young adult novel in their literature program, they must know what the genre is. Therefore sub-Saharan African adolescent literature should be made an integral part of the literature program in Africa's colleges of education and their various teacher training colleges. Teachers and prospective teachers should read widely in the young adult novel genre, primarily because familiarity with the genre will enable them to discriminate between good junior novels, mediocre ones, and bad ones. Such familiarity with the genre will obviously help teachers to recommend worthwhile novels for students. It is the literature teacher who will professionally guide the student toward the transitionary role of the African junior novel. Again, this can come through the teacher's wide and up-to-date reading in the genre.

Sub-Saharan African high school students should be taught to value good literature. Their books must relate to their natural interests, activities, and cultural environment, while keeping their sense of humanity alive and preparing them for mature and sophisticated literary studies in higher institutions. I have recently addressed a body of selected good works for African children and youth in *African Children's and Youth Literature* (Osa, 1995).

Using African Indigenous Literatures in African Universities: Curriculum Development and Research Efforts

Universities are often expected to provide leadership in creative thought and work. The stimulus of a literature is as much the job of a university as is the formulation of some new scientific law. When Martin Banham (1960) wrote of this leadership function of universities in his introduction to an issue of *Nigerian Student Verse—1959*, he envisaged the special role of higher education institutions in the emerging politically independent nation-states of sub-Saharan Africa. Africa's universities have truly played a significant role in the dissemination of literature in European languages to African students and in establishing it as a central discipline in the humanities. But much remains for the universities to do in the realm of African indigenous literatures and their use in schools. It is in the colleges and universities that indigenous literatures, both oral and written, children's literature, popular literatures, and sophisticated literature should be seriously addressed vis-à-vis other literatures of the world.

Since literature is fast becoming a multicultural discipline, sub-Saharan African universities cannot afford to isolate themselves through a sole concentration on their own indigenous literatures. Other world literatures should be taught and studied in relation to African indigenous literatures. In this regard, the reader's response approach, which is essentially rooted in the transaction between the reader and the text, should be stressed. Such an approach takes into consideration the sub-Saharan African students' backgrounds, past experiences, beliefs, and assumptions in their interaction with the texts. Until the texts are read and deciphered in the readers' minds, they do not contribute to any kind of meaning or literary experience (Rosenblatt, 1978). As R. Baird Shuman (1993) states:

The critical framework most immediately applicable, however, to elementary and secondary teachers, is reader response. It posits that all readers, by bringing their individual backgrounds and value systems to their reading, create their own texts as they shape their personal, highly individual transactions with the texts they are reading. (p. 30)

Reading then becomes a very active experience, eliciting from each African reader a response based on personal background, beliefs, and assumptions. However, before such engagement with other world literatures, their indigenous literatures, beginning with the oral tradition, should be taught and studied. The study should include their origins and place in African education, the how and why of their survival in contemporary literature, and why some scholars think they are irrelevant today.

Because most sub-Saharan African folktales deal with imaginary events of the remote past, they do not seem to be readily in touch with contemporary reality. This is why some scholars think that they are almost irrelevant to African children of today. Although Okello Oculli (1984) seems to doubt the relevance of African folktales in view of the contemporary bleak social realities and moral decadence in Africa, caution should be exercised before dismissing folktales as "fantasies" that are out of touch with reality.

Traditionally, sub-Saharan Africans regarded folktales as central to their informal way of education before the coming of Western education. When the expression, *Eguin'eifovb'okha* (The tortoise that is always in the news) is used by the Edo people to describe someone, children who know a lot of tortoise stories readily understand the import of this metaphor as a reference to a person who is always in trouble. The metaphor is rooted in the African sociocultural milieu. The folktale is not really a phenomenon of the past; it is a living tradition. Proverbs and philosophical statements are an ongoing creation from the images of the day, and in years to come the pithy sayings of today acquire the dimension of traditional proverbs.

A contemporary product can illustrate this ongoing process. The

Santana brand of Volkswagen cars is a twentieth-century technological product; and as a good and expensive car, it is associated with
wealthy people. But not all Santana owners are honorable. In a fresh
philosophical statement that draws from images of the traditional
rural past and contemporary times, the Edos say: *Eno migho ya d'e
Santana nia Odafen aghi ghere* (one who gets money to purchase a
Santana car now is regarded as wealthy). By that statement, they
essentially mean to say that appearances are sometimes deceptive.
To them the Santana owner may be an armed robber. The Yoruba
saying that also has a connection with an automobile, *Enito moto
kopa ni yo renti noba*, literally means that it is the survivor of an
auto accident that can recall later (for legal purposes or the like)
the license number of the car that hit him or her. At a deeper level,
it means that it is one who is not completely crushed in a feud or
fight over something that can make reference to the feud or fight
at a later date.

Like such sayings, deep statements are also made from contemporary personalities. For example, there are two current ones: "you
tarka me, I daboh you;" and "don't delegiwa me." J.S. Tarka, Godwin
Daboh, and Dele Giwa actually existed in this century, and a knowledge of what they stood for or represented is necessary for an understanding of the full import of the statements. J.S. Tarka was a fa-
mous African politician from the Tiv community who later served
as a federal Nigerian commissioner (a position like that of secretary
of agriculture in the United States). As a federal commissioner one
can play a major role in contract awards. Presents and kickbacks
from those who win contracts (the contractors) usually enrich the
commissioner's coffers, and friendship and other relationships are
quite strong factors in contract awards. This is why many contractors join various social clubs and fraternities to meet the people who
matter. Through such meetings and interactions they usually establish some strong foothold in the hearts of the commissioners and
their associates. While such interactions solidify friendship, they can
also destroy it. "You tarka me I daboh you" is an example. Tarka and
Daboh were friends from the same Tiv group. For a variety of reasons, Godwin Daboh swore to an affidavit accusing J.S. Tarka of
corruption and dishonesty in public office, setting off a chain of
reactions culminating in Tarka's resignation as commissioner. Obvi-

ously their friendship soured, and they ended up in bitter feuding without regard for their past happy days together. Seen against this brief background story, "you tarka me I daboh you" means a decisive resolution to retaliate.

Delegiwa is a contraction of two names—Dele and Giwa. But Dele Giwa was one man. Dele Giwa was a blunt young journalist who was killed with a mail or letter bomb in the 1980s—the first in Nigeria and in sub-Saharan Africa. He did not expect any communication parcel to be loaded with death, and therefore was a victim of deception. The expression "do not delegiwa me" means "do not recklessly deceive me or cunningly kill me." These sayings of today may be taken in years to come as traditional folk sayings. Such a phenomenon needs to be taught to sophisticated students of folk or indigenous literatures.

Indigenous Children's Literature

Like the African folk oral tradition, African indigenous children's literature needs attention. Some African literary scholars have yet to understand the literary worth of indigenous and new literature for children and young adults. They believe that this new literature belongs to the education department charged with producing teachers for the elementary and high schools rather than the literature department, even though the Modern Language Association accorded children's literature a division status over a decade ago. The observation of U.C. Knoepflmacher (1992) about the teaching of children's literature in North America is also applicable in sub-Saharan Africa:

If the teaching of children's literature is to become fully integrated into our current undergraduate and graduate programs of instruction, we will have to go beyond the parochial (or territorial) attitudes responsible for its segregation. That parochialism, however, cannot be attributed exclusively to the smugness of those who would persuade themselves that child texts are lacking in the Arnoldian "high seriousness" or the Jamesian craftsmanship of the adult classics they prefer to teach. The blame falls just as squarely on those who still welcome the isolation of the field once confined to schools of education, who continue to regard the study of child texts as a less demanding and less rigorous enterprise. It is their own devaluation of their field that has contributed to its belittlement. (p. 5)

While reputable journals like *Children's Literature* (the annual of the Children's Literature Association from the Yale University Press), the *Children's Literature Association Quarterly, The Lion and the Unicorn,* and *Children's Literature in Education* have been solidly established in North America for serious scholarship in children's literature, only one, the *Journal of African Children's and Youth Literature* (JACYL), presently exists for such studies about African children's literature.

Research and Development in Literature

If sub-Saharan African universities are to remain the institutions that provide a lead in creative thought and the stimulus of a literature, they need to be current with world development in literary studies and instruction. It is in the universities that all the various strands of literature should be synchronized for a meaningful and relevant whole. Children's literature should be seen as literature, and as an interdisciplinary subject rather than as "kiddie lit" exclusively for education departments. As Knoepflmacher (1992) would assert:

The time may not be far away when universities and colleges institute cross-curricular programs devoted to studies in childhood. Such programs would enlist the expertise of child psychologists, anthropologists, folklorists, sociologists, social historians, art historians, theologians, film and theater experts, as well as teachers of literature who might be called on to play a central role by offering their well-established courses as core studies. . . . The systematic and syncretic investigation that a program in studies in childhood would help to promote in colleges and universities can not, however, be put into place until children's literature receives the same serious attention academia expends on so-called adults texts. (p. 2)

Like children's literature in sub-Saharan Africa, African literature for adults needs to be addressed in a sophisticated manner with special attention to purpose in a multilingual Africa.

As products of European education systems, African universities are almost European university extensions. In their history and orientation African universities were European university appendages in the former colonial dominions. This is why literature curriculum and instruction was strongly British in the former British colonies like Nigeria, Ghana, Gambia, and Sierra Leone, and strongly French in former French territories like Senegal and the Ivory Coast. After independence in the 1960s the literature of the former colonial power remained strong. But, it needed a change or overhaul.

An example of a radical departure from the spirit of a traditional English department took place at the University of Nairobi in 1968. Led by Ngugi Wa Thiong'O, a group of lecturers dismantled the old English department. The primacy of English literature was demolished and replaced with African literature—oral and written. This new literature curriculum is based on the relevance of subject matter to the human conditions present in East Africa, and in the wider world as well.

But, not far from Nairobi, in Makerere, Uganda, the English department remained traditional and conservative. When Okot p'Bitek went to Makerere University in Uganda in 1979 he was made Senior Research Fellow in the Institute of Social Research, and in 1982 was appointed the first Professor of Creative Writing in the Department of Literature. Okot found the colonial curriculum in literature had not changed much in the twenty years that had passed since Uganda had become a politically independent nation. Only a few African writers were studied in special courses on African literature; the syllabus was still dominated by the literature of the British Isles. In Bernth Lindfors's words, "it was as if the revolution started in Nairobi had completely bypassed Kampala, only a few hundred miles west. Curricular neo-colonialism, instead of withering away remained in full bloom at Makerere" (1989, p. 167).

Okot p'Bitek vehemently reacted against the curriculum and instruction in English in Makerere in an article entitled, "Literature Department Needs Overhaul" published in the government-owned newspaper *Uganda Times* on May 6, 1982. The full text is included here because it reflects what is happening in various degrees, in other sub-Saharan African universities:

There is a grave crisis in the Department of Literature at Makerere. The final withdrawal of British professors [David Cook and Margaret Macpherson] has been achieved. The entire teaching staff are not merely Africans. They are all Ugandans. But the Department is still one of the whitest of literature departments north of the Cape of Good Hope. The one in the University of Malawi may just beat us in its whiteness in that books by African writers are totally banned.

If you are stupid enough to be found with any of the books of the Malawian poet, novelist, dramatist and former diplomat David Rubadiri, Ngugi wa Thiong'o, one of Africa's foremost novelists, Achebe or Soyinka or my own, you do not only lose your job, but are imprisoned.

The syllabus in the Department of Literature here seems to be deliberately designed to stultify creative talent, and to ensure that the student, after three years of literature will become so thoroughly [fed] up that he or she will think of literature only as torture. But, even more sinister, the syllabus is such that the African student is made to believe that there [are] some literatures, especially those from England and America, which are superior to those of his own people. The other day Professor Timothy Wangusa reported that poetry was not a popular subject with the students, that it was the worst paper done in the exams. How can poetry, which is the other word for song, be unpopular? A song, a story, a play is enjoyable because it is meaningful *(my emphasis). If the poetry that is being offered at Makerere is unpopular, this is precisely because it is meaningless, socially irrelevant to the society from which the student comes. Daffodils! What does this kind of lily, which does not even grow here, mean to us? They plant flowers in Europe at the beginning of a season called Spring, which comes after Winter.*

William Shakespeare's works are very interesting. At Makerere there is a whole course devoted to him. There is another course all about American Literature (20 authors). And yet last academic year, Oral Literature was not offered at all. How do we begin to rate Shakespeare, Cooper, Ellison to be superior to Adok Too, the blind poet from Lamogi near Gulu, who was jailed by the British for two years, and was hunted down by Amin's thugs, but was not caught? What of the recitals from Ankole, and the songs of Evaristo Muyinda and Tereza Kisolo at the Museum? What of the story tellers who composed the folk tales? And the wise man and woman who coined to proverbs?

In 1968 a literary revolution overthrew the Department of English at Nairobi University. It was replaced by the Department of Literature with African Literature, both oral and written, as the core of the syllabus. The syllabus did not completely exclude the literatures of other people, but the main emphasis was on African Literature. Should African stu-

dents learn what other artists have done? Of course, but after knowing their own. For only so can they begin to compare what have been produced at home with other people's works. Only so, can our future leaders have firm roots at home, something to be proud about, something they can call their own. Many of the students who take literature at Makerere are also in the Faculty of Education. When they graduate, whose literature will they teach to the children at secondary schools? Should generosity not begin at home? Thirteen years after, Makerere University's Literature Department is still essentially an English Department. What happened? Why did the revolution in Nairobi fail to reach Makerere? The answer is easy to find.

The European forces there led by the Cooks and Macphersons were still too strong. Pio Zirumu and Nuwa Sentongo and other friends on the Hill were no match. They spent their creative energy, not so much at Makerere, but at the national theater where, together with Elvania Zirimu, Robert Serumaga, Byron Kawadwa and many other talents, [they] brought about an unprecedented flowering of Ugandan theater.

What was the literary revolution in Nairobi all about? Led by Ngugi, Taban, Philip Ochieng, Owuor Anyumba and myself, we rejected the assumption that Africa should continue to be an extension, an appendage of Europe. We insisted that Africa cannot and should not be interpreted in terms of ideas, and in a vocabulary borrowed from outside. If there is need for the study of the historic continuity of a single culture, why can't it be African? Why and how do you suppose that African culture has its roots in Europe? The other fake notion we refused was the lie that there was something called Universal standards. There is no such thing. What is being paraded before us by the label from Europe is nothing more than the supposed standards of the ruling classes there. What is taught to the children of those fellows is to instill the ideas of the beautiful, etc. And these may not be what we in Uganda and Africa uphold as the beautiful.

For me, culture is philosophy as lived and celebrated in society. Human beings do not behave like dry leaves, smoke or clouds that are blown here and there by the winds. Men live in organizations such as the family, a chiefdom, a nation. He has a religion, an army, legal and many other social institutions. All these organizations are informed by, are built around the central idea of the people, that is, what they believe life is all about.

It is according to a people's social philosophy that human behavior is judged, decent woman, stupid fellow, good boy, brave solider, thief, etc. Morality and immorality, what is good and what is not good, are measured according to the people's world view. Who is a crook here may be a clever fellow somewhere else. All the creative works of man, literature, painting, sculpture, music and dance, architecture, village and town planning, etc., are all reflections of the philosophy of life of a people. It is the artist who captures and expresses this elusive "Thing" called the philosophy of life or world view in his works. He uses his voice, his musical instrument, his body as in the dance or in the theater, his pen, his gestures, etc., to achieve this. It is the artist who at the same time sustains the moral system by laughing at fools, and praising the good works of members of the society.

A Curriculum Balance

Various African universities have developed a "balance" between the old colonial curriculum and their indigenous post-colonial curriculum. But these "balances" vary. In an attempt to be very African in curriculum and instruction, content and instruction are sometimes narrowly nationalized and not internationalized. To patriotically but parochially give instruction in African literature in African universities is to get a limited view of what literature is.

As a big continent with a multiplicity of indigenous tongues, some written and some yet unwritten, a comparative study of the indigenous literatures of Africa is appropriate. Such comparative study is based on the assumption that national literatures are not islands unto themselves and that border violations between the various national domains are not only inevitable but also beneficial in the sense of a greater intellectual and aesthetic openness and an enhanced possibility of mutual understanding (Feuser, 1980, p. 100). Within even one African country like Nigeria, with its multiplicity of tongues, it is possible to comparatively study indigenous literatures.

The phenomenon of Igbakhuan in the Edo ethnic group—a spirit child born to die to torment his or her parents—is transcultural. It is called *abiku* in Yoruba, and Wole Soyinka has written a moving poem about it from his Yoruba ethnic background; J.P. Clark has written one rooted in his ethnic Ljaw background; Chinua Achebe wrote the Igbo conception of it—the *ogbanje* in *Things Fall Apart;*

the Hausa know it as *damwabi,* and among the Fanti in Ghana it is *kossanah.* Like the phenomenon of the spirit child born to die to torment his or her parents, which is transcultural, the spiritual counterpart of the human being—the Ehi in Edo cosmology is also transcultural. It is called chi in Igbo cosmology and ori in Yoruba cosmology. The transcultural nature of the Igbakhuan and Ehi (Edo) should necessitate a comparative study, which at present has not been done.

Comparative literature studies associations like the African and Comparative Literature Association of Nigeria need to be more visible, active, and responsive to the use of African indigenous literatures vis-à-vis other world literatures. Wilfred Feuser (1980) asserts that an essential precondition of the further development of comparative literature is "the total and unconditional inclusion of the continent's indigenous literatures into its purview. Collaterally, the carefully planned training of young scholars in this direction has to be given priority" (p. 107). Indigenous African literatures should be a stimulus to the study of the literature of the black diaspora—African-American, Caribbean, and Brazilian.

There is no absolute cultural divestiture between Africans and Africans in the diaspora. This is why literary works that reflect this fact need to be used in a program of indigenous literature in sub-Saharan Africa. It is like studying elements of indigenous African literatures transplanted to North America, the Caribbean, and Brazil. The Uncle Remus tales of Joel Chandler Harris, the Aunt Nancy and other folktales of the Caribbean, are a carryover from Africa. Phyllis Galembo (1992) has, in an incisive photographic study, paired Africa's Benin City and the Brazilian city of Salvador (commonly called Bahia). According to Galembo, any visitor can see that Bahia and Benin City share a special interest in the divinity of the ocean, known respectively as *lemanja/Olokun* (p. xi). The indigenous literatures of such places need comparative studies—especially since almost every facet of Bahia is still steeped in the heritage of sub-Saharan Africa. Such comparative studies should be followed by a multicultural or comparative study of African indigenous literatures and Western literatures—an exercise which has a potential for clearing errors and misconception. Nobody thinks that Scott's explication in *Ivanhoe* of the historical realities (as he imagined them) of

Anglo-Saxon and Norman culture is irresponsible or unliterary. Achebe's account of Ibo life is to be compared with Scott's tale because each is a form of historical novel (Appiah, 1992, p. 67). Such scholarly activities rightfully belong to African university languages and literature departments and education departments, which should be leaders in curriculum reappraisal.

Literary Criticism

Literary criticism cannot be ignored in using indigenous literatures. The spirit of African indigenous literatures should be visible in scholarship in African literature. Without a solid knowledge of a particular ethnic group, it is quite difficult to do a thorough exegesis and explication of a literary text from this particular ethnic group. The nuances and subtleties of expression and bodily gestures of an African ethnic group need to be known and understood before a critic can pay attention to details of a literary composition. Because quite a number of non-African scholars lack this knowledge, their scholarship sometimes fails to hit the mark; and African scholars who know their culture resent such scholarship. Chinua Achebe (1976) says, "I should like to see the word *universal* banned altogether from discussion of African literature until such a time as people cease to use it as a synonym for the narrow, self-serving parochialism of Europe" (p. 11). But, on the other hand, Reed Way Dassenbrock (1987) maintains that:

If we must be or become expert in the culture of any book we read, then we will tend to limit ourselves to our own literature. This would probably suit many African critics perfectly, since they seem to resent any outside interest in African literature. But surely it is foolish to confine each reader in a prison of only the literature that can be read expertly and surely. (p. 12)

No African critic really resents outside interest in African literature. There are some English expressions in Africa that are different from the English expressions of Britain or the United States. In a study of African English expressions in the Gambia, Edmun Richmond (1989) came up with a long list of Gambianized English items and came to the conclusion that although his collection of

Gambianized English is limited, it does point to differences in that region's development of English, and continues to demonstrate that there is not just one English, but several *Englishes* to be found on the African continent (p. 227). Truly, the continent of Africa has long been a greenhouse for the cultivation of alternate forms of the English language. There, it has flourished for several centuries, emerging as new varieties and hybrids, some of which are far removed from the original parent rootstock (Richmond, 1989, p. 223).

To illustrate, the non-African who may be a native speaker of English might misinterpret the word, "wonderful," in an African literary text. As used in Anglophone Africa, "wonderful" does not mean something "great" or "positive." It means there is something that is "strange," "unexpected," or "shocking"—something that makes one wonder. Similarly, the word "mad" does not really mean annoyance as is used in the United States. To say to an African that he or she is "mad" is an insult which is resented. With the existence of such African English idioms, it is only logical to expect that the indigenous languages of Africans can influence their expression or creativity in English. They need to be studied to have a deeper understanding of their literary works in English. For example, Edo language and literature need to be studied to understand their tales in English. Likewise, Igbo language and literature need to be studied to have a deeper understanding of *Things Fall Apart, Arrow of God,* and *A Man of the People.* This stance is defended by Daniel P. Kunene (1992):

> *There ought to be no separation of language and literature either in the minds of "African" literature scholars and teachers, or in the institutions in which such research and teaching take place. It is ironic that, in the United States, for example, "African" literatures are taught in English departments! Instead of this aberration, any genuine interest in African literatures should be reflected in a serious attempt to combine literature studies with compatible language studies. Given the will, this should not be difficult. A study of the literature of a given area should be accompanied by a concurrent study of at least one of the languages of that area. For example, Zimbabwean literature should be studied together with Shona and Ndebele regardless of whether that literature is written in English or in any of the Shona-group languages or in Ndebele (a Nguni-group language). (p. 8)*

Such academic pursuits will ensure the growth and enrichment of African indigenous languages and literatures. Without such attention, they suffer neglect and starve. Certainly, African universities' departments of languages and literatures and departments of education need to work seriously to revive and develop their indigenous literatures to complement other world literatures.

Conclusion

Like other parts of the world, sub-Saharan Africa needs to invest in its multiethnic indigenous literatures as the starting point in literary studies. The nutrients and vitality that African indigenous literatures can supply to African languages will ensure the survival of these languages as living ones escaping the fate of Latin, which is now confined to books.

Besides ensuring survival of these languages, using indigenous literatures will be invaluable in peacefully bringing together the diverse ethnic groups that make up each African nation. By providing Africans with stories—oral and written—about other ethnic groups, indigenous literatures broaden their horizon and enhance their understanding of their fellow Africans, and, by extension, their understanding of their fellow human beings. Significantly, a judicious use of indigenous literatures in Sub-Saharan African schools is a potential source of enrichment of world literatures that envision relevance, utility, and literature as an instrument for promoting the peace of the continent, and that of the world as well.

References

Achebe, C. (1958). *Things fall apart.* London: Heinemann.
Achebe C. (1964). *Arrow of God.* London: Heinemann.
Achebe C. (1966). *A man of the people.* London: Heinemann.
Achebe, C. (1976). *Morning yet on creation day.* Garden City, NY: Doubleday.
Achebe, C. (1981). Chinua Achebe: At the crossroad. In J.C. Cott (Ed.), *Pipers at the gates of dawn—the wisdom of children literature* (pp. 161–192). New York: Random House.
Adagala, K., & Kabira, M. (Eds.). (1985). *Kenya oral narratives.* Nairobi: Heinemann.
Amadi, A.O. (1981). *African libraries: Western tradition and colonial brainwashing.* Metuchen, NJ: Scarecrow Press.
Appiah, K.A. (1992). *In my father's house.* New York: Oxford University Press.
Areo, A. (1977). *The hopeful lovers.* London: Macmillan.
Banham, M. (Ed.). (1960). *Nigerian student verse—1959.* Ibadan: Ibadan University Press.
Barber, K. (1995). African language literature and postcolonial criticism. *Research in African Literature, 25*(4), 3–30.

Burton, D.L. (1980). Pop to protein? Two generations of adolescents' fiction. *Texas Tech Journal of Education, 7*(1), 7–13.

Cram, J. (1993). Colonialism and libraries in third world Africa. *Australian Library Journal, 18,* 13–20.

Dassenbrock, R.W. (1987). Intelligibility and meaningfulness in multicultural literature in English. *Publications of the Modern Language Association of America, 102*(1), 10–19.

Decker, T. (1968). *Tales of the forest.* London: Evans.

Donelson, K.L., & Nilsen, A.P. (1980). *Literature for today's young adults.* Glenview, IL: Scott Foresman.

Dunton, C. (1993, March). Africa's language problem. *West Africa, 3939,* 457, 459.

East, R. & Zaria, M.T. (1934). *Jikin Magayi.* Lagos: West African Publicity.

Ekwensi, C. (1950, January). *West African Review, 19,* 16–19.

Ekwensi, C. (1960). *The drummer boy.* Cambridge: Cambridge University Press.

Ekwensi, C. (1962). *An African night's entertainment.* Ibadan: African Universities Press.

Emecheta, B. (1976). *The bride price.* New York: George Braziller.

Fafunwa, B. (1974). *A history of education in Nigeria.* London: Allen and Unwin.

Feuser, W. (1980). The emergence of comparative literature in Nigeria. *Research in African Literatures, 11,* 100–107.

Galembo, P. (1992). *Divine inspiration—from Benin to Bahia.* Albuquerque: University of New Mexico Press.

Gerard, A.S. (1971). *Four African literatures—Xhosa, Sotho, Zulu, Amharic.* Berkeley: University of California Press.

Gerard, A.S. (1981). *African language literatures: An introduction to the literary history of sub-Saharan Africa.* Washington, DC: Three Continents Press.

Greene, B. (1973). *Summer of my German soldier.* New York: Dell.

Halpe, H. (1992). The hidden common wealth: Indigenous literatures and the commonwealth literature: New literatures in English industry. *Journal of Commonwealth Literature, 27*(1), 5–12.

Hardy, T. (1918). *Far from the madding crowd.* New York: Harper.

House, J. (1992). Modern quest: Teaching myths and folktales. *English Journal, 81,* 72–74.

Houser, G.M. (1003). Human rights and the liberation struggle: The importance of creative tension. In E. McCarthy-Arnolds, R. Penna, & J.C. Sobrepena (Eds.), *Africa, human rights, and the global system* (pp. 12–22). Westport, CT: Greenwood.

Isola, A. (1992). The African writer's tongue. *Research in African literatures, 23,* 17–26.

Jones, E.D. (1992). Myth and modernity: African writers and their roots. *African Literature Today, 18,* 1–8.

Keenan, H. (1992). Joel Chandler Harris and the legitimacy of the reteller of folktales. In G.D. Schmidt & D.R. Hettinga (Eds.), *Sitting at the feet of the past: Retelling the North American folktale for children.* Westport, CT: Greenwood.

Knoepflmacher, U.C. (1992). "Introduction" in G. Sadler (Ed.), *Teaching children's literature.* New York: MLA.

Kotei, S.I.A. (1978). Themes for children's literature in Ghana. *African book publishing record, 4,* 233–239.

Kunene, D.P. (1992). African language literature: Tragedy and hope. *Research in African literature, 23,* 7–15.

Lindfors, B. (1989). Okot's last blast: An attempt at curricular reform in Uganda after Idi Amin. In H. Maes-Jelinek, K.H. Peterson, & A. Rutherford (Eds.), *A shaping of connections* (pp. 164–170). Sydney, Australia: Kangaroo Press.

Loban, W., Ryan, M., & Squire, J.R. (1961). *Teaching languages and literatures.* New York: Harcourt Brace.

Mofolo, T. (1931). *Chaka,* F.H. Dutton (trans.). London: Oxford University Press for the International African Institute.

Mungoshi, C. (1989). *Tales from a Shona childhood.* Harare, Zimbabwe: Baobab Books.

Ngugi wa Thiong'O. (1972). *Homecoming*. London: Heinemann.

Ngugi wa Thiong'O. (1983). *Barrel of a pen: Resistance to repression in colonial Kenya*. Trenton, NJ: Africa World Press.

Ngugi wa Thiong'O. (1985). On writing in Gikuyu. *Research in African Literatures, 16*(2) 151–156.

Obanya, P. (1980). Nigeria in search of a suitable educational system. *Journal of African Studies, 7,* 48–53.

Oculli, O. (1984, November 29–30). The politics of literature for children in Africa. *The Guardian,* 6.

Okot p'Bitek. (1966). *Song of Lawino*. Nairobi: East African Publishing House.

Okot p'Bitek. (1982, May 6). Literature department needs overhaul, *Uganda Times,* p. 4.

Onadipe, K. (1963). *The adventures of Souza*. Lagos: African Universities Press.

Osa, O. (1983) Adolescent girls' need for love in two cultures—Nigerian and the United States. *English Journal, 72* (8), 35–37.

Osa, O. (1986). The sociocultural context of African children's reading today. *Reading Improvement 23*(3), 194–196.

Osa, O. (1995). *African children's and youth literature*. New York: Twayne.

Press, J. (Ed.). (1965). Preface to *Commonwealth literature: Unity and diversity in a common culture*. London: Heinemann.

Richmond, E.B. (1989). African English expressions in the Gambia. *World English, 8*(2), 223–228.

Rosenblatt, L.M. (1978). *The reader, the text, the poem: The transactional theory of the literary work*. Carbondale, IL: Southern Illinois University Press.

Rothlein, R.M., & Meinbach, A.M. (1991). *The literature connection: Using children's books in the classroom*. Glenview, IL: Scott Foresman.

Schmidt, N.J. (1981). *Children's fiction about Africa in English*. New York: Conch Magazine.

Shavit, Z. (1992). Introduction—children's literature issue. *Poetics, 13,* 1–3.

Shuman, R.B. (1993). The past as present: Reader response and literary study. *English Journal, 82*(5), 30–32.

Skinner, A.N. (1973). From Hausa to English: A study in paraphrase. *Research in African Literatures, 4*(2), 154–164.

Sutherland, Z., & Arbuthnot, M. (1991). *Best in children's books*. Chicago: The University of Chicago.

Sutherland, Z., & Hill, A. (1991). *Children and books* (8th ed.). New York: HarperCollins

UNESCO. (1987, July). *Priority needs and regional cooperation concerning youth in English-Speaking Africa*.

Wali, O. (1963). The dead end of African literature. *Transition, 3*(10), pp. 13–16.

Walsh, G. (1991). *Publishing in Africa: A neglected component of development*. (Working Papers in African Studies No. 156). Boston: University Studies Center.

Reflections on Education
in Sub-Saharan Africa

Cynthia Szymanski Sunal

Sub-Saharan Africa is struggling to provide its children with quantity and quality education. This is a struggle repeated throughout the world. Numerous stressors make the struggle extremely difficult in sub-Saharan Africa. Among them, two major stressors are a rapidly growing population and slowly growing economies. Other stressors include students' poor health, cultural reservations concerning modern, often Westernized, curricula and instructional strategies, and the need to make the curriculum relevant to the local context. These stressors have an effect on the quantity and quality of education elsewhere in the world as well. However, in sub-Saharan Africa, each stressor seems to be cast in strong relief and is extremely difficult to manage or to overcome. In other regions of the world each has an important effect on education, but frequently, the effect is not so strong.

The extreme conditions found in sub-Saharan Africa suggest that merely continuing the usual means of dealing with these stressors or importing ideas intact from other world regions will not solve all the current issues and future concerns facing the region's educational systems. Instead, some unique and innovative ideas will be required. These can emerge from the diversity found in the region. The authors of this book's chapters have described some of the ideas that have emerged in relation to six issues and future concerns which have major impact on the potential of educational systems in sub-Saharan Africa to deliver quantity and quality of education. These are: (1) the objectives of mass education; (2) funding; (3) inequities in access to education; (4) curriculum; (5) instructional methodology; and (6) research needs and efforts. These broad issues and concerns take different forms and are found at varying levels of extremity between and within the nations of the region. But patterns and trends do emerge from the authors' discussions. Their discussions indicate that Africans are developing and testing innovative approaches to education. Since all regions in the world share to an extent the same major issues and future concerns for education, African ideas should be of interest to others and may be adapted for use elsewhere.

The Objectives of Mass Education

Throughout the region there have been efforts to deliver mass education at the primary school level. Secondary schooling often has expanded as has higher education. However, the primary school is the major focus of mass education in the region. In Chapter 1, Cynthia Sunal notes two purposes usually cited for mass primary education: (1) it can make citizens literate and numerate to the extent that they can deal with problems encountered at home, and (2) it can provide a foundation for further education. She finds that these translate into educational objectives focusing on basic literacy and numeracy. She also finds objectives supporting the second purpose, preparation for the next level of schooling.

A tugging between objectives supporting each purpose is present around the world. In the United States, for example, concern has been expressed by groups such as the National Association for the Education of Young Children that early education is becoming too academic, that curricula are being pushed down from first grade into the kindergarten, from second grade to first grade, and so forth, in order to prepare students for higher levels of education (Bredekamp, 1997). The tugging occurring in sub-Saharan Africa and the solutions to this issue will be of interest to those expressing concern with the state of early education in the United States. African solutions, such as the primary school boards discussed in Chapter 1, may be adaptable to the United States or may suggest viable alternatives that could be developed within the United States.

Mass education is common throughout the world. Its objectives must fit the society supporting it, but also must prepare students for the larger, ever changing, interdependent world in which they live. As sub-Saharan educational systems determine and reevaluate their objectives for mass education, others may find ideas in the process that can be utilized.

The authors of the chapters on science, mathematics, citizenship, and literature education indicate that primary schooling includes objectives aimed at providing students with basic knowledge and competency in these disciplinary areas. Preparation for the next level dominates, however, in many of the region's schools. So, these authors fear that basic knowledge and competency among all students may be sacrificed in order to prepare some of the students for the next level of education. In this way, most students are deprived of the strong, experiential foundation needed for everyday life and future studies.

The objectives for mass education in each of these disciplinary areas are strongly influenced by objectives present in education elsewhere, particularly in Western Europe and North America. For example, movements toward the use of inquiry by students in science, the use of manipulatives in mathematics, the concept of integrated social studies rather than separate subjects such as history and geography and economics, and the use of youth literature all have roots in North America and Western Europe. The authors of the disciplinary teaching chapters address the questions of whether these movements should be, or can be, Africanized. The intention is to create mass education incorporating indigenous cultures. Citizenship education in Nigeria and mathematics education in Zimbabwe identify some uniquely successful approaches to accomplishing objectives for mass education. These will be of interest to educators elsewhere as they consider the balance between national and outside influences on the objectives for mass education within these disciplinary areas.

Higher education influences earlier levels of education, since one of its purposes is often preparation for advanced levels of education and it also trains educators. The objectives of higher education itself are being debated. The role of higher education in the region is being Africanized, yet it must also help tie the region into the world's economy, decision making, intellectual development, knowledge base, and politics. African universities reflect their nation's cultures and diversity and also reflect their ties with higher education elsewhere. Higher education faculty trained overseas bring new ideas to African higher education, but often also bring the perspectives of their overseas mentors. Faculty trained in their own country may or may not have more African perspectives; many may incorporate the perspectives of their African mentors who were trained overseas. A needed balance is being sought in sub-Saharan Africa.

Many students do not study beyond the primary school level, and many of those who complete further education work in the burgeoning informal sector of the economy. In Chapter 3, Benson Honig discusses the relationship of formal education to preparation for the informal sector. He finds efforts, along both traditional vocational and adult education tracks, and more innovative, unique tracks to use formal education to prepare individuals for informal-sector employment. Universal primary education and universal literacy and numeracy are identified as basic objectives of mass education for the informal-sector economy. Patterns are found in the objectives for mass education in sub-Saharan Africa. These include a pattern of dissatisfaction with some commonly found objectives, especially those deriving from the focus on viewing one level of education primarily as preparation for the next level of education.

Funding

Education has received a substantial share of public funding in sub-Saharan Africa. The percentage of funding devoted to education has been, in recent decades, surpassed only by the Arab States and most developed nations. Yet, when translated into U.S. dollars, the actual funding available to education has been small, because the national budget of most countries in the region is small in terms of U.S. dollars.

Available funding often has been directed at mass education's needs, usually at the primary school level. Expansion of the number of places for students in secondary and higher education has been a goal in parts of the region. To accomplish mass education and expansion of higher levels of education, buildings, classroom furnishings, teaching and learning materials, and similar supporting items have had to be built or acquired. Curriculum development, teacher training, educational research, and administrative development have been put into place and expanded. In many instances the existing educational establishment at the time of independence was small. Its expansion and Africanization have been expensive. Heavy costs are expected to continue as the population grows, and attempts to provide both quantity and quality education continue. At the same time, other public needs, such as those for clean water and adequate transportation systems, have competed for funding and will continue to do so.

The chapters discussing the teaching of four major disciplinary areas indicate serious underfunding. Science education in the region is in need of equipment, laboratories, relevant curricula, appropriate teacher training, and research on the types of scientific conceptions and misconceptions fostered by local cultures and languages. Each of these requires substantial funding. There have been efforts to train teachers in how to use local craftspeople to produce scientific equipment and how to use local materials in the making of such equipment. For example, a pan balance can be made from used plastic containers and wood doweling from local trees. Examples of other efforts to reduce the costs of science education are reported in Chapter 4. Mathematics education utilizing manipulative materials faces funding costs similar in many ways to those of science education. Citizenship education and literature education do not require large equipment outlays and laboratories, but do need library resource materials and other documents to support their curriculum. All areas must have funding for curriculum development, teacher training, and research.

Higher education requires a large outlay of funding if research and teaching are to be carried out and adequate library and computing facilities are to be available. Many institutions in the region give students living and housing allowances, maintain faculty housing, and have medical facilities and security forces. Thus, there are many fixed expenses requiring substantial funding. There are a few innovations in the region that suggest unique ways to alleviate the funding needs of higher education. Some institutions are using high technology to deliver distance education. Others are offering weekend and evening graduate coursework for working professionals as a means to generate new funding (Okebukola, 1997). Extreme economic stresses probably will spur higher education to further innovation.

There is a demand for specific types of training for the informal sector economy. Such training programs often are not expensive, but still represent some costs. Because of the demands for funding from the formal education program, informal-sector training that meets expressed needs has been of small scale and can be expected to remain small in the near future. Since it differs from traditional conceptions of the activities of formal education, it will require some changes in perspectives from educators and from the citizenry before greater funding will be supported.

The overall picture for funding is bleak because of rapid population growth combined with slow economic growth. But, there are some bright spots, such as the frequent use of local materials to make scientific equipment and the use of local storytellers in literature education programs. Both require low levels of funding and suggest structures and strategies for the use of scarce funds that may be of interest in other world regions.

It can be expected that structural adjustment policies currently in place will shift an ever increasing share of the costs of education to individuals and their families. In some of the world's regions families carry heavy burdens in educational funding. In the Far East, for example, families often pay most or all of the costs of higher education in some countries. In Latin America, many families pay for private primary and secondary education because of the limited funding for public education and the resulting perception of low quality. In sub-Saharan Africa the only viable solution may be to shift more and more of the funding of education to the families whose children are in school. However, the slowly growing economies of the region make such a shift a great hardship for many families. As a result, it can be expected that a smaller percentage of children will be able to go to primary school and have opportunities for further education. Perhaps Africans will be able to generate some compromise solutions.

Inequities in Access to Education
Inequities in access to education exist in all societies. How Africans deal with perceived and real inequities in access to education will inform others. The diversity of cultures, languages, and religious and political perspectives creates complex problems from which inequities can spring, but also creates the material out of which innovative solutions can be fashioned.

Some African populations, such as those who are nomadic, present the formal education sector with great difficulties. (This also happens in developed nations. In the United States, for example, public education in recent decades has been trying to serve the children of migrant farm workers.) The children of families living in isolated rural regions also often do not have reasonable access to education. Boarding schools have been one solution, another has been traveling teachers, and a third has been distance education via radio, television, and computers. These have been tried in sub-Saharan Africa and elsewhere with some success. None has been completely satisfactory and some have proven to be very expensive. So, the search for alternatives continues.

In parts of the region, and elsewhere in the world, girls are less likely to be educated because of cultural and religious perspectives. When educated (as with rural and nomadic children) the curriculum may be less relevant to their needs and less directed at their perspectives than it is for boys. Teachers often have different expectations and reward different behaviors in girls when compared to boys (Aldritch & Hall, 1980; Noddings, 1992). When public funding for education is severely limited and families carry increasing educational costs, girls may have fewer opportunities when decisions are made about who should go to school. There are projections suggesting that, while the actual numbers of girls in school in sub-Saharan Africa may increase with population gains, the percentage of girls attending school will decrease over the next few decades (Graham-Brown, 1991).

Children from low socioeconomic or from low-status nonmajority groups also may have reduced access to education. Families may not send their children to school because of lack of money and also because of a perceived lack of job-related benefits from schooling. These problems are found elsewhere in the world, as well.

In sub-Saharan Africa there have been numerous efforts to enroll typically underenrolled students, ranging from government mandates for attendance to public relations campaigns. Such efforts cost money and, as funding tightens, some have been reduced. New initiatives may be fewer because they require funding and because the funding may not be there for the additional students should their families want them schooled.

Past and current efforts to enroll students have sprung from the cultures of the region. These efforts offer suggestions that other regions can use as they tailor enrollment efforts to students. The diversity of the efforts underway offers a wide range of possibilities that can be considered by educators in other of the world's regions as they work to reduce inequities in access to education.

Curriculum

Africanization of the curriculum has been a gradual but strong movement in the region. This movement has been away from curricula originating in the colonial period. It has moved toward curricula that incorporate both indigenous knowledge and traditions and current ideas and knowledge representing widespread educational theory and practice. Examples are inquiry-based curricula and the use of manipulatives in mathematics. Concomitant with these movements, there has been retention of curriculum content and theory associated with the colonial period and the educational traditions of the colonizing powers. Thus, curricula often follow European models.

Immediate change to an African curriculum has not occurred. It has proven to be a process requiring time and funding. Curriculum courses of study, syllabi, materials, and textbooks are time consuming to develop, test, and implement. They are most appropriate when based on research into the types of conceptions and misconceptions the culture and language lead individuals to develop. Curriculum developers must be trained who understand the culture(s) of a nation, teaching, the disciplines and levels for which the curriculum is being developed, and national, local, and individual needs. Finally, teachers must be trained to implement the curricula.

The authors of Chapters 4, 5, 6, and 7 address these issues in their discussions of four major disciplines in the curriculum. They point out the need for a balance between indigenous knowledge and knowledge from elsewhere. They support the use of locally relevant examples, materials, and knowledge in the curriculum.

Typically, the most Africanized curricula are found at the primary school level and in informal-sector education. As students move into secondary and higher education, the curricula are less Africanized and often very much like curricula found elsewhere. Indigenous languages are fostered most often in the primary school, whereas other languages such as English, Arabic, and French often are used in curriculum materials after the primary school level. Some authors, such as Osayimwense Osa in Chapter 7, argue for heavy use of indigenous material at the secondary school level. Dr. Osa's chapter describes the complex forces acting on curriculum development in the region and the balancing that is necessary, but hard to accomplish. While he argues for the use of indigenous literature at the secondary school level, a move toward Africanization, he also argues for the use of youth and young adult literature, a movement representing worldwide trends at the secondary school level. He discusses modern, written indigenous literature for youth and advocates its use along with youth literature from elsewhere. This represents a break with traditionalists who may favor the use of indigenous and other adult literature. In this break, Dr. Osa has the company of literature educators in many other parts of the world. Dr. Osa also notes the existence of narrow interpretations of Africanization in some of the region. He finds that curriculum developers sometimes focus on the indigenous literature of their country and exclude literature from other African nations.

Since Africanization appears to be strongest at the primary school level, and this is the level beyond which many African students do not progress, some questions result. If students will receive no further formal education, do they not need to be given a foundation of knowledge about the world outside their own culture and nation? How much should they study about their culture and nation? neighboring nations? other parts of the continent? other regions of the world?

Curriculum has many definitions in the literature (Jackson, 1992). It has few clear guidelines for developers anywhere in the world. Curriculum is heavily impacted by tradition and certainly by the perspectives of its developers. The questions and quandaries faced in sub-Saharan Africa occur everywhere. In the United States, for example, cultural diversity is an issue that is being argued in terms of curricula. How much world literature should be in the curriculum? Do students from a Puerto Rican background in the United States need different examples from students of Polish background or students from a Lebanese background? Do some groups perform poorly because the curricula are very different from the cultural and knowledge background of their home? As Africans work through similar questions, their curriculum development processes and philosophies can be expected to inform and interest developers in other world regions.

Instructional Methodology

Instructional methodology is an issue in sub-Saharan Africa and else-where. Traditions in African societies have fostered in children a strong respect for adults. Children are welcomed into families, well loved, and enjoyed. They are expected to be obedient, to carry their part of family responsibilities, to be polite, and not to question adults. Tra-ditional teaching has been dependent on apprenticeship and, in for-mal settings, on lecture, memorization, and recitation, particularly with younger students. Throughout the region, adults frequently discuss issues and ideas thoroughly and attempt to reach consensus. But such discussion is uncommon in formal education, with some exceptions in higher education. Even in higher education there is an emphasis on lecture, with the teacher serving as the textbook.

Chapter 2 discusses the emphasis on the teacher as textbook. Students take notes as nearly word-for-word as possible, memorize the notes, and are not surprised when asked on an examination to "give the notes on . . ." (Rufai, 1997). There are variations across higher education, of course, but the teacher as textbook is common. In many parts of the region the most reliable sources of information are the teacher and the chalkboard. This occurs because of the short-age of funding for library and other resources, and unreliable elec-tricity, which limits the use of overhead projectors and other tech-nology. Thus, lecture and memorization are fostered, especially in commonly found large classes.

Many of the same problems are found in primary and second-ary schools. With few resources other than the teacher, the instruc-tion becomes focused on lecture, memorization, and recitation. Par-ticularly in primary schools, there are many underqualified teachers. Such teachers fall back on lecture and recitation and cannot cre-atively use local resources, materials, and examples (see Chapter 1). Unfortunately, poor performance is common among students on international tests. The research base often finds a link between poor instruction and a lack of meaningful learning, which may be re-flected on international tests (Sunal, Sunal, & Haas, 1996). It also is suggested as a major cause of a high rate of repetition in grade level in many areas of the region, resulting in the dropping out of stu-dents who are not succeeding academically.

In the four chapters on teaching disciplinary areas, the authors acknowledge the strength of passive student roles during instruction in the region. Yet, as content specialists familiar with the types of thinking skills used by professionals in their fields, the authors describe the need for active discussion, problem solving, and decision making if students are to comprehend these fields in a manner that will enable them to compete equally with students from other regions of the world. They also indicate that the nations of the region need scholars in these fields who can assist the development of their country and can do so only if they are equals of their peers in the developed world. How to arrive at a balance that respects traditional student roles, yet assists students in understanding the content field from current worldwide perspectives is a problem not yet solved in the region but one that is being investigated throughout it.

There are questions raised regarding the instruction of girls and of minority student groups. Research in the developed world suggests many girls do best in cooperative group learning situations and in classrooms where there is a lot of discussion (Noddings, 1992). Chapter 4 raises concerns about the instruction of girls in the region in science. African girls see few models of women scientists and may find the common lecture, recitation, and memorization strategies limiting. Research needs to be done to determine what types of instruction best suit girls in the region and the modifications needed to current practice. There have been successes elsewhere. In the United States, the number of girls beginning science and engineering programs has risen dramatically in the last decade during which many efforts were instituted to foster girls' interests in science and mathematics (Sunal & Sunal, 1997).

Relatively little research has been carried out in sub-Saharan Africa regarding appropriate instruction for minority groups. Since most countries in the region are conglomerations of a variety of different groups often speaking many different languages, appropriate majority and minority instruction will need to be investigated within each country or portions of countries. This is a time-consuming and expensive task. It has begun and should continue in order to establish guidelines for appropriate instruction.

Informal-sector education should utilize a wide range of instructional methodologies. Adults are able to identify specific objectives they wish to meet. Many of these are narrow and task oriented. Such training does not help most adults meet their objectives when delivered through lectures. This is an area where much needs to be done in the training of the trainers.

Instructional methodology presents complex problems everywhere in the world. There often seems to be some dissatisfaction among educators and among the populace with the manner of instruction. Both traditional and nontraditional forms of instruction have been under attack, but each has strong support within the region. The diversity found in sub-Saharan Africa complicates problems found in less diverse societies. But, it also offers opportunities for new ideas.

Research Efforts

The research base on education in sub-Saharan Africa is small but growing. Some nations in the region have a number of educational researchers. On a quarterly basis, the African Studies Association reports each doctoral dissertation dealing with Africa. Dissertations on education topics have averaged between twenty and thirty each quarter in reports during the 1990s. Every chapter in this book cites an existing research base. The research base is most limited with respect to informal sector education. Each chapter also indicates the need for much more research in the region on its topic.

The future of educational research in the region is limited by slowly growing economies. Funding problems encourage some "brain drain" of researchers to other regions. The supports needed for research are lacking and require funding. For example, in much of the region, some computers are found but computer repairpersons and parts are hard to find and expensive. Intermittent and/or fluctuating electrical voltage make computing hard to do and can damage sensitive equipment, so alternatives such as motorcycle batteries are sometimes used to power equipment. Such problems make research more difficult to accomplish in sub-Saharan Africa than in developed nations. African researchers generally have less time and energy in which to do research because of the demands of daily living, ill health, low salaries, unstable governments, frequently closed universities, and other problems found less often outside the region.

Despite all the problems, educational research is being carried out. There are strong associations of researchers in the region that foster research. They give researchers opportunities to meet with each other to discuss their field and their work. These groups and other vehicles for facilitating research in the region suggest means for fostering research even when the stressors impacting it are extreme.

Conclusion

Sub-Saharan Africa is diverse, yet patterns and trends emerge in education across the region whether it is examined through the lens of level of education or through the lens of disciplinary content area teaching. There are strengths that emerge from the diversity and the similarity between peoples in the region. These cannot easily be translated to other societies, but suggest means by which educational issues can be addressed. Their diversity is enabling Africans to take many different paths in addressing educational issues. In this process they are offering the world unique ideas. The world may benefit from an examination of these ideas.

References

Aldritch, M., & Hall, P. (1980). *Programs in science, mathematics, and engineering for women and girls in the United States: 1976–1978.* Washington, DC: American Association for the Advancement of Science.

Bredekamp, S. (1997). NAEYC issues revised position statement on developmentally appropriate practice in early childhood programs. *Young Children, 52*(2), 34–41.

Graham-Brown, S. (1991). *Education in the developing world: Conflict and crisis.* New York: Longman.

Jackson, P. (1992). Conceptions of curriculum and curriculum specialists. In P. Jackson (Ed.), *Handbook of research on curriculum* (pp. 3–40). New York: Macmillan.

Noddings, N. (1992). Gender and the curriculum. In P. Jackson (Ed.), *Handbook of research on curriculum* (pp. 659–686). New York: Macmillan.

Okebukola, P. (1997, April). Personal interview. Chicago, IL.

Rufai, R. (1997, April). Personal interview. Kano, Nigeria.

Sunal, D., & Sunal, C. (1997, April). *Teaching about energy.* Paper presented at the annual meeting of the National Science Teachers Association, New Orleans, LA.

Sunal, C., Sunal, D., & Haas, M. (1996, Spring). Meaningful learning in social studies through conceptual reconstruction: A strategy for secondary students. *Inquiry in Social Studies, 32*(1), 1–16.

Reference Books in International Education

Edward R. Beauchamp, Series Editor

Education in the People's Republic of China, Past and Present
An Annotated Bibliography
by Franklin Parker and Betty June Parker

Education in South Asia
A Select Annotated Bibliography
by Philip G. Altbach, Denzil Saldanha, and Jeanne Weiler

Textbooks in the Third World
Policy, Content, and Context
by Philip G. Altbach and Gail P. Kelly

Minority Status and Schooling
by Margaret A. Gibson and John V. Ogbu

Teachers and Teaching in the Developing World
by Val D. Rust and Per Dalin

Russian and Soviet Education, 1731–1989
A Multilingual Annotated Bibliography
by William W. Brickman and John T. Zepper

Education and Cultural Differences
New Perspectives
by Douglas Ray and Deo H. Poonwassie

Contemporary Perspectives in Comparative Education
edited by Robin J. Burns and Anthony R. Welch

Education in the Arab Gulf States and the Arab World
An Annotated Bibliographic Guide
by Nagat El-Sanabary

International and Historical Roots of American Higher Education
by W.H. Cowley and Don Williams

Education in England and Wales
An Annotated Bibliography
by Franklin Parker and Betty June Parker

Chinese Education
Problems, Policies, and Prospects
edited, with an introduction by Irving Epstein

Understanding Educational Reform in Global Context
Economy, Ideology, and the State
edited by Mark B. Ginsburg

Education and Social Change in Korea
by Don Adams and Esther E. Gottlieb

Three Decades of Peace Education around the World
An Anthology
edited by Robin J. Burns and Robert Aspeslagh

Education and Disability in Cross-Cultural Perspective
edited by Susan J. Peters

Russian Education
Tradition and Transition
by Brian Holmes, Gerald H. Read, and Natalya Voskresenskaya

Learning to Teach in Two Cultures
Japan and the United States
by Nobuo K. Shimahara and Akira Sakai

Educating Immigrant Children
Schools and Language Minorities in Twelve Nations
by Charles L. Glenn with Ester J. de Jong

Teacher Education in Industrialized Nations
Issues in Changing Social Contexts
edited by Nobuo K. Shimahara and Ivan Z. Holowinsky

Education and Development in East Asia
edited by Paul Morris and Anthony Sweeting

The Unification of German Education
by Val D. Rust and Diane Rust

Women, Education, and Development in Asia
Cross-National Perspectives
edited by Grace C.L. Mak

Qualitative Educational Research in Developing Countries
Current Perspectives
edited by Michael Crossley and Graham Vulliamy

Social Cartography
Mapping Ways of Seeing Social and Educational Change
edited by Rolland G. Paulston

Social Justice and Third World Education
edited by Timothy J. Scrase

Politics of Classroom Life
International Perspectives on Classroom Management
edited by Nobuo K. Shimahara

Schooling in Sub-Saharan Africa
Contemporary Issues and Future Concerns
Cynthia Szymanski Sunal

Index

216, 225, 227
academic freedom, 47
administration, 48–49
campuses, 40
curriculum, 50–51, 61–64, 67, 205, 207
diversity, 46–47
dominant teaching styles, 59–63
enrollment, 40, 41
evaluation, 67
funding, 43–44, 46–47
instructional methodology, 53–54, 66,
    67, 213
instructors' motivation for teaching,
    58, 59–63, 65
libraries, 41
literature education, 213, 216
needs assessment, 67
non-African institutions, 49–50
outreach programs, 49
rewards, 57, 62, 66
staff development, 52, 57, 61–64, 66–
    67
student admission, 40
student roles, 57, 61–63
student views of teaching, 59–63
university closings, 43
women, 46
Hodzi, R., 158
home environment, 12
homework, 21
Hopeful Lovers, 207
House, J., 205
Houser, G.M., 190
Hughes, W., 121
Hurry, L.B., 119

Igbo, 190, 216, 217, 219
illiteracy, 27
indigenous
    children' literature, 211
    education, 172
    language, 156, 195, 196, 230
    literature, 101, 189, 193–198, 196, 231
    mathematics, 160–162, 163
    science, 111, 113, 121, 126
industrial education, 78
informal sector, 72, 227
    formal education, 73
    skill acquisition, 81
informal sector education, xiii, xv, xvii, 3,
    103, 226, 233
inservice programs, 11, 21, 25, 28–30,
    52, 105, 107, 114, 141, 145

nonformal education, 84, 85
science, 123
social studies, 187
instructional methodology, xiv, xvi, xviii,
    xxiii, 11, 21–22, 26, 96, 114, 117,
    123, 126, 223, 232, 234
gender, 233
higher education, 53–54, 59–63, 67,
    213
indigenous language, 108
inquiry, 111, 119, 124, 154, 174, 200
mathematics, 153–154
recitation and lecture, 11, 26, 108,
    123, 129, 145, 149, 154, 232
science, 123, 124, 126
social studies, 185, 186
thinking skills, 28
International Association for the Evalua-
    tion of Educational Achievement
    (IEA), 7
International Institute for Children's
    Literature, 206
International Labor Organization, 81
International Monetary Fund, 105, 140
International Youth Library, 206
Inuwa, A.R., 52
Ivory Coast, 9, 213

Jaji, G., 148, 153, 158
Jamaica, 86, 87, 89
Jegede, O.J., 106, 122
Jikin Magayi, 193, 194
Jones, N., 121
*Journal of African Children's and Youth
    Literature,* 212

Kabira, M., 204
Kawadwa, B., 215
Keenan, H., 194
Kenya, xviii, 10, 12, 72, 79, 80, 116,
    171, 190, 195, 215
Kenya Oral Narratives, 204
Kikuyu, 190
King, K., 75, 78
Kisolo, T., 214
Knoepflmacher, U.C., 211, 212
Korea, 90, 91
Kpelle, 158
Kunene, D.P., 194, 219
Kuchemann, D., 138, 139, 142

labor market segmentation theory, 79
Lagos Plan, 105